PUBS AND RESTAURANTS

An Industry Accounting and Auditing Guide

PUBS AND RESTAURANTS

An Industry Accounting and Auditing Guide

Grant Anthony

Zahir Fazal

Ted Sloper

Clark Whitehill

Accountancy BOOKS

Accountancy Books
Gloucester House
399 Silbury Boulevard
Central Milton Keynes
MK9 2HL
Tel. 01908 248000

ISBN 1 85355 738 2

Cover photograph: The Prince of Wales Public House, Green Tye, Nr Much Hadham, Herts.

British Library Cataloguing-in-Publication Data.

A catalogue record for this book is available from the British Library.

Throughout this book the male pronoun has been used to cover references to both the male and female.

Typeset by LBJ Enterprises Ltd of Aldermaston and Chilcompton
Printed in Great Britain by Bell & Bain, Glasgow

Contents

Preface and acknowledgements

There have been many exciting developments in the pub and restaurant sector over the last 10 years, however, it remains fiercely competitive.

Our objective in writing this book is not only to provide a reference book for auditors and accountants with an interest in the industry but also to provide useful practical information for the operators of both single and multi-site outlets. The marketplace is constantly changing and the operator needs to keep pace with those changes in order to survive and subsequently to prosper. Failure is more likely where tight control is not maintained over the operational financial management of the business or where the accounting systems are not adequate to provide proper accounting information. In a business notorious for poor record-keeping the importance of keeping proper books and records cannot be exaggerated.

We felt that a book was needed to cover these issues and intended it to be both practical and technical in content. We also wanted to emphasise the importance of planning for the future and, with this in mind, we have included a chapter on strategic planning which covers such issues as preparing a strategic business plan and considering ownership succession. We hope that this may encourage the owner/manager to set goals and targets which are not only financial in nature.

In writing this book we sought the advice and help of a number of people working in the industry. Particular thanks go to Tony Hill and Clive Eplett of Surrey Free Inns and Chris Philips of Front Page Pubs who provided us with detailed comments on earlier drafts which proved to be invaluable.

We are indebted to all the Clark Whitehill partners and staff who provided input on a number of chapters and to Paul Barrington-Gibbs of MICA International for writing the Information Systems chapter.

Finally, and perhaps most importantly, a big thank you to Lorna Bunn who uncomplainingly typed draft after draft of the manuscript.

Grant Anthony
Zahir Fazal
Ted Sloper
May 1997

Foreword

In the last decade the pub and restaurant sector has been a fertile breeding ground for smaller companies. Some, like Wetherspoon and Regent, have progressed rapidly to become significant fully listed companies; others, like Pelican and Tom Cobleigh, have been engulfed by the majors. A host of others now contribute to the UK economy as small and medium-sized enterprises. They create both an opportunity and a challenge for the profession.

Transparency and best practice are unlikely to characterise the accounting policies of smaller companies. An examination of published accounts in this sector will frequently find silence on key issues and perhaps obfuscation. My experience suggests this is often not because of an intent to hide or mislead, but more because of the pace of commercial life and a genuine lack of financial understanding.

This book addresses a need for a comprehensive review of the sector's accounting and auditing issues and considers them against a backcloth of the principles of financial management and strategic planning. It has a value for the senior management of operators who are growing or have such aspirations. It sets out clearly the financial subject matter they need to appreciate in order to guide their companies through the pitfalls of the public arena. In addition, it covers all of the technical issues which are current and important. As such, it will be of value to the student or professional practitioner.

Clark Whitehill have made a significant contribution to my company's improvement in reporting and corporate governance as we have progressed towards a full listing, currently planned for autumn 1997. Their hand in this book is likely to influence financial standards throughout the sector. There is also a clear signal of movement towards best or better practice evident in Wetherspoon announcing depreciation of freeholds and Regent Inns retreating from its sum of digits depreciation policy.

No one should approach the book as if it is an encyclical. Unsurprisingly, the authors are influenced by the profession's current baggage. In contrast, my own FD, an accountant rounded by commercial experience, has repeatedly drawn attention to the dangers as well as the benefits that prescriptive accounting standards can create in specific industries. FRS 3, as an example, was for the most part a welcome step forward. Unfortunately, it suffers from quirks which in our industry generate absurdities in the accounting treatment of profit upon disposal which, frankly, does a disservice to the intellectual perception of the profession. The commercial world will totally disagree with the book's acceptance that a pub or restaurant should be valued as a property rather than as a business. The implications upon valuation, upward or downwards, impact on P & L in ways which have no relevance to 'true' profitability and must obscure the real measurement of performance. Happily, the book is not marred by evangelism and properly offsets its views against the dialogue of fact and interpretation, leaving the reader to reach an informed opinion.

Tony Hill
Managing Director, Surrey Free Inns

Chapter 1 – Overview of the pub and restaurant industry

1.1 Introduction

In 1995, the catering sector was worth £39.26 billion, of which £5.86 billion was serviced by fast food chains and £5.29 billion by 16,900 outlets of other restaurants and cafés. Keynote Limited estimate that in the same year there were approximately 33,000 pub businesses with turnover of approximately £14 billion (including pub restaurants).

This chapter sets out the nature of the pub and restaurant industry today and the significant changes in the last decade. It provides an outline of the different types of pubs and restaurants which service the consumer from city to country locations and the move towards speciality or themed pubs and restaurants. It is intended to furnish the reader with an overview of the types of establishment serving the consumer and the marketplace in which they operate.

1.2 Restaurants

The industry is characterised by frequent closures and changes of ownership. Many operators manage single outlets and are tempted into the industry by the relatively low barriers to entry. It is not uncommon for retired people to use their savings to purchase an outlet, but many find to their cost that the industry is very competitive, and without due care an investment can soon lose its value.

With the introduction of expanding restaurant chains which have acquired prime high street sites, and fast food outlets which have recently expanded aggressively into out-of-town sites, the margins of the small single outlet operator have been squeezed. This process was accelerated by the recession during the early 1990s which reduced the average spend per head particularly in medium to high priced restaurants. This has caused a polarisation in the market with the small operators serving a niche local market offering something different in order to survive and the larger chains gaining a higher proportion of the total eating out expenditure.

1.2.1 Restaurants by type

'Restaurants' is a generic term which covers a broad range of catering establishments from roadside cafés to up-market restaurants with internationally renowned chefs.

Most restaurants are licensed to sell alcohol, and those which do not usually allow the customer to supply their own and charge a nominal amount for corkage. If a restaurateur wishes to sell alcohol, he can apply to a licensing court for an on-licence which will be granted at the discretion of the magistrate. The licence may be granted without restrictions or it may be limited to certain alcoholic beverages and/or restricted to certain times of the day or night. If a variation or extension to licensing hours is required, a separate application must be made.

Generally, restaurants which achieve acclaim for the highest quality food through inclusion in food guides such as Egon Ronay, or by the award of Michelin stars to the chef, are at the top end of the market in terms of both price and quality. These restaurants are designed to appeal to the customer who takes his food seriously and is willing to pay not only for the quality of the cuisine and service but also for the kudos attached to eating in a prestigious establishment. Indeed, in very expensive restaurants the exclusivity which comes with the high prices adds to the attraction for the target customer – lower prices could actually lead to a fall in demand.

The roadside café, in contrast, is positioned at the other end of the market and is typified by very low spend per head, low costs and high volumes. Both the up-market restaurant and the roadside café have clearly defined separate markets.

In the middle are the restaurants which have a broader appeal based on the quality and price of the service they offer. These are dominated by chains of restaurants and include fast food outlets and themed restaurants.

Broadly, restaurants fall into one of the following categories:

- traditional restaurants;
- self-service restaurants;
- fast food and take-away restaurants;
- pub restaurants; and
- theme or concept restaurants.

Traditional restaurants

Traditional restaurants will provide waiter service and offer both a lunchtime and dinner menu. Very often they are independent but may specialise in a particular cuisine.

Self-service restaurants

Self-service restaurants provide fast and inexpensive meals for those looking for convenience. Usually, they are located in supermarkets, department stores and motorway service stations. Most offer a wider range of meals, sandwiches and snacks than fast food outlets.

Fast food and take-away restaurants

Fast food and take-away outlets have grown significantly both in number and type in recent times. They appeal to the consumer that requires low cost and fast service and are attractive to the operator because of the high returns, limited menus and high customer turnover.

The market is dominated by the major chains such as McDonalds, KFC and Pizza Hut. All now have prime high street locations and, more recently, out-of-town sites. The more traditional take-away outlets such as fish and chip shops, Indian and Chinese take-aways are growing more slowly. The growth in the pizza market is showing signs of stagnating as the market becomes saturated with many different operators providing a very similar product which is difficult for the customer to differentiate.

Pub restaurants

Pub restaurants, which include branded outlets such as Harvester (Bass), Chef & Brewer (Scottish & Newcastle) and Beefeater (Whitbread), are also major players in the market. The introduction of restaurants into pubs has become ever more important to the brewers and the independent pub companies as the sales of alcohol and other drinks have diminished. Until recently, pub restaurants had a down-market 'steak house' image. As a result, the major operators introduced investment programmes to change the image, making them more appealing and creating a wider customer base by introducing family-oriented and heavily branded outlets. Some pub restaurants now have branded children's play areas, for example, Whitbread's Brewers Fayre chain is annexed by Charlie Chalk Fun Factories. The brewers have relied on advertising to ensure the down-market steak house image of the pub restaurant has been replaced with a more consumer friendly, family image in the minds of the public.

Theme or concept restaurants

Theme or concept restaurants offer the customer a brand with which they can identify. Not only do these restaurants aim to provide quality food at reasonable prices, they also encourage customer loyalty due to the uniqueness of the surroundings. The restaurant may be based around a particular theme, such as Planet Hollywood or the recently launched Fashion Café, or a concept, such as Conran's Quaglino's or Mezzo, where huge capacity provides a fun atmosphere combined with high quality food. Both offer the customer more than food; they provide a unique eating out experience.

1.2.2 Restaurants by location

With increasing levels of competition, the importance of location to the success of a restaurant cannot be overemphasised. The location best suited to the restaurant will depend on the type of outlet envisaged.

City centre

Historically, city centre locations, particularly high streets, have been considered as the prime sites and commanded a high premium. If the location is right, a restaurant may be able to cater for business lunches as well as servicing the evening trade. However, the downside for any restaurant targeting the business community is that demand is likely to be flatter in the evening and potentially non-existent at the weekends. On the other hand, a restaurant which is able to attract business trade at lunchtime and perhaps theatre/cinema trade in the evening is likely to enjoy consistent levels of demand at lunchtime, evenings and weekends.

Usually, the lunchtime menu will be different to the evening menu and it is probable that alcohol sales and the spend per head will be higher in the evening session.

Out of town

Out-of-town locations typically service a catchment area with high proportions of local customers. If the demographics of the area are favourable, restaurants can command a high degree of customer loyalty attracting both lunchtime and evening trade. Fast food operators are now targeting out-of-town sites, attracting customers who are more concerned with convenience than glamour.

Other

Other locations include small villages or rural areas. Restaurants located in these areas are dependent on their reputation to build customer loyalty. The Roux brothers' Waterside Inn, for example, has established a reputation and achieved great success in spite of its rather out of the way location. In some cases, the surrounding countryside or local interest may add to the attraction. One of the challenges which country restaurants face is the likely seasonality of sales; a restaurant in a sparsely populated local beauty spot may be popular in summer and empty during the winter months.

1.3 Pubs

Pubs have been an everyday part of life in Britain for centuries. Traditionally, pubs have sold large quantities of beer, although increasingly the sales of other alcoholic and soft drinks have assumed more importance. Today, many pubs provide amusement machines both with and without prizes, including juke boxes, pool tables and fruit machines; some provide live entertainment and most serve bar snacks including crisps and nuts. A few offer accommodation, but the most significant advance recently has been the growth in the number of pubs providing a restaurant service.

The principal suppliers to pubs have been, and continue to be, the national brewers although there have been substantial changes in the nature of the relationship in recent years (see **1.4** below).

1.3.1 Pubs by type

Pubs can be broadly sub-divided into one of the following categories:

- tenanted houses;
- managed houses;
- free houses.

Tenanted houses

Until recently, tenanted pubs were owned by the brewers. However, the Monopolies and Mergers Commission Report (MMC Report) and subsequent Beer Orders in 1989 (see **1.4.1**) have resulted in the sprouting of non-brewing pub companies which have acquired tenanted pubs. Under a tenancy agreement, the pub is leased or rented to a tenant who runs the pub as his or her own business, enjoying the profits or suffering the losses. Typically, tenancy agreements are now of up to 21 years' duration. The drawback for the tenant is that in exchange for the tenancy at a reduced or below-market rent, he is tied to that brewer for beer purchases (except for one guest cask conditioned ale), usually at full market prices which are substantially above the discounted prices that can be negotiated by free house operators. Even where a brewer no longer owns the pubs the new pub companies tend to have supply agreements with the major brewers.

Since the Beer Orders, the tenant has been free to purchase all other drinks from a source other than the brewer to which he is tied.

Managed houses

Managed houses are run by the owner's employees for the benefit of the owner. All profits or losses are enjoyed or suffered by the owner of the house. The manager will earn a salary and usually a bonus based on the profits/turnover achieved. In some cases the manager may be allowed to run his own food operation.

In recent times there has been a move away from tenancies towards managed houses by the major businesses. For example, in 1992 Scottish & Newcastle had 1,000 tenanted/leased public houses and 850 managed houses; by 1996 it had 940 and 1,845 respectively (source – *Publican Newspaper*). Many non-brewing pub companies have also acquired significant estates of managed houses.

Free houses

Free houses are, by definition, not tied to any brewer so can buy their beer from any source. The free house, therefore, has more bargaining power than a tied tenant and as a result can negotiate barrelage discounts. To counteract this, brewers have sought to create exclusive supply agreements by offering renovation 'loans' to free houses at preferential rates. This has become known as the 'loan tie'. Free houses are often favoured by the serious beer drinker as they are able to offer a wide range of beers including real ales.

1.3.2 Pub locations

The location of a pub is key, as the local demographics including the age and social class of the population will influence the type of outlet most suited to the local environment. Themed pubs appeal more to the younger age group who expect all-round entertainment. The more traditional pub is still popular amongst the older clientele.

1.4 Recent developments in the pub sector

The tied house system of vertical integration has played a major part in the pub sector for more than two hundred years. Under the system, brewers acquired pubs and created tenancies the terms of which included an exclusive supply agreement which guaranteed effective distribution of their products. The tenant agreed to buy the brewers' products at full price, on the understanding that the rent would be correspondingly reduced to reflect the anti-competitive nature of the supply agreement. As part of the deal, the tenant would also receive financial, marketing and technical support from the brewer. A second form of tie was also created whereby the brewer targeted independent pubs (free houses) requiring finance and offered preferential interest rates on a loan in return for an exclusive supply agreement for their products.

This section reviews the recent developments in the pub market and how the changes have affected the industry.

Specific issues to be covered include:

(a) the Monopolies & Mergers Commission Report and the resulting Supply of Beer Orders 1989 (the Beer Orders);
(b) the European Commission block exemption under Article 85(1); and
(c) the recent Office of Fair Trading investigation.

1.4.1 The Monopolies & Mergers Commission Report and the Beer Orders

Historically, the tied estate system has been justified on the grounds that it gave the brewer a guaranteed outlet for a product with a short shelf-life, while the reseller was compensated with low rental costs. However, in 1989 the Director General of Fair Trading considered that the arguments had moved sufficiently against the tie to refer it to the Monopolies and Mergers Commission. When the Monopolies and Mergers Commission reported, they found that aspects of the beer tie were anti-competitive and therefore against the public interest. As a result, they made a number of recommendations including:

(a) the abolition of the loan tie;
(b) the prohibition against any brewer holding more than 2,000 on-licensed premises; and
(c) the right to purchase non-beer items from other suppliers.

Although these recommendations were watered down in 1989, two statutory instruments collectively known as the 'Beer Orders' were issued. Perhaps surprisingly, the loan tie was not abolished, although the Beer Orders stated that any loan tie had to be capable of redemption on three months' notice. The most far-reaching effect of the Beer Orders, however, was to restrict the number of tied houses owned by any one brewer. In simple terms, the Beer Orders forced all brewers to reduce their estate of tied houses by one for every two tied houses that they owned in excess of 2,000. The Beer Orders also allowed tenants to purchase at least one brand of draft cask conditioned ale from whomsoever they chose.

The Beer Orders caused an unforeseen change in the nature of tenancy agreements. Prior to the Monopolies and Mergers Commission investigation, the majority of agreements were short-term three-year non-transferable tenancies at a low rent, with the tenant required to purchase beer and other supplies from the brewer landlord. In 1990 the Landlord and Tenant (Licensed Premises) Act 1990 was introduced, with the intention of protecting the tenants' rights. However, this together with the Beer Orders in 1989 prompted the brewers to introduce new commercial full repairing leases of up to 21 years' duration, with the tenant having the responsibility to insure the property. Tenants were still required to purchase all their beer from the brewer landlord but were threatened with eviction unless they agreed to the terms of the new long-term lease. Despite this the tenancies were at a substantially increased rent in comparison to the traditional three-year tenancies.

In 1972 when the UK joined the European Community it became subject to European law. Article 85 of the Treaty of Rome controls agreements which 'prevent, restrict or distort competition' and Article 86 prohibits abuses of a dominant position. In 1983 the European Commission, after considering the advantages and disadvantages of the tied house system, granted a block exemption from Article 85(1) for certain categories of exclusive supply agreements and included special provisions for beer supply. Under both UK and European Law, therefore, the tied house system was legal.

However, the European Commission's block exemption was due to expire on 31 December 1997, putting the future of tied house systems again under the spotlight, with the European Commission considering whether the block exemption should be renewed. In January 1997 brewers were given a two-year reprieve as a final decision has been put on hold until 1999. In the meantime, a Green Paper has been issued from Brussels on which comments are invited before July 1997. None of the proposals set out in the Green Paper would mean the complete end to the tie, making it likely that small brewers will be allowed to keep the tie.

For the block exemption to be valid, the brewer/landlord must provide the tenant with a 'special, commercial or financial advantage' to compensate for the fact that the tenant is required to purchase beer from the brewer/landlord at full price whilst free houses are able to negotiate a discount. The 'special, commercial or financial advantage' historically was passed on to the tenant through below-market rents, financial, marketing and other support from the brewers. However, many tenants believe that they have now been saddled with both high rents and high product costs. Although many tenants would welcome a decision to end the tied house system, there are fears amongst them that the brewers would be forced to heavily discount their product in order to maintain market share in a free market, and would seek to recoup their lost profit by increasing the rent charged to tenants. Therefore, in practice, the bargaining power of tenants may not be significantly increased whatever the final decision from Brussels.

1.4.2 Inntrepreneur Estates Limited

In 1991 Inntrepreneur Estates Limited was formed as a joint venture between Grand Metropolitan and Fosters making it the largest pub owner in the UK. At the same time, Grand Metropolitan divested its brewing arm selling it to Courage (owned by Fosters). Inntrepreneur Estates Limited was the amalgamation of public house estates owned by Grand Metropolitan and Fosters.

When Inntrepreneur was formed, it negotiated an exclusive supply agreement with Courage and offered its tenants long leases to replace the existing short-term tenancies. These leases have been the subject of significant industry comment suggesting that the leases do not meet the requirements of the block exemption. As a result, Inntrepreneur has asked the European Commission to grant its leases specific exemption. In 1993, the Commission announced its intention to grant specific exemption, on the grounds that it considered that the Inntrepreneur lease 'contributes to an improvement of distribution while allowing consumers a fair share of the resulting benefits'.

From comments received by the Commission from interested parties, it became clear that the prices charged by Courage to free house customers and those charged to Inntrepreneur tenants were significantly different. The Commission commented that:

'this wider differential in prices must preclude the operation of the tied pub on the level playing field. If so, it is questionable whether the . . . conditions for granting an exemption under Article 85(3) are fulfilled.'

The Commission was also concerned that the differential had widened across the UK brewing industry and so invited the Office of Fair Trading (OFT) to investigate the matter. The OFT reported in May 1995. They found that price differentials of up to 13 per cent for beer and 19 per cent for lager existed but concluded that the differentials generally did not put the tied trade at a competitive disadvantage to the free trade. Therefore, no further action has been taken. At the time of writing, the European Commission has not made a decision in respect of the Inntrepreneur lease.

At the time of its formation Inntrepreneur Estates was required to give a number of undertakings to the OFT before the joint venture was permitted to proceed. As a result it is committed to freeing its pub tenants from the Courage tie and to manage no more than 20 pubs out of the 2,900 it currently owns by 1998. However, in February 1997 the Government agreed to release Inntrepreneur Pub Company Limited (formally Intreprenneur Estates Limited) from its undertakings to the extent that it will be able to tie lessees beyond March 1998, but must allow its tenants to buy beers produced by brewers other than Courage. Inntrepreneur argued that it should have the same rights as other pub groups to negotiate large supply agreements, particularly as Courage has now been sold by Fosters to Scottish & Newcastle (see **1.4.3** below). As a result Inntrepreneur has introduced a package of discounts called Retail Link on the basis of discounts negotiated with various brewers which it believes will benefit its tenants.

1.4.3. Fragmentation of the pub market

The introduction of the Beer Orders in 1989 has had a significant effect on the composition of the market. The intention was to create competition in the marketplace by reducing the power of the major breweries. Arguably, it has had the opposite effect.

When the MMC reported, there were six major brewers; that number has now been reduced to four and potentially to three. The significant corporate activity in this area is listed below:

(a) Grand Metropolitan divested itself of its brewing operations to Courage, but formed Inntrepreneur Estates Limited with Fosters.
(b) In 1992 the Monopolies and Mergers Commission allowed a merger of the brewing operations of Allied Lyons (now Allied Domecq) and Carlsberg to form Carlsberg Tetley.
(c) In 1995 Scottish & Newcastle was allowed to acquire Courage from Fosters. The effect was to reduce the number of major brewers from five to four with more than 50 per cent of beer sales in the UK

produced by Scottish & Newcastle and Bass. In order for the transaction to proceed, Scottish & Newcastle had to give a number of undertakings, including reducing its tied estate by 115 to 2,624 within one year. Given that the brewing capacity of Scottish & Newcastle increased greatly as a result of the acquisition of Courage the decrease in the number of tied estates, however small, was significant.

(d) In the summer of 1996 it was announced that Allied Domecq had accepted an offer from Bass for the sale of Carlsberg Tetley, subject to clearance from the OFT/MMC. At the time of writing clearance is still pending.

Perhaps the most significant effect of the Beer Orders has been the creation of non-brewing pub companies. The Beer Orders resulted in large numbers of unprofitable pubs being placed on the market as the brewers were forced to reduce their portfolio of tied estates. These enforced sales created opportunities for a new breed of company. Independent multiples such as Enterprise Inns, Discovery Inns and Magic Pub Company (since acquired by Greene King) have all benefited either directly or indirectly from the fallout from the Beer Orders. Some of these pub companies are in fact ex-brewers such as Greenalls and Boddingtons (now owned by Greenalls). The regional brewers also benefited from the national brewers' enforced reductions by purchasing pubs which fitted their location and portfolio requirements.

1.4.4 Tenanted v managed pubs

There has been a move away from tenanted to managed pubs, as companies have realised the benefits of the greater profit potential for managed pubs as opposed to tenanted pubs. There are now a number of pub companies which are quoted either on AIM or the main market. The increased potential of managed over tenanted estates is clearly reflected in the stock market prices.

1.4.5 The threat from the single market

With the increased level of competition, there is a downward trend in the number of pubs. There has also been a steady decline in the consumption of beer in pubs in the 1990s. This is partly a result of the recession, partly due to the increased propensity to drink at home and partly due to the threat from the introduction of the single market in 1992. Historically, beer sales have held up well during recessionary periods, often actually increasing as people find solace in a pint of beer at their familiar local pub. The latest recession has put a brake on that trend, but of more fundamental concern to the brewers and publican alike is the threat posed by the introduction of a single market. In the absence of import duty, individuals are now able to purchase alcoholic drinks on the Continent at significantly lower prices for consumption at home. The unfortunate side effect has been to create a black market for imported, low duty, alcohol. Inevitably, the bootlegger has seized upon the opportunity to purchase and offer for sale duty-free alcohol to the unscrupulous publican who can then reduce his prices to the disadvantage of those purchasing from legal sources.

The industry is lobbying the Government to reduce the duty on beer to put UK on-licensed premises on a more even playing field with European outlets. In recent years the Chancellor has halted the increase in duty which has provided some respite but many believe that the duty should be decreased to European levels. There have been a number of campaigns organised by interested parties to bring the publican and brewers' plight to the public's attention.

1.4.6 Other developments

The changes brought about by the Beer Orders and the declining level of alcohol sales, particularly beer consumption, has meant that the industry has had to react quickly to the changes in the marketplace. The pub sector has needed to adapt in order to maintain its share of the public's leisure pound.

Apart from the fallout from the Beer Orders and the threat from the single market, there have been two other significant developments in the early 1990s:

- the rise in the number and popularity of themed or branded pubs; and
- the increased incidence of pub restaurants.

Traditionally, pubs have been male dominated drinking establishments with little effort made to attract the female consumer or family unit. Many of the traditional pubs with smoke-filled rooms and limited seating have now been converted into more family-oriented areas with a brighter feel and more comfortable seating. Some now have air-conditioning and no smoking areas. The introduction of children's certificates is a further step in the evolution of pubs into areas of family entertainment, although many in the industry believe that the conditions which a publican has to meet before a children's certificate is granted are unnecessarily onerous and will therefore limit the number of pubs which can allow admission for children under 14 years.

There is a general awareness in the industry that people no longer view pubs as simply a place to drink. They are demanding a higher level of entertainment. The industry has reacted to this by creating pubs with a particular ambience or atmosphere. There are now chains of concept, branded or theme pubs, from sports bars to super pubs. Some are based around a particular culture, such as Irish pubs. Other chains are branded with a particular name, with each outlet having similar design concepts which are instantly recognisable to the consumer and therefore create brand loyalties. Many of these pub chains have become very successful and can command high values, illustrated by the sale of the Pitcher & Piano chain to Marstons for £19.5 million in July 1996. The chain itself was based in London and consisted of only seven outlets. Marstons are hopeful that the number of outlets can be increased, expanding and extending the life of a successful brand name.

Many pubs now include quiz nights, karaoke, satellite television and other live entertainment. These have proved to be very successful with the consumer although karaoke may be in danger of over-supply.

1.5 Summary

While there has been activity in the restaurant market with a move towards theme restaurants and the increasing popularity of fast food and pub restaurants, the most significant changes have been in the pub sector.

In summary, the pub sector has fragmented into three principal sections:

- national and regional brewers
- expanding pub companies with mixed tenanted, managed and franchised estates; and
- smaller independent units and free house chains.

The Beer Orders forced the major brewers to rethink their strategy. There are now four national brewers, which are likely to reduce to three, plus a number of regional brewers. An immediate result of the Beer Orders was to put large numbers of the less profitable public houses on the market. This created an opportunity for a new breed of pub company to acquire managed and tenanted public houses. One of the negative results of the Beer Orders has been the closure of a number of country, village and town pubs which had relied on support from the national brewers.

The industry has been under threat from the increase in the level of home entertainment, the recession in the late 1980s and early 1990s and the threat from the single European market. The industry has adapted to the resulting change in demand of the consumer and there are now a number of very successful pub chains based on a particular concept, brand or theme. The extension of permitted hours and Sunday openings have also helped the publican without the feared increase in the level of alcoholism and alcohol-related crime. The working time directive, which imposes a maximum 48-hour working week, and the threat of a minimum wage present the publican and restaurateur alike with further challenges for the future.

The tied estate debate will continue for the medium term as the interested parties campaign in the run up to the European Commission's decision following the Green Paper on whether to renew the block exemption after December 1999.

Chapter 2 – Operational financial management

2.1 Introduction

The purpose of any business is to make a profit. However, more businesses fail as a result of insufficient cash than through lack of profits. In order to ensure the survival of a business it is important to manage the cash flow as well as maximising income and minimising costs. Once the basic working capital management is in place, it will create a more suitable environment in which to make key business decisions to maximise the profit potential of the business. This chapter covers the following issues:

- working capital management;
- what information is required to make informed business decisions?
- how can operational performance be assessed?
- what decision-making strategies/tools are available?
- when should decisions be taken and implemented?

2.2 Working capital management

Working capital is the means by which a restaurant or pub finances its trade on a day-to-day basis. It consists of net current assets, i.e., those assets which are easily convertible into cash, net of current liabilities.

The key is to manage working capital so that the level of cash and cash equivalents is sufficient to run the business efficiently. Where a pub or restaurant holds too much cash it is not utilising its resources in the most profitable way and will become vulnerable to predators. A business in this situation is said to be undertrading. On the other hand, if a pub or restaurant invests heavily in stock or uses short-term financing for long-term investments, i.e., new outlet fit-outs, then meeting its liabilities as they fall due may become difficult. In this situation the business is said to be overtrading and its prospects for survival are poor unless corrective action is taken quickly.

In a pub, current assets consist principally of stock and cash, usually with little or no debtors. In some circumstances credit may be given to regular customers but this is becoming less common. Most restaurants and some pubs accept credit cards as a means of payment, and where this is the case, the level of debtors will be higher. Current liabilities represent amounts payable to suppliers and other amounts repayable within one year, such as any bank overdrafts.

2.2.1 Measurement of working capital

The most common measure of the adequacy of working capital is the current liquidity ratio, which measures the ratio of current assets against current liabilities. It provides an indication of the short-term financial position of the enterprise. A ratio of more than one indicates that current assets exceed current liabilities and vice versa.

Example

The Red Lion Pub has the following current assets and current liabilities at 31 December 1996:

	£		£
Stock	1,000	Bank loans and overdrafts	200
Debtors	700	Creditors	1,700
Cash at bank	–	Accruals	200
		Tax	500
	1,700		2,600

$$\text{Liquidity ratio} = \frac{\text{Current assets}}{\text{Current liabilities}} = \frac{1{,}700}{2{,}600} = 0.65$$

A pub or restaurant would expect to have a low liquidity ratio as the level of cash sales is high and stock is financed by credit taken from suppliers, i.e., high level of creditors. Therefore, a ratio above 1.5 may be indicative of undertrading. Indeed, it is usual for pubs and restaurants to have net current liabilities and therefore a liquidity ratio of less than one. Whatever the ratio, it is important that a close eye is kept on any movements, as a sudden fall in the ratio could signal future cash flow problems. An expanding group will need to ensure that the costs of new outlets do not have a detrimental effect on the working capital available for the existing business.

2.2.2 Managing cash flow

The most important component of the working capital is the cash flow. If cash is not properly managed a business will not survive. The main areas of concern should be:

(a) The level of working capital needed to finance the business. Any increase in requirements needs to be factored into the cash flow. Usually, working capital requirements will vary in line with turnover.

(b) Any expected one-off payments such as the repayment of a loan or purchase of a capital item. Fit-out costs for new outlets or premiums paid for new leases should be factored into the cash flow. VAT and rent payments are other major costs which should be reflected in the correct period.

(c) In a pub or restaurant there may be sudden and substantial swings in the cash balance due to factors such as, for example, the seasonality of sales. For instance, in January there is likely to be a major cash requirement to pay suppliers for stock delivered over the Christmas and New Year period whilst falling cash receipts reflect declining demand during January.

Nowadays, pub companies and restaurant chains have investment programmes for new openings. However, it is important that any expansion plans should remain as flexible as possible and postponed or even curtailed if necessary. The risk increases as the size of the investment in an individual outlet, relative to the size of the company, increases. Until the project is finalised and earning an income stream, it represents a cash drain on the operation. Any large projects should be undertaken with caution.

Once the cash flow has been prepared, the restaurateur or publican will be able to see whether the business can remain within the facility limits in place. It is important that the cash flow is analysed on a month-by-month basis and in some cases more regularly so that any peaks and troughs can be identified and arrangements made for additional financing where necessary. The manager should also make plans to ensure that the troughs are properly managed. The single most controllable cost in a pub or restaurant is labour, therefore, it is important that staff scheduling is planned carefully.

By setting up proper procedures for cash flow budgeting and monitoring actual cash flow on a regular basis it should be possible to prepare cash flow forecasts which are reasonably accurate. This will enable the publican or restaurateur to manage the cash flow so that it combines efficiently with the other components of working capital.

2.2.3 Managing stock

There is a cost to stockholding; this includes the cost of storing stock and the interest cost on money used to purchase stock. It should be management's aim to keep stock levels as low as possible without running the risk of stock-outs with the detrimental effects they can have on consumer satisfaction and loyalty. Where goods are perishable, the risks of holding too much stock increase, i.e., ensuring that a restaurant purchases the optimum level of fresh food will have a significant effect on profit margins achieved. To manage stock efficiently a publican or restaurateur will need to know the relative popularity of stock items. For these purposes it is useful to know how many times stock turns over in a given period. This is usually measured by dividing the cost of sales by the value of stock at cost; the more times that stock turns over in a period the more efficiently the business is being run, provided stock-outs are kept to a minimum.

A typical pub might expect total stock to turn over at least 20 times a year, however, this will include beer stock which may turn over once a week or more frequently and spirits which will turn over more slowly. Restaurants would normally have higher stock turnover particularly where food is freshly prepared. Restaurants will be reliant on techniques such as volume forecasting in order to keep wastage of food to a minimum. Pubs with restaurants will obviously have the same concerns regarding wastage although wet sales are less of a problem, the obvious exception being beer, which will need to be kept in the right environment and used in the short term to avoid it spoiling.

In calculating the optimum level of stockholding, fluctuations in the level of demand and the lead time for ordering must be taken into account. Seeking to minimise the stockholding costs must be balanced with the increase in delivery and other costs if frequent orders are made. The aim should be to keep stocks low in order to minimise the stockholding costs, but there comes a point where the additional administration and delivery costs of frequent orders equal the savings made by holding fewer stocks. This point, known as the economic order quantity, provides a theoretical optimum order level. However, there may be other factors such as quantity discounts, rebates and expected price changes which should be taken into account before a final decision is taken on the appropriate order quantities.

Once the quantity has been finalised management will need to decide when to place the order. This decision should be based on the expected lead time and the amount of stocks expected to be used during the lead period. This ensures stock is delivered 'just in time', i.e., immediately prior to a stock-out, although it is sensible to allow for a buffer stock to be absolutely certain that stock-outs only occur infrequently. In many cases such a theoretical approach may not be possible especially in a tied pub where weekly deliveries, usually on a Friday, will be agreed with the brewery in order to avoid stock-outs over the weekend.

2.2.4 Managing debtors

The management of debtors is critical in many businesses but should not be of major concern to a publican or restaurateur as the level of debtors should be negligible. The only significant debtors should be from credit card sales, however, provided proper vetting procedures are followed the risk of bad debts is borne by the credit card company and the accounts are normally settled within a month of the transaction.

2.2.5 Managing creditors

The proper management of creditors will help working capital requirements, but care must be taken to ensure the right balance is struck between taking extended credit and paying within the supplier's stated terms. If creditors are paid slowly it will benefit the cash flow in the short term, but at what cost? If suppliers are constantly chasing payment they may refuse to meet orders until payments are made and will be far less inclined to provide an efficient service or to provide emergency requirements when needed. The result will ultimately be customer dissatisfaction when orders are not met on time. On the other hand there may also be a cost to settling balances too early if cash flow is weak – it may be beneficial to take as much credit as possible foregoing any settlement discounts. Management should decide whether it is better to pay early to take advantage of settlement discounts or to take the maximum credit in order to benefit the cash flow. In any event, to help cash flow budgeting the manager should try to negotiate prices which are guaranteed at a specific level for a minimum period of time.

To keep track of credit taken, the number of days' purchases represented by trade creditors (creditor days), can be calculated:

$$\text{Creditor days} = \frac{\text{Trade creditors}}{\text{Cost of trade purchases for past year}} \times 365$$

Any significant fluctuations in creditor days from one period to the next should be investigated. If the number of days' purchases outstanding are increasing it may be a sign that the business is overtrading. If this is coupled with a sudden loss of major suppliers the problem may be serious and corrective action should be taken immediately.

2.3 What information is required to make informed business decisions?

2.3.1 Management information

For a business to function properly management must have up-to-date financial information on which to base its decisions. Care must be taken to ensure that the information is not only accurate but is timely and relevant.

As a minimum, every business should produce monthly profit and loss accounts and cash flows. This should be presented in a set format and be subject to formal procedures so that the information provided is consistent from month to month.

A typical monthly management information pack for a pub or restaurant should include the following:

(a) detailed profit and loss account;
(b) basic balance sheet;
(c) separate analysis of wet and dry:
  (i) turnover;
  (ii) margins;
  (iii) stock turnover;
(d) analysis of working capital including cash flow forecast;
(e) analysis of labour costs as a percentage of turnover;
(f) analysis of controllable and uncontrollable costs (for multi-site operations this information should be prepared on an outlet-by-outlet basis).

Included at Appendix 1 is an example of a detailed profit and loss account extracted from a typical management information pack.

A manager will also need more regular up-to-date information for day-to-day decisions. Trading conditions may change rapidly; for example, an unexpected period of hot weather may result in higher than anticipated lager sales. If daily sales figures are not reviewed the opportunity for increasing supplies to meet the extra demand may be missed. A manager should be aware of any significant fluctuations in sales or costs, so that remedial action can be taken when necessary or advantage taken of unexpectedly favourable trading conditions.

The detail required will depend on the volatility of the business – where volumes and margins change regularly detailed sales information will be very important. In more expensive restaurants the proportion and relative cost of fresh food will be high. As a result it is important that the manager, chef and buyer keep track of the most and least popular items on the menu so that, where necessary, adjustments can be made to the buying order. For example, grilled salmon steak is likely to sell well when the weather is hot but suffer a decline in sales during cold spells.

On a day-to-day basis the headline sales and cost information will form the basis for any short-term decision. An analysis of the relative popularity of items on a restaurant menu will provide the manager with information to assist in volume forecasting. This is dealt with later in this chapter.

A chain of pubs or restaurants will require daily sales returns from its outlets. More detailed weekly returns, showing full receipts and payments and other relevant information such as the number of covers, should also be submitted to head office in a standard format. The task of producing management information from the detailed returns can then be carried out centrally.

2.3.2 Budgeting

Budgeting procedures are critical to the decision-making process. Budgets can be useful for planning purposes, as a means of assessing actual performance and as a motivational tool. Listed below are some examples of specific applications.

Planning
Budgeting can be used for resource scheduling to ensure that the maximum use is made of employees, reducing the risks of under or overstaffing during periods of variable trading conditions. Depending on the mobility and flexibility of employees, it may be possible to move staff from one outlet where trading is poor to another outlet where trading is expected to be more favourable. A comparison of budgets prepared for different outlets will highlight the possibilities. Proper resource management is vital in the pub and restaurant trade where labour is a major component of an outlet's costs.

Assessing actual performance
By comparing actual results to those budgeted, a manager will be able to react to unexpected variations.

Motivating staff
Provided the relevant staff are involved in the budgetary process and made responsible for costs/profit centres within their control, budgets can be a useful motivating tool.

2.3.3 Basis of preparation

Different businesses have different methods of preparing a budget but the method they choose will be a derivative of either the bottom-up or top-down approach. In a multi-site operation, the bottom-up approach involves the manager of each outlet preparing a budget with input from the staff responsible for meeting it. On completion, each outlet passes its budget to head office for review and collation into an overall 'group' budget. The top-down approach, as the name suggests, requires that head office first prepares the key determinants of the budget, e.g., overall sales, from which the component budgets are prepared.

Generally, a budget should be prepared for a period of one year, analysed monthly.

It is common practice for a budget to be based on the previous year's results. Although this is a useful indicator of the likely trends in any 12-month period there may be a number of reasons why the sales for the following year may differ. To avoid a budget based on the previous year plus or minus a given percentage, it is useful to start from a zero base. In other words the budget is prepared from scratch although the previous year's trends should not be discounted.

For the avoidance of confusion, assumptions should be made about the trading environment. For instance, those involved in preparing the budget should be told to assume that, for example, the weather for the following year will be average. Also, for budgetary purposes expected price increases or decreases should be set by head office and the various operations informed.

2.3.4 Sales

For both pubs and restaurants, sales will be the driver in the budgeting process. Inevitably, there will be factors which limit the sales that can be achieved. For instance, restaurant sales will be limited by the number of covers and pub sales by the size of the outlet. Although a restaurant's capacity is limited by the number of tables available it may be possible to increase sales by serving more than one sitting or by adding tables to expand the seating capacity. A pub may be able to expand by creating a beer garden.

The budgeted sales figures should be as realistic as possible. However, some managers deliberately set higher budgeted sales in order to motivate staff to achieve better results. Whatever the intended purpose of the budget there are a number of considerations which must be taken into account in compiling the budgeted sales figures. For a pub or restaurant those considerations will include:

- the effect of changes in eating trends, e.g., nouvelle cuisine;
- the market as a whole;
- how sensitive demand is to changes in price;
- the effects of planned price increases or reductions;
- the effects of proposed sales promotions;
- the effect of changes in sales mix;
- the effect of known seasonal variations, e.g., sales at Christmas and New Year;
- the target market and the effect of demographic changes;
- expected growth – planned new outlets;

- the immediate competition;
- the effect on demand of refurbishment;
- the effect on demand of refurbishment of a competitor's outlet; and
- the effects of food scares, e.g., BSE on the sales of a steak house.

Other income may be crucial to the profitability of the business and should be budgeted for. Many pubs rely on machine and other income to generate bottom line profit. The machine income should be based on past experience and would normally be calculated as a percentage of the budgeted sales.

2.3.5 Variable costs – direct raw material costs

The budgeted sales should be compiled in such a way that sales can be analysed between different products or groups of products. This is important as the sales mix will have a significant impact on the margins achieved. The manager with the assistance of the buyer should be able to estimate with reasonable accuracy the margins achievable for each product, or product group. Inevitably, estimating the margins achievable will focus on historical data as well as:

- market conditions for principal supplies;
- expected price increases/decreases;
- changes in recipes;
- changes in portion sizes.

In preparing the budget, the manager should bear in mind the margins that need to be achieved in order, firstly, to cover fixed overheads (see **2.3.7** below) and, secondly, to make an adequate level of profit. If during the budgeting process it becomes clear that the margins achievable, based on the prices set, are inadequate then it will be necessary to rethink the pricing strategy and consider the knock-on effect on demand. Typically, this concern is overcome by operating a cost-plus pricing policy whereby a set margin is added to a standard cost to give the sales price. Where a cost-plus pricing policy is used the budgeted margin will drive sales price rather than vice versa.

There may not be any potential for raising prices without losing significant custom, in which case the manager will need to review his buying costs and if possible switch to cheaper suppliers or take advantage of trade discounts. In preparing the budget and considering the margins achievable, the manager will need to consider any likely retrospective discounts that will be achieved based on the budgeted sales. A new pub or restaurant will not have the buying power of a more established concern and so is likely to achieve lower margins making the control of fixed costs more important.

Managing the cost, preparation and pricing of food is a difficult balancing act, and will depend on the individual circumstances of the operation. In smaller operations where it is not practical to produce a detailed sales budget, it should be possible to prepare an overall sales budget on which an estimated gross profit can be calculated based on an expected margin. The direct costs will be the balancing figure.

2.3.6 Variable costs – labour

The number of staff required by a restaurant or pub will depend on factors such as:

- the size of the outlet;
- the level of turnover in each outlet;
- the mobility of staff between outlets.

For any outlet there will be a finite number of staff needed after which there will be diminishing returns as, for example, bar staff begin to get in each other's way. On the other hand there will also be a minimum number of staff required whatever the turnover of the outlet. The aim should be for staff to be as productive as possible by keeping idle time to a minimum. Inevitably, there will be periods of fluctuating sales due, for example, to seasonal variations. The number of staff needed will depend on their flexibility. The more part-time staff that can be used during busy periods whilst maintaining core staff levels, the more efficient the resourcing is likely to be. For multi-site operations it may be possible to move staff between locations according to the peaks and troughs in the demand of the individual outlets. Again this should reduce idle time. However, when preparing the budget it is prudent to allow for some idle time.

2.3.7 Fixed costs

Fixed costs are those costs which do not vary to any great extent with the level of turnover. As a result it should be possible for a manager of a restaurant or pub to estimate the level of overheads over a 12-month period. To avoid the temptation of making fixed costs the balancing figure in order to achieve a pre-determined net profit, the fixed cost budget should be prepared as a separate exercise based on the manager's knowledge of the business. Typically, the fixed costs of a pub or restaurant will include the following:

- Property costs:
  - rent and rates;
  - repairs;
  - heat, light and power;
  - insurance.

- Operating costs:
  - cleaning;
  - uniforms;
  - equipment repairs;
  - cutlery, glasses, etc.;
  - equipment hire;
  - consumables;
  - laundry.
- Administration:
  - print, postage and stationery;
  - depreciation and amortisation;
  - motor and travel;
  - telephone.
- Legal and professional:
  - accountancy and audit fees;
  - stocktaking fees;
  - licensing costs;
  - other legal fees.
- Advertising and promotions:
  - music and entertainers;
  - promotional costs;
  - advertising.
- Financing costs:
  - bank charges and interest;
  - credit card charges.

Some fixed costs will be incurred directly by an outlet, others may be recharged from head office. For performance measurement, it is important to distinguish between those costs which are controllable by the outlet and those which are not. For these purposes a manager of an outlet will consider costs for which he is responsible to be controllable and those recharged by head office, or which head office impose, to be uncontrollable. There will also be costs such as rent and rates over which the manager will have little control. However, it should be borne in mind that a manager is less likely to attempt to negotiate lower costs if he is aware that head office have identified those costs as uncontrollable and therefore as having no bearing on the value of his bonus. When assessing the performance of a particular outlet for appraisal purposes, it is important only to take into account the costs which can be controlled by that outlet. Controllable costs should be identified during the budgeting process so that sensible comparisons can be made between the relative performance of different outlets.

In setting the budget for rent, leases should be reviewed to ensure that there are no imminent rent reviews. Proper advice should be taken when a lease is signed and careful consideration given to onerous clauses. If the landlord has the power to enforce increases, particularly where they are based on turnover, the viability of the business should be questioned before the lease is entered into. In any event, expected increases or decreases should be budgeted for.

2.3.8 Reviewing the budget

When the budget has been collated it should be reviewed to ensure that any assumptions made are reasonable and that it is achievable. The key areas will be:

- sales;
- gross profit and gross profit margins; and
- net profit.

In any business the first concern of management will be to make a contribution to overheads. The composition of the gross profit may include menu items, which are making no contribution, i.e., they are making a gross loss. Unless it is part of a business strategy management should seek to redress the position immediately. At times it may be worthwhile to continue to sell drinks or menu items at a loss if there is a knock-on beneficial effect on other items sold by the outlet.

If the budgeted gross profit is insufficient to cover the budgeted fixed costs the business will have a budgeted net loss.

By focusing on these areas the manager will gain an overview of the budget and where necessary can look behind the figures to the detail, making adjustments to the budget as appropriate.

When the budget has been completed it should be subject to a final review by the manager who should be satisfied that the budget is achievable and is consistent with his expectations.

2.3.9 Revised budgets

During the year the budget should be compared with the actual results. Variances should be investigated and appropriate action taken. If it becomes clear that there are significant variances and that the conditions that resulted in the variances are likely to prevail, the budget will need to be revised.

2.3.10 Cash flow budget

Having prepared a budgeted profit and loss account, the preparation of a cash flow budget should be relatively straightforward. However, care should be taken to ensure that non-profit and loss items such as capital expenditure or changes in financing are properly reflected. Non-cash flow items such as depreciation must, of course, be excluded. Cash flow is considered in more detail in Chapter 5.

> ***Tip***
>
> To check that a profit and loss and cash flow is reasonable prepare a simple budgeted monthly balance sheet which will highlight any unusual movements such as an ever-increasing creditor balance.

2.3.11 Capital expenditure

Finally, it is sensible to ensure that a capital expenditure budget is prepared for each site. In any case, all capital expenditure during the year should then be questioned before it is carried out.

2.4 How can operational performance be assessed?

It is not enough to have accurate historical information and detailed budgets. The managers must be able to interpret the figures and make business decisions accordingly. This section considers some of the ways in which a manager can measure performance and the following:

- variance analysis;
- competitor and market analysis;
- margin analysis;
- daily/weekly/monthly sales;
- covers served/seats turnover;
- average spend per table/head; and
- menu/bar mix.

2.4.1 Variance analysis

Budgets on their own are a useful tool for ensuring management focus on the proper planning of the business, but when compared with other management information they become an essential tool. By analysing the differences between budgeted and actual figures, known as variances, a manager can keep up to date with the changes in the trading conditions of his business so that business decisions can be made in a timely and effective manner.

Sales variances
The more specific the sales information available the more useful it will be to management. Therefore, food and drink sale should be allocated

different profit centres so that the performance of each centre can be closely monitored.

Sales variances can occur for a number of reasons. For instance, a negative sales variance could result from any of the following:

- a fall in sales volumes; or
- a fall in sales price; or
- a change in sales mix.

If detailed budgets have not been prepared, the reasons for a fall in sales value may not be apparent. For instance, prices may have been cut leading to an increase in demand for a particular menu item, albeit not enough to recover the reduced revenues from lower prices. If the sales budget cannot be broken down into its component parts it will not be possible to identify whether variances in sales value are due to a change in quantities sold, a change in price or a different sales mix.

Example

Sales volumes at Luigi's restaurant have consistently beaten budget for the first nine months of their financial year ended 30 June but in the first month of the final quarter the trend has reversed. Budgeted sales for the month were £40,000 but only £32,000 was achieved. Management is surprised but believes that some of the decline may be due to the weather being slightly below the seasonal average. On closer examination they find the following:

	No of covers	*Spend per head* £	£
Budgeted sales	1,000	40	40,000
Actual sales	914	35	31,990
Total adverse sales variance			8,010
Analysis of variance:			
Covers served variance	86	35	3,010
Spend per head variance	1,000	5	5,000
			8,010

The reasons for the fall in the spend per head can be analysed in more detail. It may result from lower prices, a tendency to purchase cheaper menu items or a propensity for customers to buy less, e.g., no starter. If the budget has been prepared in sufficient detail based on standard prices (and costs) it will be possible to pinpoint the exact reasons for the fall in average spend, which may be a combination of factors.

By analysing variances in this way the manager is able to identify the reasons for the unexpected adverse sales variances and may be able to take corrective action.

Gross profit and cost of sales variances
An increase or decrease in the gross profit margin may have a significant impact on the profitability of the business. The reasons for the change in margin may not be immediately obvious without undertaking variance analysis, for instance, margins may improve despite a fall in sales prices. An increase in margins may arise for one of the following reasons, or a combination of all of them:

- higher sales price;
- lower direct costs;
- change in the sales mix;
- improved recipe yields;
- reduced wastage.

Higher sales prices will directly impact on margins provided there is no compensating increase in direct costs and assuming the increased revenues are not offset by declining volumes.

Changes in direct costs may have been caused by a switch to a cheaper supplier, increased discounts, or price decreases negotiated with existing suppliers.

A change in the sales mix from low margin products to higher margin products will feed through to the gross profit achieved provided there is not a compensating fall in the quantities sold.

Improved recipe yields may result from more efficient food preparation or a better quality of food reducing wastage. Alternatively, changes in the recipe *per se* could provide higher yields.

Labour variance
Pubs and restaurants employ high numbers of staff. After direct food and drink costs, labour represents by far the largest single cost. When comparing actual to budget the variance analysis should take into account not only the rates of pay but also the productivity achieved.

Flexed budgets
In calculating cost variances, the budget should be flexed to take into account actual quantities sold. By so doing, that part of the cost variance which is dependent on the performance of the sales staff is eliminated. For instance, an increase in a restaurant's food costs due to higher volumes

sold than budgeted is not within the control of the chef, but higher costs due to variations in standard recipes or increased portion sizes are within the chef's control and he should be held responsible for any such changes. Flexing the budget ensures that responsibility for services is focused on the staff responsible for the costs concerned.

Use of budgets as a motivator
If it is intended to use a budget as a target to motivate staff members, it is important to involve those staff members in the budgeting process. By so doing it is more likely that the staff will feel that they are an integral part of the business and that they will work hard to achieve the budget which they have participated in setting.

The final responsibility for the budget should be taken by senior management. This will avoid the temptation for staff members to under-budget to provide themselves with easy targets. On the other hand, if budgets are set too high it will increase the temptation for staff to overstate results in order to meet targets, or the budget may be perceived by staff members as impossible to meet and will become demotivational. As a result rather than increase productivity the budget may have the opposite effect.

A properly prepared budget can be a valuable motivational tool provided its aims are clearly communicated to the relevant staff members.

2.4.2 Competitor and market analysis

Accurate financial information and proper budgeting procedures are important for the decision-making process. It is also necessary to have up-to-date information on competitors and an analysis of the current market. Comparing the level of sales, gross margins and overheads with those of competitors will help to highlight where, if at all, the business is under-performing. Care must be taken to ensure that the information being compared is consistent. This should be borne in mind when analysing competitors' statutory accounts.

Equally important will be a knowledge of the current market. If the restaurant manager or pub operator anticipates trends before his competitors he may open a competitive advantage which will be difficult for his rivals to close.

2.4.3 Margin analysis

As all businesses will seek to maximise gross profit, margins are a useful benchmark for assessing the relative performance of a business. Margin analysis can be used as:

(a) an indicator of changing trading conditions;

(b) a means of comparing similar businesses; and
(c) a means of identifying the least and most profitable stock lines or menu items.

Fluctuations in gross profit will be one of the first indicators of improving or deteriorating trading conditions. Where possible, it will also be useful to compare gross profit margins with those of local competitors or to compare results to an accepted industry average margin which may highlight areas where improvements could be made.

By carrying out margin analysis on a line-by-line basis the manager will be able to identify the most profitable products and develop a sales strategy accordingly. The object should be to maximise the gross profit, therefore it is important to isolate those products which are both fast moving and have a high margin then seek to maximise their sales.

Care should be taken in focusing on high margin stock alone as low margin products may make a greater total contribution to bottom line profit.

2.4.4 Daily/weekly/monthly sales

As a regular routine, a manager should review his outlet's takings on a daily basis. These statistics may provide an early warning signal of a decline in demand or an unexpected rise in demand. Either way the manager will be able to react by decreasing or increasing orders of food or drink while keeping stocks to the minimum needed to run the operation efficiently.

2.4.5 Covers served/seats turnover

The number of covers a restaurant is able to serve will dictate its capacity and therefore its sales volume. The manager of a restaurant should keep accurate records of covers served so that trends can be analysed and comparisons made with other local restaurants/pubs. By dividing the covers served by the total seating capacity the manager can ascertain the seat turnover. Some of the more expensive restaurants may only serve one sitting whereas others will plan on several sittings in any one session. The number of courses served and the seat turnover will provide the manager with a useful indication of the throughput of people and therefore the volume of business.

2.4.6 Average spend per table/head

Dividing an outlet's total revenue by the covers served during a particular period gives the average spend per head. Using seat turnover and average spend per head as complimentary measures of throughput and volume allows the restaurateur to monitor the fluctuations in trading. The same performance measurements can be used in a pub or restaurant but for bar sales the approach has to be less scientific. A pub manager will instinctively know whether he is having a good session, however, he is unlikely to know how many people visit his pub during that session. At the end of the session his analysis will be based on the total revenue taken and the volume of drink sold.

2.4.7 Menu/bar mix

In any given menu there will be differences between the margins achieved on different dishes. The number of each dish sold during a session will give a general indication of the relative profitability of the session. The same is also true of wet sales, for example, margins on soft drinks such as orange squash are higher than the margins on beer.

2.5 What decision-making strategies/tools are available?

Variance analysis and other performance measures provide the catalyst for business decisions. In the following paragraphs we consider some of the strategies which are available to the pub or restaurant manager to improve the performance of the business.

2.5.1 Pricing strategy

It is important that the restaurateur or pub manager establishes a coherent pricing strategy. The strategy should be formal but not inflexible so that account can be taken of specific circumstances.

The most common form of pricing strategy within the restaurant and pub trade is cost-plus pricing. In its purest form this means adding a margin to the standard cost of a product. If a mark-up of 60 per cent is required, for example, then the sales price would be 160 per cent of the cost price. Assuming a cost of £1.00, the selling price would be £1.60 and the gross profit £0.60. This represents a gross profit margin of 37.5 per cent measured by dividing the sales price by the gross profit (0.60/1.60 × 100%). A more typical gross profit margin for the pub trade, of say 60 per cent, could be achieved if a mark-up of 150 per cent were made, i.e., a drink costing £1.00 is sold for £2.50 giving a gross profit of £1.50. The gross profit margin is again calculated by dividing the gross profit by the sales price (1.50/2.50 × 100%).

Whilst this is a useful benchmark it would be dangerous to adhere to this strategy rigidly without taking into account such other factors as:

- price elasticity;

- prices charged by the competition; and
- the beneficial effects of loss-leaders or other promotions.

The elasticity of a product is the measurement of how sales are affected by a change in price. The more price-elastic a product the greater the effect on demand of a change in price. Conversely, a product which is price-inelastic will not be significantly affected by a change in price. Empirical evidence shows that products which were once thought of as inelastic are becoming more elastic. Inevitably, there will be some recipes and some drinks which are more price inelastic than others making it ever more important that the pricing strategy is appropriate. For instance, a menu may contain a number of high cost main course items with some lower cost side orders. A small increase in the price of a fish dish may be enough to dissuade customers from ordering it in favour of cheaper alternatives on the menu. However, a higher percentage increase in the cost of a side order may go relatively unnoticed and have little effect on its demand.

In setting a price, due consideration will need to be given to the amounts charged for the same or similar products by the competition. The level of influence that a competitor's price should have over prices charged by the manager or restaurateur will depend on the degree of differentiation between the products as well as the immediate location of the competitor in comparison to the catchment area served by the outlet concerned.

It may also be appropriate to sell a product at or around cost for promotional purposes or as a loss-leader. Such a strategy can be very effective if it achieves its objectives of bringing people through the door. Care should be taken in undertaking any promotion to ensure that the expected increase in demand which will accrue from the promotion is sufficient to outweigh the cost of the promotion itself. For this purpose, systems should be set up to identify as accurately as possible the additional sales which result from the promotion.

Whatever the strategy adopted the pricing structure must be robust enough to allow for some increase in supplier costs. It is bad customer relations to change menu prices for each incremental increase in food costs.

2.5.2 Volume forecasting

It will not always be possible to pass on cost increases to the customer, therefore, the control of costs is paramount to the effective running of the business. In order to ensure costs are kept to a minimum the restaurateur will need to estimate the demand for a particular product. This is of most significance for dry sales. If a restaurateur or pub manager is unable to predict with a reasonable degree of accuracy the level of demand for specific menu items there is the danger that supplies will be over or under-ordered. Over-orders will lead to wastage, particularly where fresh foods are concerned and under-orders will lead to customer dissatisfaction and ultimately loss of business.

Volume forecasting is particularly important where the raw materials are perishable. The more accurate the estimate of sales of menu items containing perishable food the less waste there will be. Additionally, if the total number of covers is accurately estimated, the scheduling of staff for the preparation of the food is easier with the result that idle time is minimised. By the same token the number of waiting staff can be scheduled according to the level of business expected.

The restaurateur should base forecast volumes on sales in recent weeks and use personal experience to allow for expected seasonal or other fluctuations.

By compiling information on the eating habits of its customers, a restaurant or pub will be able to form a database of up-to-date sales information which will not only assist with volume forecasting but will also have other decision-making applications. The sort of information that can be compiled includes:

- sales of individual menu items;
- customers that drink wine with their meal or other alcoholic beverage;
- customers that take all three courses;
- customer profiles;
- elasticity of demand for particular items; and
- the levels of business per session and during sessions.

Additional information can be obtained by holding a monthly prize draw, the winner being selected, for example, from a pool of business cards deposited by customers. Many outlets use the information to mailshot customers with news of special promotions.

The advantages of volume forecasting for wet sales are not quite so clear-cut. Whereas restaurants will invariably use perishable fresh foods on a daily basis, most drinks have a fairly long shelf-life. Beer is an exception but an experienced pub manager will be able to predict with a certain amount of accuracy the level of beer sales in the short term subject to unexpected weather changes.

2.5.3 Change of suppliers

Raw materials are a major part of any pub or restaurant business. Once the quantities required are established according to the expected level of demand, the order can be actioned. However, there is little point in establishing controls to limit the wastage of food if there are no controls over its purchase. To manage the cost properly the restaurateur and publican will need to ensure that there are controls at each stage of the purchasing cycle. There will be important decisions to make regarding who should supply the raw materials, whether to buy in bulk or on a 'just-in-time' basis, whether to have a regular contract or buy on an ad hoc basis and the standard of quality required to make the product both marketable and cost-effective.

Many restaurateurs allow their chef to purchase fresh food. The chef's first priority will be to ensure that food is of good quality. Care should be taken to make sure that economy is not sacrificed in an effort to improve the standard and reputation of the food unless the increased costs can be recovered through higher sales prices. Where the chef is given the responsibility for buying fresh food he should also be made responsible for the relevant budget and made to explain variances where they occur.

Where supplies are purchased by contract they should be put out to tender regularly to ensure competitive prices. However, in the pub trade it is common for managers to purchase sundry items from cash and carry businesses or supermarkets and remain loyal to that one supplier. In many cases this is a reasonable compromise.

If food is purchased by contract, a full specification of what is required should be given and items checked for quality at the delivery stage. Subsequently, care should be taken to ensure that items are immediately moved into appropriate storage.

2.5.4 Staff scheduling

After raw materials, labour costs will be the most significant part of a restaurant or pub's costs. It is important, therefore, that the productivity of the staff is maximised. The restaurateur or pub manager should seek to match the staff numbers with the level of demand.

The labour costs as a proportion of turnover should be kept to a minimum. As a general rule of thumb, a publican should expect labour costs to be around 20 per cent of turnover and a restaurateur can expect costs to be in the range of 20–40 per cent of turnover. The precise labour costs as a proportion of turnover will depend on the type of establishment, for example, a restaurant pub will inevitably have higher wage costs than one which offers no food. If the percentage of labour costs as a percentage of turnover increases, it may indicate a fall in staff productivity. On a day-to-day level, costs can be monitored by using timesheets completed by each member of staff indicating the number of standard hours they have undertaken and overtime. These statistics can be compared with the number of covers they have served during the period. If these measures are used to assess an individual's performance then factors such as the overall level of demand must be taken into account. A lower than normal productivity rate may indicate a fall in demand rather than a decrease in the efficiency of an individual member of staff. Comparing each member of staff may give a more accurate assessment although, again, it should be remembered that productivity may be a function of the customers assigned to each one.

For a pub manager, a direct comparison is more straightforward as in theory each member of staff has an equal chance of serving each customer. The extraction of the relevant information to make this comparison will be more difficult without an EPOS system although this problem can be overcome by allocating staff to individual tills which are reconciled at the end of each shift. In analysing the information the manager should not discount the importance of glass collection to customer service. So care should be taken in interpreting the information.

For the restaurateur, and for the pub manager who offers a food service, the labour costs in preparing food will also be significant. In most cases food is prepared freshly on the premises due to the perishable nature of the raw materials. Therefore, staff have to be available for each shift as there may be only limited opportunities for preparing food in advance. The benefits of accurate volume forecasting to keep idle time to a minimum cannot be overemphasised.

In multiple site operations where it is possible to move staff between locations, significant savings can be made. The more flexible the staff both in geographical terms and in the hours they are prepared to work the more likely it is that labour can be used efficiently. The pub operator or restaurateur will need to assess whether the likely higher labour rates required to achieve this flexibility are outweighed by the increased level of productivity.

2.5.5 Menu options

We have discussed the need to keep costs to a minimum. Ensuring that the optimum level of raw materials is purchased and wastage is kept as low as possible are primary objectives based on the menu offered and the forecast volumes. Carefully choosing the items on the menu will help to meet these objectives.

The menu offered will be dictated to a degree by the type of restaurant. For example, a restaurant offering traditional English food may be expected to serve steak and kidney pie irrespective of the availability of the raw materials. In these circumstances, if the raw material prices increase substantially, it is unlikely that the restaurateur will be able to pass the whole increase on to his customers. However, the wider the choice offered to customers, the more food that has to be bought to meet potential demand and the greater the potential for wastage. Therefore, it is good business sense to limit the number of items on a menu and where possible those choices should be limited to dishes containing key ingredients. To give variety, recipes can be changed without altering the key ingredients. Limiting the number of dishes available has proved a successful formula for 'Clarke's' in Kensington, where the customer is limited to a single dish per course each day but attracted by the reputation for outstanding food.

2.5.6 Standard recipes

Standard recipes and standard portion sizes can also provide the restaurateur with greater control over costs. Recipes can be standardised by a system of trial and error to find the ingredients which provide the highest yield while maintaining the quality of the dish. Depending on the size of restaurant each dish can be checked by the chef prior to delivery by the waiter to ensure uniformity of portion sizes.

2.5.7 Space utilisation

Traditionally, income from pubs and restaurants has been limited to the earnings from lunchtime and evening sessions. With the constant pressure on achieving adequate returns it is becoming more common to measure success in terms of income or profit per square foot. Any method of increasing profit by encouraging custom outside the traditional pub or restaurant hours is therefore worthy of consideration.

Lighting is an important feature in any outlet. Carefully installed, it can enable a publican to change the atmosphere of an outlet from a café to a pub to a nightclub, offering obvious benefits in terms of space utilisation. Lighting is not the only important factor, the size of the outlet and the fittings installed will also be important; paying attention to the design details during construction of a new outlet is critical.

2.5.8 Repositioning the outlet in the marketplace

In some extreme cases it may be possible to change the target market for a restaurant or pub. An outlet which is failing to cover its overheads may be aimed at the wrong customer. Factors such as the type and level of competition for a particular target market should be researched. With a greater tendency for themed or branded outlets there is a higher risk that the concept will become tired and demand will fall off as fashion changes. Whatever the reason it may be possible to refocus the outlet to attract different customers or to encourage the original customers to return. Such a move should only be made with extreme caution as a drop in demand and declining profitability may be a function of a more fundamental change in the demographics of the location, e.g., the relocation of a major business in the area affecting both the lunchtime and evening trade. Conversely, the opening of a major new entertainment complex or shopping mall may substantially increase the passing trade.

2.5.9 Outsourcing the catering

With the growth in tendency towards restaurants in pubs the importance of dry sales to the pub trade is increasing. The growth in popularity has arisen as a result of the move towards more family-oriented pubs with a lighter, airier feel. In order to tap into this market, it is important to provide good quality food at a reasonable price. Improving the eating facilities may also result in increased wet sales by attracting new custom.

Setting up a properly staffed, well-managed food operation can be costly and involve additional administrative duties for the manager. By outsourcing to a private catering company a pub may be able to provide the same service without the additional administration costs of setting up an in-house operation. It will also give the manager greater flexibility should sales be disappointing. The degree of autonomy given to the contracted catering company will depend on the agreement reached. The alternatives are:

(a) the catering company rents the kitchen space in the outlet paying separately for utilities but has complete control over the restaurant operation enjoying all the profits and suffering any losses; or
(b) the catering company is employed on a fee basis but again has complete control over the restaurant operation although the profits or losses are taken by the pub operatives.

To ensure that the pub gains maximum benefit from the success of the restaurant the fixed fee should be based on a percentage of turnover or profit. Equally, where the catering company is being charged for rent and utilities it may be possible to base the rent on the level of turnover or profits achieved so that the pub receives some of the benefits of the restaurant's success.

In both these scenarios the catering company assumes the risk for wastage, scheduling of staff, volume forecasting, etc. so that the pub manager is left to concentrate on running the pub operation. In a multiple outlet operation it may be more beneficial for the company to appoint a consultant to oversee the catering in each of the outlets.

2.6 When should decisions be taken and implemented?

Achieving optimum sales is half the battle, however, managing the cost of the business is just as important to achieving high profitability. The raw material and labour costs can only be effectively managed if there are proper procedures in place for forecasting demand. Although a comprehensive review of the overall operations can be effectively undertaken on a monthly basis by assessing management information, it is vital to the business that sales figures are reviewed on a daily basis and appropriately analysed. By so doing it should be possible to predict with a reasonable accuracy the level of sales on a product-by-product basis, e.g., beer sales or individual items on a menu. Using this information the appropriate numbers of staff can be scheduled for each session, orders can be adjusted to reflect the variations in demand and the food preparation managed to take into account the likely levels of demand for each of the items on the menu.

The more accurate, up-to-date and useful the information, the more likely that an outlet will be able to minimise losses due to unexpected falls in demand or take advantage of opportunities due to unusually buoyant trade.

Volume forecasting is of prime importance on a day-to-day basis. However, in the longer term using sales analyses any trends in demand will become more obvious. The manager that recognises these changes and adapts accordingly will gain a competitive advantage over his rivals. In so doing, he may gain market share which others may find difficult to recover subsequently.

Managers should be prepared to act quickly but not impetuously. A snap decision could result in changes brought about by one-off blips in demand. However, a manager that reacts too slowly may lose market share to his competitors or suffer unnecessary losses. In particular, the timing of decisions will depend on the availability of information, the stability of the market and the experience of the manager.

2.7 Summary

In order to run a profitable pub or restaurant business it will not only be necessary to generate a high level of sales but also to keep control over costs. The level of sales achieved will depend on a number of factors:

(a) the type of outlet and its suitability for the demographics of the area;
(b) the ambience created within the pub or restaurant both in terms of decoration and the friendliness and efficiency of the staff;

(c) market conditions generally; and
(d) the level of competition.

The decisions regarding the type of establishment, the decoration and the target customers are vital to the performance of the business and due care should be taken before they are finalised. Changing all these factors after the event is likely to be prohibitively expensive. The pub or restaurant manager will have more of an ongoing role creating the right ambience within the confines of the furnishings of the pub or restaurant he is running. When taking over an existing site, proper research should be undertaken to ensure that the local market conditions are understood. It is dangerous to ignore the underlying business which may have been built up over a long period of time and could be crucial to the initial cash flow. In any outlet the training and ability of staff is of prime importance. The customer is now demanding more, he is no longer satisfied simply with buying a drink, he expects to find well-mannered and friendly staff, combined with pleasant surroundings. It is up to the manager to ensure that the customer's demands are met.

Chapter 3 – Measuring success

3.1 Introduction

This chapter provides a brief outline of some of the methods that are available to assess the effectiveness of pub or restaurant operations and the techniques that can be used to make investment decisions.

3.2 How effective is the operation?

In general a business may be considered to be effective if it is profitable and cash flow positive. More specifically, measures of a business's effectiveness include:

(a) *Profitability*. How much profit before and after tax has the operation made?
(b) *Return on shareholders' funds*. A measure of the profitability of a company in relation to the amount the owners/shareholders have invested in the business.
(c) *Return on capital employed*. A measure of the return achieved from the assets employed in the business.
(d) *Market share*. Is the target to be the biggest in the area, country or the world?

Which of these measures is appropriate will depend to some extent on the sort of operation.

3.2.1 Profitability

The profitability of a pub or restaurant provides a useful measure of an operation's success or failure, however, it becomes more useful as a tool if it can be compared with the results of similar operations. A meaningful comparison can only be made if there is consistency of approach in preparing profit and loss accounts between different operations. Listed below are some of the items which may lead to inconsistencies in approach and so may require adjustment. Net profit may be stated after charging:

- depreciation;
- management charges/directors' bonuses;
- exceptional expenditure, for example fire damage;
- interest on short and long-term loans; and
- cost of raw materials – drinks and food.

Depreciation

The depreciation charges will depend on the age of the properties and other fixed assets concerned, and on the depreciation policy adopted. Any inconsistencies between different operations may have a significant impact on the charge recorded in the profit and loss account. Consider the following example.

> ***Example***
>
> Business A has 10 restaurants that were built some 15 years ago and cost £1 million. The company policy is to depreciate all property by 2% per annum. The depreciation charge in the current year is £20,000.
>
> Business B has 10 properties that were built some 15 years ago and cost £1 million. The company revalued all property five years ago at £1.4 million and is now depreciating the revalued amounts over the remaining 40 years. The depreciation charge for the current year is £35,000.
>
> Assuming the same turnover and the same level of efficiency then a review of the financial statements would show a significant difference, all because of the effects of the revaluation and the depreciation policy adopted.

Management charges

Different companies may have different method of charging management costs to subsidiary companies. For instance, a management charge may be a means of moving profit from one company to another and may not represent a recharge of costs incurred or a genuine charge for services provided.

Directors' bonuses

Dependent on the policy of the business there may be a variety of ways of arriving at the remuneration package for the senior management of a company. In an owner-managed business paying bonuses could be a more efficient way of removing profit from the business than paying dividends. This would distort a comparison with a similar business which adopted different policies.

Exceptional expenditure

While accounting standards attempt to ensure consistency in the way unusual expenditure is disclosed in the accounts, it may be necessary to take into consideration any unusual items in order to make meaningful comparisons between accounts.

Interest charges

The interest charge will depend on the amount borrowed to fund the business. In a small business the owner may have sunk life savings into the operation and borrowed nothing while another may have borrowed most of the money to fund the operation. The first should expect to recover the cost of the investment in terms of lost interest and still make a profit, the second is actually allowing for this cost in arriving at the profit figure.

Cost of raw materials
At first sight, a manager would expect costs to be comparable, however, if a comparison is to be made between the accounts of an owner-managed pub and the accounts of a chain of pubs owned by one of the big breweries, it is necessary to consider the transfer pricing policy adopted. An owner-managed operation pays what it is charged by the brewery. A chain of pubs owned by a brewery may be charged more or less for the drinks supplied by the brewery based on where the overall group would wish to see a profit. While accounting standards attempt to eliminate these problems they still exist. For instance, in the mid-1990s one major brewery chain reassessed its transfer pricing policy, adding some 10 per cent to the profit of the managed estate division.

To make meaningful comparisons a manager will need to review the profit and loss account of the businesses and adjust the profit for any inconsistencies of approach. Once this has been done, the manager will be able to review the relative profitability of the businesses and consider areas in which he could make improvements.

3.2.2 Return on shareholders' funds

An operation's effectiveness can be measured by comparing the profit after tax with the amount of money that has been directly invested into the business.

Comparing total shareholders' funds as shown by the balance sheet with the profit as shown in the profit and loss account provides a percentage return. The result can be used to compare similar operations and, therefore, as a basis for deciding whether the management of the business is using the shareholders' funds to best advantage.

This method of assessment is only effective when considering operations where it is comparatively easy for the shareholder/investor to realise their investment in the business. An investor who is not satisfied with the return can transfer his investment into a business or project offering a higher return.

$$\text{Return on shareholders' funds} = \frac{\text{profit after tax}}{\text{shareholders' funds}} \times 100\%$$

3.2.3 Return on capital employed (ROCE)

ROCE is net operating profit expressed as a percentage of capital employed and gives an indication of how hard the assets are working for the business. To arrive at net operating profit it is necessary to adjust the disclosed profit figure for items which distort the ongoing profitability of the operation. The capital employed must then be clearly defined and identified.

Capital employed is usually interpreted in simple terms to mean those items described on the balance sheet as fixed assets and current assets. Fixed assets will include not only the bricks and mortar of the pub or restaurant but also all the furniture and fittings, and this is often a very large proportion of the total value of the operation. The expression 'current assets' would include such items as:

- stock;
- debtors; and
- cash.

Each of these areas is discussed in detail in Chapter 2 on financial management. The ROCE is calculated as:

$$\frac{\text{Operating profit}}{\text{(Fixed assets \& current assets)}} \times 100\%$$

Using ROCE, management will be able to assess whether the operation is making an adequate return on the assets of the business or if improvements could be made to increase the return. An increase in profits due to the opening of a new outlet may not tell the full story. The ROCE may be lower than for other outlets in the group which may be indicative of teething problems. In this situation management should monitor the position regularly. Once the outlet has reached a 'normal' trading pattern the ROCE should be more in line with the rest of the group, any material differences should be investigated and appropriate action taken if necessary.

However, this measure is similar to the ones based exclusively on profit, in that it is influenced by how the figures in the financial statements have been arrived at and thus what appears in the equation. These are considered in more detail below.

Current assets

The items making up this figure are not too contentious in terms of value, but need to be considered so that a consistent interpretation is arrived at.

Cash

The pub and restaurant trades are traditionally cash or near cash businesses and as such it is comparatively easy to establish the cash figure.

Debtors

In general, the only debtors are likely to be credit card payments, since only those organisations with a significant 'function' business are likely to allow debtors. Even if the business under review has a significant amount of its turnover derived from functions, the debtors figure published in the accounts is likely to be fairly insignificant when compared to other assets.

Stock

The stock of food for restaurants, and beer and spirits for pubs, should be comparatively small in relation to turnover since these items have, in general, a fairly short shelf-life and therefore are unlikely to represent much more than a few days' sales.

Stocks of wines are likely to present more problems. Stock is valued for accounting purposes at the lower of cost or net realisable value, but poor storage methods or even something as fickle as a thunderstorm could render the contents of a wine cellar worthless. In any event the value of a wine cellar will be more difficult to assess where a high proportion of fine wines are held. In general, however, the valuation of stocks, particularly where stock checks are carried out by independent stocktakers, should be straightforward. So, for ROCE purposes it is practical to assume that current assets can be extracted directly from the accounts.

Fixed assets

Whole books have been written on the problems associated with the valuation of fixed assets, which is of particular concern to the pub and restaurant trade. However, it is appropriate that this matter is reviewed, as the policy adopted will have a significant effect on the ROCE reported. The two principal problems concern:

- age of an asset; and
- any revaluation of an asset.

Age of asset

In comparing one group of pubs or restaurants with another, the length of time each has owned its properties is important. If the pubs or restaurants have been owned by the operation since, say, 1900, the cost value will be significantly lower than outlets bought in 1988, for example. Not only will the cost be lower but the net book value will also be lower. The net book value is the amount disclosed in the accounts after allowing for depreciation. Freehold/long leasehold property is normally depreciated at 2 per cent per annum so properties acquired in 1900 will only reflect the cost of land. The two sets of accounts could show substantially different net book values for their estates (provided neither has revalued their assets, see below) which would distort the relative ROCE calculations and render them non-comparable.

A review of accounting policies will be necessary to take into account such matters as the way that fixtures and fittings are accounted for and the depreciation policy adopted for freehold properties.

Revaluation
The problems described above can be further aggravated by policies in relation to revaluation of land and buildings. To put different operations on a similar footing each would have to use the same basis for revaluing their estates.

Within the pub sector this has resulted in widely disparate and non-comparable ROCE calculations.

It is even more difficult to obtain meaningful comparisons of ROCE in the restaurant sector since the valuation of restaurants is fraught with difficulties. Whilst it may be possible to revalue land and buildings on the basis of changes in the property index, the effect is to produce 'a new set of figures' which takes no account of such matters as:

- a change in status of the site being revalued due to population movement;
- a change in value due to other local developments; or
- any other unforeseen matters.

Therefore, the best policy may be to look at the organisation in relation to trends in profitability relative to similar businesses and their trends. Again, to ensure consistency of approach any items which distort the ongoing profitability of the business should be adjusted for.

3.2.4 Market share

Market share is often seen as a measure of the relative success of an operation. Increased market share and therefore size can lead to economies of scale and ultimately to higher margins. However, care should be taken to ensure that the reasons for aspiring to increased market share are properly thought out, as the costs of meeting the target may outweigh the advantages associated with a larger slice of the market.

3.2.5 Other measures of efficiency

Included at Appendix 2 is a list of other ratios that can be used to assess an organisation's profitability and effectiveness. It also includes an explanation of the ratios concerned.

3.3 Investment decisions

This section looks at the factors that should be considered in making investment decisions within the pub or restaurant sector and examines the tools that are available to assist with the decision.

The easiest way to follow this sort of problem is to consider an example.

Assume that a business is considering a significant investment to add a function room alongside the main restaurant. The steps that should be considered are:

- market research;
- cost estimate; and
- expected net revenues.

Market research
The organisation should have considered the need for such a facility at the particular location. This market research may be in the form of commissioned research by a specialist agency or by the internal department of the organisation.

The research should take account not only of existing demand but also of future expected demand which may arise as a result, for instance, of a new urban development or new industrial development.

Cost estimate
When costing a major project there should be evidence that all aspects have been fully researched and that all areas have been included, not just the obvious costs such as materials and labour.

The sort of items that are easily forgotten and yet are significant costs within a new development might include:

- preparation of architect's plans;
- submission costs for planning permission;
- disruption of existing trade;
- costs of hiring or recruiting extra labour to run the new facility;
- advertising costs to launch the facility including costs of launch events, etc.

Not only do these and other costs need to be identified but some effort should be made to identify when the costs will arise so that appropriate financing can be arranged.

Expected revenues
When estimating expected revenues once the new facility has opened, it is important to estimate when the future revenues will arise, thus enabling a forecast of future cash flows to be prepared and financing arrangements made to cover any anticipated shortfall.

We consider below some of the methods which can be used to assess the viability of a project or investment decision.

3.3.1 Return on capital employed

Consider the following example.

Example

Fagan's restaurant has been operating for six years on the edge of a small urban development. Market research has shown that with the proposed development of a new industrial park there will be a need for meeting rooms for day conferences and training events. Additionally, there is a shortage of suitable venues for evening dinner dances and wedding receptions in the area. Therefore, business on Friday and Saturday nights could also be served by a new facility.

Capital expenditure:	£
Architects' fees and associated costs	10,000
Building costs	450,000
Fitting-out costs	40,000
	500,000

It is estimated that construction will take approximately four months and that fitting-out will take a further two months

Lost revenue during the construction phase is estimated at £5,000 per month which results in a total loss of £20,000. Additional overheads will be incurred from the new rooms, amounting to £7,000 per month excluding any allowance for depreciation.

Monthly revenue estimates:

Revenue sources	*Revenue per month*	*Operating profit percentage*	*Estimated operating profit*	*Total per half year*
	£	%	£	£
Room hire	3,000	85	2,550	
Day delegate	8,000	35	2,800	
Dinner dance	20,000	35	7,000	
Weddings	12,000	40	4,800	
			17,150	
			× 6	102,900

It is estimated that in the first full 12 months of trading (i.e., months 7–18 from the date that construction began) only 50% of revenues will be achieved and in the second year (months 19–30) 80%. Thereafter (month 31 onwards), 100% of revenues are achieved. Therefore, it is only two and a half years after capital expenditure commenced that the revenue from the investment reaches its full potential.

Summarised profit forecast:

		Six-monthly profit £	*Estimated annual profit* £	*Cumulative profit* £
Year 1	Months 1–6	(20,000)		
	Months 7–12	9,450[1]	(10,550)	(10,550)
Year 2	Months 13–18	9,450		
	Months 19–24	40,320[2]	49,770	39,220
Year 3	Months 25–30	40,320		
	Months 31–36	60,900[3]	101,220	140,440
Year 4	Months 37–42	60,900		
	Months 43–48	60,900	121,800	262,240
Year 5	Months 49–54	60,900		
	Months 55–60	60,900	121,800	384,040

Monthly profit is arrived at as follows:

[1] ((50% × 17,150) – 7,000) × 6 = £9,450
[2] ((80% × 17,150) – 7,000) × 6 = £40,320
[3] ((100% × 17,150) – 7,000) × 6 = £60,900

Based on the budgets, the expected average annual ROCE by the end of the fifth year will be:

$$\frac{384{,}040}{500{,}000} \div 5 = 15.4\%$$

The problems with this as a method of project appraisal are:

(a) no account has been taken of the financing for the project;
(b) no account has been taken of providing for equipment replacement; and
(c) no account has been taken of the timing of the flows of money.

3.3.2 Payback method

This involves calculating how long it would take to return all the capital to the investors. In the above example (at **3.3.1**) we can see that the investment would be fully 'repaid' in the sixth year when the cumulative profit exceeds the £500,000 cost of investment. This is an excellent way of assessing what may be considered to be a risky project because it focuses the mind on how long the capital is at risk.

3.3.3 Discounted cash flow (DCF) method

This is a method of project appraisal that takes account of the future value of funds. The point can be illustrated by way of example. If £100 was invested in a safe investment at the beginning of a year we would expect it to be worth, say, £108 at the end of the year. The reverse of this is that £100 received at the end of the year is the equivalent of receiving, say, £93 now. We call the factor which we used to calculate 'future values' the discount factor and it is calculated by using the following formula:

Discount factor = $1/(1+i)^n$
Where i = the discount rate
n = the number of years from the initial investment.

For the example given above, assuming a discount rate of 11.9 per cent and assuming the profits are surplus funds, the discounted cash flow would be as follows.

Example

	Cash flow £	*Discount factor* £	*Present value* £
Capital investment net of inflows	(500,000)	1.000	(500,000)
Year 1 outflow	(10,550)	0.894	(9,432)
Year 2 inflow	49,770	0.799	39,766
Year 3 inflow	101,220	0.714	72,271
Year 4 inflow	121,800	0.638	77,708
Year 5 inflow	121,800	0.570	69,426
Year 6 inflow	121,800	0.509	61,996
Year 7 inflow	121,800	0.455	55,419
Year 8 inflow	121,800	0.407	49,573
Year 9 inflow	121,800	0.364	44,335
Year 10 inflow	121,800	0.325	39,585
Net present value			647

The viability of the project is dependent on it providing a positive net present value over the period of assessment set by management. In this example, a 10-year period has been assumed. We could assess the new facility over a longer period but 10 years would seem to be reasonable on the basis that economic cycles may span up to 10 years.

In this case, based on a discount rate of 11.9 % there is a positive return on the investment. Management would now need to consider if this was an adequate return in the current economic environment.

Having decided that the project is viable based on the assumptions made it is important to ensure that these assumptions remain valid. Therefore, every effort should be made to complete the project on time and within budget.

3.4 Project management

Unless the organisation has extensive experience of project management it may be appropriate to assign this task to a specialist, such as the architect responsible for the original plans who should have experience of managing similar projects.

There are, however, a number of factors that should be considered by management which are discussed below.

3.4.1 Time penalties

The contractor should be made aware of the time constraints. Usually, a 'liquidated damages' clause is built into the contract penalising the contractor should deadlines not be met.

3.4.2 Monitoring

Architects' certificates should be obtained at regular stages of the contract in order to validate that the work completed to date is of a satisfactory standard.

3.4.3 Fitting out

The project leader needs to ensure that all fixtures and fittings and other equipment arrive on time and in good condition so that delays are not encountered elsewhere because of quality control problems. A critical path analysis should be tabled by the contracts manager and discussed with the pub or restaurant manager to ensure that potential delays are anticipated and avoided where possible.

3.4.4 Contingencies

A contingency period needs to be allowed for in the project to avoid the embarrassment and associated costs of a delayed launch. Any such delays could have a significant impact on the first impressions that customers form.

3.4.5 Cost monitoring

All costs associated with the project should be continually monitored and compared against budget so that decisions can be taken quickly to rectify any overruns.

3.4.6 Staff training

Allow for time to train staff before the outlet is officially opened to ensure that customers receive the service they expect.

3.4.7 Health warning

Try and avoid making changes during the project. These are always the ones that cost the most money. If a contractor is running up against cost problems they may be inclined to recover their overruns by charging exorbitantly for changes to the specification that are requested during the contract.

3.5 Summary

There are two key areas to consider in monitoring the effectiveness of a chain of pubs and restaurants. Firstly, is an operation making adequate returns and, secondly, are new investment decisions taken after proper consideration? In this chapter we have focused on whether the assets of the business are being used and managed in the most effective way. However, there are many other considerations to take into account, for example, a manager should not ignore his most important assets, namely the staff he employs. He should review the operation's procedures for training and developing staff and should ensure that appropriate monitoring of their performance is undertaken. This part of the leisure industry is particularly dependent on the level of service provided to the customer.

It should be remembered that there are other methods to assess the success of a business. Sales per square foot, a common performance indicator in the retail sector, is becoming a popular method of comparing different outlets in the pub sector.

Likewise, in making investment decisions, different methods of appraising a project may be appropriate in different circumstances. This chapter has touched on this subject briefly but it is only intended to be an introduction to investment appraisal. Over time managers should develop their own methods depending on the individual circumstances of the operation concerned.

Chapter 4 – Information systems

4.1 Why have a computer system?

The expression 'pubs and restaurants' covers a wide range of businesses, ranging from the small wayside 'Ye Olde' pub with limited bar food to a large top-flight restaurant. As a consequence, the considerations for deciding on a computer system are very different. The trend towards computerisation is increasing at a very fast rate in all fields of the leisure business. It follows that owners and managers of all establishments must:

(a) be aware of and keep up to date with information technology developments;
(b) maintain an open mind on the practical applications of information systems (IS) in pubs and restaurants; and
(c) evaluate whether and how computerisation can help achieve business objectives.

Surprisingly, a recent survey indicated that 47 per cent of pubs and restaurants do not yet have any sophisticated computerised equipment. Whether you are operating a pub or a restaurant, the use of IS can be divided broadly into EPOS and food and beverage management systems.

There is a lot of jargon associated with information technology. Appendix 3 includes a glossary of the most common terms.

4.1.1 Electronic point of sale (EPOS)

EPOS systems are rapidly replacing older style cash tills in bars and restaurants. Easy to use and attractive in design, the degree of sophistication depends on the needs of the organisation and, of course, the available budget.

Designed for fast food restaurants where speed is paramount, touch screen technology has dramatically reduced staff training time and ordering errors.

As the EPOS is at the heart of all food and beverage operations, it is important to understand the benefits of such systems. With an increasingly large choice of products to sell to customers, it is important to deliver the product quickly and correctly priced.

To speed up the ordering process, orders can be printed remotely either in the kitchen or in a dispense bar, so helping to speed up the service to the customer. Hand-held terminals that duplicate the EPOS terminals are also available from some suppliers. This means that waiters spend more time in the restaurant with guests, instead of having to go to and from the kitchen and bar to place orders. The screen displays the customer choice in the form of an order which is entered through one button entry keys, making the system very simple to use, whilst overcoming the problem of illegible handwritten notes.

Listed below are some modules and functions not normally associated with traditional point of sale:

(a) Credit card authorisation – with people carrying less cash these days, taking and authorising credit cards is becoming standard.
(b) Smart card customer loyalty schemes – tracks promotions for marketing statistics.
(c) Interactive dispense monitoring – tracks drinks, both draught beers and optics, that are not paid for.
(d) Kitchen management screens – kitchen monitor touch screen showing total orders in progress.
(e) Reservation/waitlist system – could replace the old manual diary. The system maintains a waiting list with the customer's name, the number of guests in their party and their smoking preference. The system is also used to keep track of reservations. Overdue reservations are brought to the attention of the management, with the option to either cancel or extend them.
(f) Database management – easier access to and faster delivery of information.
(g) Networking – having the system installed on a network gives you greater flexibility and reliability.
(h) Training – on screen help and prompting reduces training time and decreases operator error.
(i) Designer screens – the system-generated screen formatting automatically reconfigures the touch screen keypad when you add an item into the EPOS.
(j) Interactive EPOS/PC – allows the user to switch from the EPOS mode to PC applications.
(k) Instant online reports – allows a manager to print any control reports up to the minute.

4.1.2 Food and beverage management systems

A successful operator is one who can control his costs. There are a number of management systems available such as:

- stock control;
- recipe costing;
- purchasing;

- menu planning;
- production planning;
- accounts payable;
- time costing and rosters.

To benefit the manager, the systems must either be integrated as one system or have a two-way interface between the EPOS and the management control system. As an example, when items are recorded as sold on the EPOS the information is sent automatically to the stock control system, deducting the item from the stock. Products are recorded by actual delivery size, enabling the stock re-ordering system to prompt when minimum stock levels have been reached. Prices that are entered in a recipe control system are transferred to the EPOS to update automatically the prices at the tills, eliminating the time-consuming task of manually reprogramming each till when prices change.

Whatever the size of the organisation, somebody has to decide on staffing requirements and see that these are met. It is a key function. IT facilities cannot do this for you but they can certainly help to make life easier. With very little effort staffing schedules can be produced, staff records maintained, timesheets recorded. The results are simply transferred to a payroll system. Since we are talking about the lifeblood of any pub or restaurant – 'people' – it pays to formalise the procedure and see that it is followed. Appraisals should form part of any staff monitoring system.

Manual ledgers are out, computer records are in. Anyone who has had to keep books of accounts in the past can heave a great sigh of relief. That said, the same care and attention is required, albeit in a more friendly computer environment. Management needs to decide what records, budgets and actual data are needed and how it is presented. More accounting systems now have graphical facilities to help make presentations. With the correct links in place, charts can be updated automatically every few minutes, if required. Again, like most systems, accounting software can be bought in a modular format.

4.1.3 Sales and marketing

One of the keys to successful marketing is an up-to-date knowledge of the customer base. In larger concerns statistics showing responses to promotional efforts are essential to future planning. Information systems provide great benefits in this connection through the ability to:

- identify and develop the best sources of business;
- monitor promotions and product sales; and
- assess the profitability of menus.

With minimum effort it is possible to code and identify sales of different types of dishes or drinks via the EPOS. Using daily or monthly sales reports, it is possible to identify trends for certain products to assist in forecasting. Most of the EPOS systems can download their data into third party products such as Microsoft Access, a database software package which can be designed to your own requirements.

To give you an example of sales and marketing; the large superstores such as Tesco and Safeway know that, if the temperature outside is between 17°c and 19°c, more sandwiches will be sold and fewer Cornish pasties will be required. How do they know this? By analysing the products sold on a daily basis and correlating that data with the weather. This helps the store forecast what to buy and wastage is kept to a minimum. This forecasting practice is called inventory or yield management. Yield management is a forecasting tool that utilises historical data to manage the selling of consumable products.

You may ask, how can this benefit a pub or restaurant? There are a number of applications that it can be used for. The first area is your stock level. If you know that, between the months of November and March, your spirits consumption will be lower than in the other months, you can plan either to lower your stock level or organise promotions to help boost sales. The same applies for restaurants. If, during the winter months, smoked salmon is a non-mover, but the profit margin is greater than anything else on the menu, it can be sold at a reduced rate through promotions.

You can only make these decisions on historical data. Keeping your sales reports in a spreadsheet on a daily basis, you can spot emerging trends and therefore make a sound business decision rather than a 'toe in the water' judgement.

4.1.4 Customer service

Customer service can be judged in many ways: the attitude of staff, the environment, waiting times, the quality of food or drink and value added service. Information technology will not directly figure in this assessment but will be there helping to meet customer requirements. It must be remembered that it is a tool and not the business answer to success. It is easy to blame the system, either the software or hardware. At the end of the day, it is the staff and the quality of the product that will make the business a success. Information systems can help alleviate the manual day-to-day processes and allow the staff to pay more attention to customer needs. Customers are becoming more demanding and expecting greater value for money. They are more widely travelled than the previous generation, so have more experience and appreciation of what constitutes good service. If a customer cannot pay by credit card, they will not visit the establishment again; if the service is poor and the bill incorrect, they might send a letter to the local newspaper complaining.

One of the most common customer complaints is that staff tend to keep their eyes down on the computer rather than looking up at the guest. A number of establishments try and hide their computers from the customer. The most popular 'hidden' position is the embedded screen within a desk. Why they do this is surprising because everyone knows what a computer looks like and accepts the need for it. There are a couple of ways to correct this approach. One is to buy a laptop rather than a normal desktop computer. They are small computers but as powerful as their cousins. Another way is by making sure that the computer is placed is such a position that members of staff can see both the monitor and the guest with little head movement. This is nothing to do with the system, rather paying proper attention to ergonomics and training.

In pubs equipped with EPOS, how often does the member of staff have to go to the system to get a total of a bar bill? In the 'old days' the staff member would know exactly to the penny how much the drinks were while serving. No need to go to the cash register, it was all in the head. Nowadays you have to wait for your drinks to be poured and then wait again for the bar person to go to the EPOS, clock in their identity code and enter in the items. Is that customer service? The problem can be rectified by placing mini pads by the dispensers which are in turn linked to the main EPOS for billing and control.

In summary, why have an information system? Because it makes good business sense to employ modern business techniques. One of the main reasons people run pubs and restaurants is to make money. Information systems can help you improve not only your profit margin but your customer care.

4.2 How to select a system

There are now many owner-managed businesses in the pub and restaurant trade. Installing the right computer system will improve the management information and potentially enhance the earnings of the business.

Selecting the system is as important to a first-time purchaser as it is to seasoned users updating or enhancing their existing facilities. In both cases it is of vital importance that any system selected must be chosen on the basis of servicing the requirements of the business rather than for any technical features which, on the face of it are impressive, but which may have little or no relevance to the actual needs of the pub or restaurant. Clear foresight is needed when selecting a system. Information technology is moving at a rapid pace so the system you are selecting must be flexible both to external and internal changes. With the installation of any system certain objectives will need to be achieved that will be discussed later, but the most important factor is how it will change the way the company operates.

4.2.1 Feasibility study

It is clear that systems requirements for running a single pub or restaurant will be different from those required for running a chain of pubs or restaurants. In either case it is of utmost importance that you first determine why you want to install a computer system and what you expect from it. Conducting a feasibility study in the early stages will reduce the risk of ending up with an over-complicated system that may do more than you require but not necessarily what you require. In a recent study, it was found that users only utilise 70 per cent of a system's functionality.

If you are a first-time purchaser it is probable that you will not be fully aware of the systems available and what can be expected from them. If you already have a computer system installed and wish to upgrade it, you will be well aware of its inadequacies and you will be seeking to find a system that will fill the gaps. In both cases, the first part of your feasibility study is to determine exactly what software there is available on the market that caters specifically for the pub and restaurant business. You will find that the choice is wide and that, of the systems available, most will perform basic accounting, price-lookup and stock-control activities.

Without some sort of planning process, there is a danger that individual systems will be implemented which:

(a) do not provide the expected benefits and/or are not cost-effective;
(b) are incompatible with each other;
(c) are hostage to a single supplier;
(d) do not allow a 'corporate' view of how the organisation is doing;
(e) do not provide the required results at reasonable cost; and
(f) are technically led and do not satisfy 'business' and user requirements.

4.2.2 Reviewing your business requirements

Identifying the specific functions you require the system to carry out is essential and, having selected the individual functions, writing down the benefits you expect to achieve from them is important. Analyse the things that go wrong in your business, either frequently or infrequently or those administrative chores that take up too much of your time, and look at where improvements could be made. When faced with new technology, certain working practices will be exchanged for new faster practices. It may be a change of culture, from manual to automated functions. In the case of multi-site restaurants or pubs, chains linking each outlet's accounts modules via a modem to the central office is faster and more productive than recording each outlet's results on a manual spreadsheet. The group accounts can be consolidated more quickly, making decision-making easier and more effective. This will leave the managers of the units more time to focus on their jobs and the business.

One approach is to draw up a list of the activities of your operations and the benefits you would like to achieve by installing a computer system. The following list is an example of some of the benefits:

(a) customer service – flexibility and speed of use;
(b) staff training – ease of use;
(c) till control – daily reports showing voids;
(d) cash control – right price charged and right change given;
(e) reduced staff cost – hand-held terminals;
(f) management reports – sales reports at any time;
(g) smart card technology – increased sales via promotion and loyalty schemes;
(h) reduction of administration time – integrated systems;
(i) maximise sales – prompting to sell on; and
(j) menu change – quick and easy to configure.

4.2.3 Statement of requirements

Once you have your specified requirements clearly listed it is time to approach potential suppliers. Probably one of the best ways is to seek recommendations from other pubs or restaurants as actual experience is invaluable. Trade associations, such as the Systems Managers Association specialising in hotel information technology, are another possibility for gathering information. Failing this, your trade magazines will carry advertisements and if there are any trade shows on, they would be worth a visit. All the major suppliers are at the shows and it is a valuable arena to visit and see first hand the different systems. Try and assess whether the supplier of the system is still going to be in business for the foreseeable future.

Having selected the suppliers to approach, a lot of time and effort can be saved by sending each of them your specific requirements. The most suitable method takes the form of a statement of requirements (SOR).

The document should not attempt to cover every function requirement in depth. Instead, it should concentrate on those issues that have been identified as crucial.

An SOR has three main purposes:

(a) It concentrates the mind so that you and your supplier are absolutely clear what is required. Suppliers are only human and, if their software does not provide everything you have specified, they may attempt to talk you out of certain requirements and into others more appropriate to their product. By adhering strictly to your SOR you can reduce the risk of disappointment.
(b) When a supplier is demonstrating their software, the SOR can be used to ensure that all the functions you require are not only present in the product but actually provide the desired effects in the manner you anticipated. Remember, however, that the demonstration is taking place in a controlled environment. In the case of food and beverage management systems this is unlikely to be a concern, but for EPOS greater care is needed. Ask the supplier to take you to an existing user, preferably in a similar business environment to yours, where you can see the system at work in a normal business environment.
(c) It will highlight the features or functionality that may not be available from the supplier. This will help to either negotiate a better price for the system or obtain a commitment from the supplier to add these features on at a later stage.

Your SOR should include any supporting material that you think will aid the supplier such as:

- number of restaurants, bars and kitchens;
- number of covers in each outlet;
- number of staff, full/part-time;
- number of items on the menus and on the wine/bar list;
- current promotions;
- number of meal periods, opening and closing times;
- average turnover per day/month;
- number of suppliers, food and beverage; and
- current PC hardware and software installed.

It is important to mention at this stage that many software suppliers favour certain types of hardware for their food and beverage management systems. It is not unusual for them to recommend their equipment as part of the package. You can, of course, insist on other hardware equipment but be sure your reasons for doing so are sound. Once you deviate from a supplier's package deal you stand the risk of weakening your position in the event of any subsequent breakdown. It is also wise to get the supplier to draw you a schematic of where the hardware should be located as well as the cabling runs. A schematic will show a plan of the pub or restaurant displaying the terminals and printers. This will give you a better idea of the installation and whether all the areas are covered. This service should be given free as it will help both parties in the planning stages.

4.2.4 Cost

Like car prices, the variations in computer system costs are wide and in the end you tend to get what you pay for. It is obvious that the more sophisticated the package, the higher the cost. The following example indicates some of the points to be covered:

(a) Hardware cost – a total breakdown of each item such as PCs, printers, EPOS terminals including any peripheral equipment such as network cards, modems, tape streamers, UPS, security keys for the EPOS, either data or telephone cabling (ISDN) and delivery charges.
(b) Software cost – the initial software package plus any third party products that will be needed such as spreadsheets, word-processing, database, network and Internet software. There might be an added charge for interfacing one product with another.
(c) Software licenses – sometimes a hidden cost that may not be included in the software cost.
(d) Hardware maintenance – either via the supplier (EPOS) or a dedicated maintainer (PCs) or both.
(e) Software support – the supplier of the system and a dedicated maintainer (Novell, Windows NT).
(f) Training – the cost of the training at the implementation stage for the system plus extra training on any third party products such as Microsoft Windows. There might be an added cost of restructuring the workforce. Allow enough in the budget for extra training by the supplier after implementation.
(g) Architectural cost – due to the new system, the staff workplace might have to be redesigned. A dedicated room might have to be used to store the equipment in a safe place with the correct air conditioning, racking and fire safe.
(h) Insurance cost – make sure that the extra hardware and software is covered by your existing policy.
(i) Stationery cost – new printer rolls, ribbons and laser toner cartridges will need to be budgeted for.
(j) Marketing cost – you might want to notify your customers and suppliers of the changes.

As is often the case, the art is in the negotiating skill of the buyer. There are often cheaper systems available which, whilst capable of fulfilling an adequate job, will tend to be limited in the extent of their functions.

Equally, there are often more expensive versions available which possibly provide more than you require. You know your budget and it is sensible housekeeping to work within it.

4.2.5 Invitation to tender

The last document in a computer selection that you need to compile is an invitation to tender (ITT). This document sets out how the tendering process is conducted. Some typical ITT headings are:

- purpose of the document;
- response to the ITT;
- background and overview of the requirements;
- the timetable;
- format of response;
- selection criteria; and
- the statement of requirements (SOR).

All the suppliers you approach should be asked to put forward their quotations based on the criteria contained in the ITT and SOR. That way you can help to ensure that direct comparisons can be made between rival quotations.

Try to limit the number of companies you select to provide quotations. A preliminary telephone call outlining your requirements should enable you to weed out all but the most suitable potential suppliers. Try and restrict your final ITT to a maximum of five companies. The ITT places you in the driving seat. Insist that you will not accept an all-in price quotation. Every item must be individually identified and priced. This ensures you are able to make direct comparisons between competing suppliers. Set a time limit by which suppliers should provide their tender. A clear four weeks should be more than adequate.

4.2.6 Demonstrations

Having received the tenders, the next important step is to eliminate those suppliers who fall short of your specified requirements or whose costs fall outside your budget. The remaining contenders should now be asked to demonstrate how their product meets your requirements. Ask for the answers to any points requiring clarification to be made in writing by the supplier.

The demonstration should be based on your SOR and it is up to you to ensure that all criteria stipulated are met. The demonstration is effectively the culmination of all your pre-planning and, if you are not happy at this stage, the chances are you will be a lot less happy if you adopt the system on the basis that 'it will be alright on the night'. It almost certainly will not be.

The demonstration should be held at the offices of the supplier. Please remember that this is a demonstration in a controlled environment. Ask questions and write the answers down so that they can be followed up at a later stage. Do not be rushed into making a decision and try to have a colleague or two to join you for the demonstration.

4.2.7 References

Once satisfied with the outcome of the demonstration, you are reaching the final stage of selecting your supplier. It is a wise precaution to ask him to provide a full list of his customers. Any reluctance to do so should be treated with the utmost suspicion. Try and find customers with similar set-ups to your own and give them a call. Ask about the potential strengths and weaknesses of the system you are considering and the suppliers themselves. The responses may not always be favourable (there are bad customers as well as bad suppliers) but a consensus of opinion should enable you to form a view.

4.2.8 Contracts

The supplier will naturally have their own standard terms and conditions. The following points might help identify some pitfalls:

(a) Make sure that the SOR covers the entire functionality of the system. Make amendments to the SOR where necessary. Without a detailed and accurate functional specification of the system, it is very difficult to sue in the event the system is found to be flawed or inadequate.
(b) Ensure that the number of users referred to in the software license are current users of the system and not the number of physical terminals attached to the system.
(c) Ensure that the licenser/supplier indemnifies you against any claims which may be made on them, e.g., infringement of copyright, trade mark, etc.
(d) Do not be bullied by the supplier. The supplier will need payment for any hardware that they have bought on your behalf, however, the software should be conditional on your acceptance. Keep part of the payment back until you are confident that the system works to your satisfaction.
(e) The delivery date of the system must be set and agreed to. If the supplier fails to meet the targets, you may include a penalty clause in the contract. If it is found that due to bad project management on your behalf the time schedules have slipped, then this part of the contract becomes null and void.

4.2.9 Acceptance testing

To have a successful installation, whatever the size, you must have the following:

(a) A logical plan, setting out the milestones, timing and the people who need to be involved at each stage. These should not only include the supplier's staff but more importantly your own personnel. Include your employees in the planning stages and discuss the target objectives. If your staff are not aware or not interested in the project, they can hinder the time schedule dramatically.

(b) An environment that will house the testing system before the full installation. In the case of a group installation there should be a pilot site for testing the configuration. In the case of a single site, a spare room should be set aside for testing. You must also identify key personnel within your operation who will help train the rest of the staff after the live date. Do not skimp on training. You should take time out to show the benefits of the new system to encourage and motivate the staff. Monitor the training schedules and help staff that may be wary of the changes. Also, make sure that the standard of training provided by the supplier is of an adequate standard.

(c) The configuration of the system will have been set out in the SOR. Make sure that the items that you want to appear on the system are logically written up step by step. For example, if Menu A has three courses, make sure in your documentation that the relevant dishes will print on the correct kitchen printer (main, larder, pastry). Each item should have the correct description, price, VAT, any modifier that it may have (no salt, with onions) and the printer number. In the case of beverages, make sure that all the draught beers will appear on the same screen in half and full pints. This documentation can take some time to collect and organise, but will be the backbone of the system.

(d) Once the system is in its testing stage, be thorough. Allow time to go through all the stages that you are faced with during operations. The testing environment should reflect a scaled-down version of your operation. Allow different scenarios to be tested and write down the results. During this stage you may find that the functionality you hoped for does not work in your environment. It is better to clarify during testing time why a certain procedure is not working rather than after the installation.

4.3 Systems management

One of the most common mistakes after buying and installing any system is thinking that the system will run itself. All the time and effort that was taken up writing the SOR and on the selection process could be wasted if system reviews are not followed up. It is important to log and report any 'bugs' or errors with the supplier. It is also important to ask for any enhancement that you may wish to see on the system. Depending on the size of the user base and the value of the enhancements, most suppliers will take note of points raised. Have monthly meetings with either the supplier's account manager or better still with the user group to share and document your problems.

Procedures need to be in place prior to installation on the systems management needed. In some cases the supplier will furnish the customer with a brief résumé of the tasks, but at the end of the day, it is up to the management to make sure that the 'good housekeeping' practices are carried out.

4.3.1 Maintenance support agreements

Be very careful what you sign for when buying a new system. Hardware and software support agreements are the most expensive 'ongoing' charges. The normal cost for hardware or software support ranges from 10 per cent to 20 per cent of the total cost of the packages. The high maintenance costs reflect the labour content rather than the cost of parts. Because the industry operates 365 days of the year, 24 hours a day, high levels of support and services are needed by the supplier.

The agreements need to be closely scrutinised and negotiated hard by the customer. Software maintenance agreements are the lifeblood of many suppliers. Prior to buying a system, visit the supplier's offices to have a look at their operations. Note the number of personnel on the support desk as well as the general impression of their operation.

A checklist of the things to consider when selecting a maintenance company are:

(a) what is the response time for call-outs?
(b) what are their standard hours of support?
(c) does the supplier have emergency support hours outside the standard hours?
(d) what is the cost of the emergency support?
(e) how many support personnel do they employ?
(f) how many programmers do they employ full-time?
(g) is there an account manager as the focal point of contact?
(h) does the supplier keep a log of all faults reported and review the monthly calls with the customer?
(i) does the supplier have a user group?
(j) can the customer keep any spare equipment on site?

(k) what are the termination terms?
(l) what are the escalation procedures if a problem is not rectified immediately?
(m) can they perform remote diagnostics and software 'fixes'?

4.3.2 Post-implementation reviews

The post-implementation review should be held every six months after the installation of the system. The post-implementation review will clarify whether the expected benefits have been achieved and if not, why not. Reasons why the benefits may not have been achieved include:

(a) policy and procedures have not been changed since the installation;
(b) the software could not carry out the functions required as stated in the SOR;
(c) the benefit is a long-term rather than a short-term gain.

In the course of the review meetings, new benefits and objectives may be added to the list originally anticipated. The supplier should be aware of the outcome of these meetings and it may be appropriate to send the supplier minutes of those meetings.

4.3.3 Daily and monthly housekeeping

A lot of money has been lost as well as man-hours wasted by businesses which have not regularly backed up their data. Some suppliers have written an automatic command into their software that will prompt the user to back up the system during the auditing stage of the day's business. Clear and precise procedures should be adhered to by all who use the system.

There are a number of methods to back up a system, but the most common is the use of data tapes. These come in various sizes and capacities. The most expensive tapes (digital) will hold at least eight gigabyte of data, more than enough for any pub or restaurant system. You should keep daily tapes on a rotation period for a least seven days. At the end of the financial month, make and keep a monthly tape. These tapes as well as the system disks should be kept in a fire-proof safe and clearly labelled. It would be wise to keep the monthly tapes off site, the most common place would be in a bank deposit box. The tapes can be used for up to 12 months before they should be replaced. Check that your tapes are actually backing up your data – do not wait to find out when it is too late!

4.3.4 Viruses

Over 7,000 different PC viruses are currently known to exist. So what is a computer virus? It is simply a computer program written by an ill-intentioned programmer. A computer virus becomes active when you run an infected program or start your computer from an infected disk. Once active, the virus spreads by attaching copies of itself to other programs.

There are three ways that a virus can infect your PC. Installing programs or files from a diskette or CD–ROM, downloading files from the Internet using a modem or using a local area network or wide area network.

The solution is to load anti-virus software onto your PCs and keep the software updated. Once loaded, the software will detect known viruses that may already exist on your computer, prevent known and unknown viruses from infecting your computer and monitor for activities that may indicate an unknown virus.

4.3.5 System auditing

Every system will provide a host of audit trails, from who logged into the system to who took cash from a particular table. You should print these reports either to paper or to file for later reference. Make sure that when employees leave, their ID and passwords are deleted from the system. Items or menus that are no longer sold in the operation should also be removed from the system.

4.3.6 System maintenance

There are a number of utilities that can be used depending on the software platform. Most products will have their own in-built maintenance utilities. A number of suppliers hold courses on systems management (at extra cost) and it is a worthwhile investment. The utilities range from configuring a new PC to rebuilding the databases. It is important to keep the system manageable. If these procedures are not done over a period of time, the system will become sluggish and in some cases there might be either data loss or corruption.

4.3.7 Documentation

Make sure that you have received all the documentation from the different suppliers – hardware and software. Keep it in a safe place where it is easy to retrieve in case you need documents in an emergency. In some cases it would be worthwhile to create a synopsis handbook of the major functions of the systems. You will note that most system reference manuals have been written for the software engineers and not the average lay system user. The handbook could then be used as either a training manual or for system troubleshooting. Make sure that it includes a contact list of the names and telephone numbers of persons required in case of emergency. Other areas that need to be documented are:

- location and description of equipment;
- equipment physical and network identity;
- location and address of the cable points;
- spare equipment on site;
- staff security and passwords;
- network configuration;
- listing of the software loaded on each PC;
- disaster recovery plan;
- data backup procedures;
- system passwords.

A disaster recovery plan helps secure your data in the case of a fire or flood. If all the above points are followed, your hardware is secure from theft or malicious damage, and you should be in a better position than many other businesses.

4.3.8 Training

As previously mentioned, training and re-education will be very important during and after implementation. Take time out to follow up on the progress of members of your staff. Within the first couple of weeks of the installation you might hear of a number of complaints about the system. Instigate daily meetings to try and clear the problems up quickly.

As time moves on, there will be a dilution of knowledge because of staff turnover. This is where proper training procedures are important. Whenever a new employee starts, allow at least two weeks for them to be trained on the different systems. After a period of one month, review the skills and knowledge gained and if required, arrange further training.

4.3.9 Data Protection Act 1984

Under the Data Protection Act 1984 data users who control the content or use of personal data which is processed automatically must register the details with the Data Protection Registrar. It is an offence not to do so or to operate knowingly or recklessly outside the terms of the registration. A restaurant with a marketing database containing personal information will need to register the details with the Data Protection Registrar and must be careful to ensure that the information contained on the database is not misused.

4.4 The future

Our daily lives have changed dramatically in the last 10 years due to the advancement of IT. The microchip has become such a powerful part of our work and leisure that many of the functions we take for granted today could not be achieved without the aid of a computer.

What will the next 10 years bring us in the catering industry? In the 'Internet age', the gathering and delivery of information will be paramount. The term 'word of mouth', which has traditionally been the best sales and marketing tool in the industry, will be replaced by 'Word on the Web'. More investment will be focused on sales and marketing on the Internet than either the face-to-face approach or the printed publication. Pubs and restaurants will advertise and react to their customers' needs on their local interactive Internet service.

The demise of hard currency will no doubt happen. Smart cards will debit our accounts in all retail outlets. Smart card security will be foolproof with photo and fingertip signature. Smart cards will store our financial as well as our personal data and may help the service providers to ascertain further proof of credit. On the other hand, the service providers will have to give a faster and more reliable service and customers will become more demanding for quality and improved service. You will no doubt see individual tabletop ordering systems that will allow the customer to choose their meals and drinks without a need for human intervention. A card swipe prior to the order will guarantee payment for the service, and the only human you will see will be the waiter bringing and clearing your food or drinks. Personal service will be charged for accordingly and will be seen as an expensive luxury for the lucky few.

IT in the next millennium will increasingly shape the society we live in. More time for leisure activities will be taken because computers will be able to do the work faster, more cheaply and more efficiently than humans can. Whether the future will provide a better existence than the present, only a computer simulation can predict!

Chapter 5 – Risk management

5.1 Introduction

There are risks involved in running any business which, if not properly managed, could undermine an otherwise healthy operation. This chapter considers what these risks are and how to minimise them. The areas covered are:

- identifying the risks and introducing controls in the sales cycle;
- preventive controls – food and wet sales;
- detective controls – food and wet sales;
- preventive and detective controls – costs;
- physical and other controls;
- other specific issues.

It is incumbent upon a manager to identify the risks inherent in his business. By so doing the manager will be able to consider the controls needed to minimise the risk identified. The need for, and the extent of, the controls required will depend upon the perceived level of risk and the maximum financial impact in the event that the risk crystallises. It will also depend upon the type of risk identified. Some risks will result in a direct financial loss whilst others may result in poor or insufficient management information on which to make informed business decisions.

Having identified the types of risk and their potential effect, the manager will need to consider whether it is cost-effective to implement controls. It is important to realise that risk cannot be eliminated altogether, it can only be minimised. The control needed to reduce the risk in a particular area may be out of all proportion to the potential cost if the risk should materialise. In this case the resources would be best employed elsewhere.

Assuming that controls have been introduced to the manager's satisfaction, how can he be sure that they are operating properly? Where there are changes in systems employed or in the size or nature of the business, controls should be reviewed to ensure that they are still operating as intended. Any breaches in controls should be properly investigated and appropriate action taken to avoid a culture whereby avoiding or ignoring controls becomes typical. There should also be controls which monitor the overall performance of the business and highlight where preventive controls have failed or have been avoided.

The pub and restaurant trades are typified by a high volume of low value cash transactions and perishable stock which is easily pilfered. The manager will need to take account of these factors in identifying the areas of greatest risk.

5.2 Identifying the risks and introducing controls in the sales cycle

In the sales cycle, two significant difficulties need to be addressed:

(a) the inability to carry out pre-sale checks as each transaction is made instantaneously;
(b) the inability to separate out the sale from the receipt;

The manager should bear in mind that weak controls will create an environment for the opportunist thief and, conversely, that a high risk of detection will put off the potential fraudster. Therefore, controls should be obvious to all employees and should be seen to be operated at all times.

Strict controls should be maintained over the tills. This can be achieved by introducing a float system and carrying out reconciliations of takings to till rolls at the beginning and end of every shift. Any discrepancies should be investigated immediately. This process will be made easier if each member of staff is required to use the same till during a shift, or an EPOS system (see **4.1.1**) operates which allows each transaction to be recorded under the name of the relevant bar staff. Nowadays, most bar staff are given personalised keys or other devices which must be used to operate the tills. These controls should reduce the incidence of petty theft and error.

With the introduction of EPOS, the recording of each transaction can automatically update the stock records and identify the bar staff responsible. It should be recognised, however, that these systems do not eliminate the risk of fraud or error. It is still possible for staff to under-ring tills or water down drinks, but the information which is available to the manager from EPOS is useful as an early warning signal. Provided this information is properly interpreted, significant losses are much more likely to be detected early, for example, by reviewing the gross margins achieved on individual stock lines and comparing them to prior periods, any unusual variances will be highlighted and can be investigated. Although it may not be possible to identify an individual member of staff responsible, the fact that management is investigating is likely to discourage future dishonesty.

In many organisations the introduction of EPOS may be prohibitively expensive and may outweigh the possible benefits, at least initially. In these circumstances more basic controls will need to be introduced which are more appropriate to the circumstances.

5.3 Preventive controls – food and wet sales

Sales in pubs and restaurants are similar in nature. In pubs, cash is usually taken over the bar for food and wet sales although it would be normal for separate tills to be used. The restaurant trade is slightly more sophisticated in that sales are based on an ordering system, initiated by a waiter, passed through the kitchen and completed by the cashier.

The risks at this stage are two-fold:

- the sales are not correctly recorded, e.g., under-ringing of tills;
- the customer is overcharged, e.g., drinks are watered down.

5.3.1 Wet sales

Under-recording of sales

The control of sales is dependent to an extent on the calibre and honesty of the staff involved. The nature of the industry is such that there is a high level of staff turnover with many employees only working part-time or employed on a casual basis. Typically, the staff will be low paid but may have a high level of responsibility handling cash on a day-to-day basis. Unfortunately, it is not practical or cost-efficient to vet the character and integrity of each new member of staff, so managers should develop their own criteria which have to be met before a person is employed, whether full or part-time. Ideally, the recording of a sale and the receipt of money should be segregated, a practical impossibility in a crowded pub. Given these difficulties, a manager will need to devise other methods of reducing the risk of unrecorded sales.

To minimise the demotivational effects of low wages staff could be offered a bonus based on performance. Provided that all staff benefit equally, there will be less incentive for those on low salaries to under-ring the till and pocket the difference particularly as other employees are more likely to notice, given their own self-interest.

At a higher level, the remuneration of pub managers and restaurateurs should be based on the profit achieved by the outlet concerned. However, costs which are not under the manager's control should be taken out of the calculation so that he is not disincentivised by escalating costs which are controlled by head office.

If the manager and staff are motivated to ensure that all sales are recorded, the chances of petty theft will be reduced. However, care should be taken to ensure that this does not introduce the risk that sales are over-recorded. The manager may be tempted to inflate sales so that targets are met and his bonus secured, only for the sale to be reversed in the next period.

> ***Tip***
>
> To reduce the incidence of petty theft or error introduce staff incentive schemes which benefit all relevant staff equally.

Overcharging customers

Whilst designing controls to minimise the risk of direct theft or error is the manager's first priority, he should also be aware of the implications of staff overcharging customers. For instance, a member of staff may provide a customer with a glass of sparkling wine but charge him for the champagne he requested, pocketing the difference. Alternatively, the barman may simply add a small erroneous amount to a customer's bill which may go unnoticed if that customer orders several drinks. If the staff member is careful, he can ensure that the takings reconcile to stock movements making the theft from the customer difficult to detect. The best control in these circumstances is the customer as he will not want to pay for drinks he did not receive, but a staff member may gamble on the customer not noticing and apologise for an 'honest' mistake if the customer spots his ruse. If the practice continues it may result in adverse publicity and loss of customers. Whilst it is not possible to monitor every sale made, the risk of this type of dishonesty will be reduced if prices are publicised so that they are visible to all customers. This again makes the likelihood of detection higher and will act as a deterrent to the staff.

Another practice which will have a detrimental effect on business is the watering down of drinks and charging for a full measure. Not only will the pub suffer from loss of custom if the practice is discovered, it is also likely to be fined by the Weights and Measures division of Customs & Excise.

To ensure that these 'tricks' are not widespread it is sensible to employ professional 'customers' who will order drinks in the normal way whilst watching for any sharp practice. Each visit made by professional 'customers' should be a surprise to staff but they should be made aware that professional 'customers' are used in this manner.

> ***Tip***
>
> Ensure that staff are aware of controls that have been introduced as a deterrent to fraud.

5.3.2 Dry sales

Food sales, where waiter service is offered, are easier to control because the recording of the order, the provision of service, the invoicing and the cash collection can all be segregated, minimising the opportunity for fraud or error. However, it should be recognised that this will not always be possible in a pub unless the restaurant is run as a separate operation.

There are a number of systems commonly used in practice which all involve the recording of the sale on a multi-part order pad. For example, a waiter takes a customer's order using a sequential three-part order pad. The order is then passed to the cashier for authorisation and distribution. The cashier keeps the top copy to use for preparing the bill at the end of the meal, one copy is passed straight to the kitchen and the final copy kept by the waiter so that he is able to fulfil the order. If the system is properly managed the chances of an individual acting alone in overcoming controls for personal gain is eliminated, although there is still the possibility of collusion between staff members. Any form of collusion is very difficult to prevent, but the risks are reduced if staff rotas are prepared so that, where possible, members of staff do not work together on a regular basis.

Credit card sales

It is becoming increasingly common for restaurants and pubs to accept credit cards. Therefore, staff must be properly trained in the procedures for accepting credit card payments. Care must be taken to ensure that authorisation is received at the point of sale and the card being used is not one reported as stolen. If these simple procedures are followed the risk of bad debts is borne by the credit card company.

5.4 Detective controls – food and wet sales

Given that preventive controls cannot eliminate the risk of financial loss to the business or fraud on the customers, the manager will want to detect any cash or other losses as soon as possible so that they can be investigated and stopped. There are a number of detective controls which act as early warning signals, flagging problems as they arise.

This form of control is particularly important in the pub trade where the vast majority of transactions are made in cash. Very often, the manager will not become aware of a problem until he reviews the results for a given period. However, the results will be of no benefit unless he is able to compare them firstly with what was expected, i.e., budgeted results, and secondly with an equivalent historical period.

5.4.1 Budgetary controls

Implementing budgetary procedures has two advantages. Firstly, it is an important business tool which enables the manager to plan in a focused and detailed way and, secondly it provides a regular method of monitoring the performance of the business. Variances from budget may give the first indication of a breakdown in controls and a financial loss to the business. Unusual fluctuations or variances should be properly investigated and followed up. If, after taking into account expected fluctuations, sales are still below budget further investigation will be necessary. Variances may arise due to a difference in price, quantity, or sales mix, compared with budget. All these variances should be separately analysed.

It is important to use up-to-date management information when analysing variances against budget. Any delays in producing monthly management figures will delay the necessary corrective action or prevent the manager cashing in on an unexpected opportunity. Budgetary procedures are covered in more detail in Chapter 2.

5.4.2 Gross margin reviews

Gross margin analysis will be important at all levels of operation but particularly important for the smaller operations. The tenant or manager of a single outlet will use sales and gross margins as the barometers of the financial health of their business. Many small businesses are successfully managed by focusing almost exclusively on this information. Both Customs & Excise and the Inland Revenue maintain details of expected margins according to the location and type of operation. To ensure the accuracy of the gross margins, stocktakes must be accurate and regular. In this situation, a professional stocktaker who has the advantage of independence, should be used if at all possible. The information that can be obtained is discussed in more detail in **5.5.2** below.

The under-ringing of tills cannot be detected by performing a reconciliation of takings to till rolls but will result in a reduced margin. The greater the sophistication of the system in place the easier it will be to identify the lines affected. With a full EPOS system it may be possible to carry out a review of margins on all stock lines or print out an exception report for all stock lines where there are significant variations from expected margins.

If the outlet does not have accurate records and only reviews margins on an irregular ad hoc basis, the pilfering of stock or under-ringing of tills could continue for long periods only to be discovered when it has had a serious impact on the cash flow of the business.

5.4.3 Sales trends

The same food and drinks sold in pubs and restaurants can be purchased from supermarkets, so it would be relatively easy for a manager or member of staff to purchase identical stock and sell it through the outlet of their employer at the normal selling price. Preventive controls may not be sufficient to eliminate the problem, but a sudden apparent fall in demand for a normally profitable stock line is worthy of investigation.

5.4.4 Reconciliation controls

As well as undertaking till reconciliations daily or by shift, there should also be regular bank reconciliations prepared by appropriate members of staff. In multi-site operations the bank reconciliations will usually form part of a weekly return made by an outlet to head office. It is important that these reconciliations are carried out on a regular basis so that any discrepancies can be followed up quickly. Daily banking sheets should be received from each outlet and compared with the amounts actually banked.

5.4.5 Control checks

Once all the controls over food and wet sales are in place, care must be taken to ensure that they are operating as intended. In larger chains, occasional visits to individual outlets can be carried out by internal audit departments to ensure that controls are not being circumvented. The regular use of 'mystery' customers may uncover examples of theft, and staff knowledge of the procedure is likely to reduce the incidence of theft. As previously discussed, an employee of the company or an outside contractor specialising in the area is paid to act as a customer whilst observing the bar staff for under-ringing of tills, overcharging and any other means of defrauding the customer or the company.

5.5 Preventive and detective controls – costs

The two principal costs in the pub or restaurant trade are the payroll costs and the raw material costs of food and drink. Common sense dictates that controls should be focused on these areas.

5.5.1 Payroll costs

Typically, pubs and restaurants have a high turnover of low paid staff. Many of the staff are employed on a casual basis which creates its own problems not least from a PAYE perspective. The tax implications of casual staff are considered in Chapter 6.

With relatively large numbers of staff often working different shifts, some working part-time, there is a need to keep track of the hours actually worked. In many instances it may be difficult for a manager to record the hours worked, particularly if changes are made to staffing at short notice as a reaction to unexpected increases or decreases in activity. The introduction of a time-recording system will ensure that time spent by each staff member is recorded by them on periodic timesheets. By so doing the manager can review any time over and above standard hours and ensure that any overtime has been approved by an appropriate member of staff. He will also be able to carry out comparisons between the volume of business and the number of hours worked. If the control is operated properly staff can only be paid for the time worked.

In a group of pubs or restaurants it will be difficult for head office to keep track of staff on the payroll as new names are added and old ones removed. With so many expected changes it creates the perfect environment for 'dummy' employees to be added to the payroll or past employees to be improperly left on the payroll.

Proper records of standing data must be kept and only authorised personnel should have access to that data in order to reduce the chances of an employee altering the details for personal gain. Regular checks should be undertaken to ensure that all staff members recorded on the payroll are still employed. Checks should also be carried out on the rates of pay and other standing data on an ad hoc basis.

Payroll bureaux are increasingly popular as they can offer an efficient and cost-effective service. However, the tendency is for managers to believe that the chance of errors or fraud has been eliminated because the payroll is carried out by an independent third party, but it should not be forgotten that the accuracy of the bureau's output is dependent on the integrity of the information received as input. All the controls that are relevant to an in-house payroll system regarding employee numbers and standing data are just as relevant to a payroll administered by a bureau.

For computerised systems powerful interrogation software packages such as IDEA are available, which can highlight unusual items, duplicate items or can cross-match data to other files on the system. For instance, payroll bank details could be cross-matched with supplier details. Any positive matches should be investigated.

It is common practice to employ foreigners to work as waiters or bar staff. This can create problems if the staff do not have the appropriate working visa or they are illegal immigrants. The Government has plans to make it a criminal offence to employ immigrants with the result that restaurateurs and publicans could be fined £5,000 if they fail to check the status of their employees. Therefore, it is wise to undertake proper vetting procedures before employing anyone to avoid problems in the future.

5.5.2 Raw material costs

The main suppliers to pubs and restaurants are breweries, food and drink retailers/wholesalers and cash and carry outlets. For a pub or restaurant to be successful it will need to ensure that its suppliers are reliable and provide good quality stock at a competitive price. Many pub managers are responsible for the purchase of soft drinks and food and tend to be reliant on one supplier, usually a cash and carry outlet, for these items.

To identify the risk areas it is necessary to consider the different stages of the food cycle from the original order to the payment for the goods, through to the storage and finally the preparation of the menu items.

- order;
- receipt of goods;
- payment of invoice;
- storage and movement of stock; and
- preparation of food.

Food and drink orders

Due to the perishable nature of food the level of stock held will depend on its shelf-life as well as its popularity. While large quantities of beer and other alcoholic beverages may be purchased from one reliable supplier by different outlets in the same chain, fresh food is often purchased locally by individual managers.

Often the chef will be given the responsibility for making these purchases. It is important that control is exercised over this process. Unless the chef is made responsible for the level of these costs he may sacrifice economy for quality. Whilst it is important to maintain the quality of the food a manager should not lose sight of the need to make a profit. This is particularly true where it is difficult to pass price increases on to customers, for instance, pub food is often relatively price-elastic as customers do not expect, or want to pay for, *haute cuisine*.

The fresh food costs as a proportion of food sales should be monitored and the chef made responsible for the results. More generally, purchases should only be made from authorised suppliers and credit limits should be set which cannot be breached without senior approval. Orders should only be raised after a check has been made to ensure that the credit limit has not been breached.

For many stock items, where a perpetual inventory is kept, stock can be reordered automatically once a pre-set economic order quantity has been reached. The amounts ordered are crucial particularly for perishable food (which will normally be ordered on a day-to-day basis). Pursuing discounts for volume purchases are unlikely to be cost-effective in the long run. Effective ordering will be made significantly easier by the introduction of an EPOS system which can automatically flag stock lines for reordering.

Where appropriate, prices can be agreed with the supplier in advance. If this is not possible staff should only be allowed to buy within certain parameters. Within the organisation, appropriate staff should be given authorisation limits above which more senior approval is required before an order can be made. In any event, regular reviews of monthly management information (or more frequent for headline information) should be made and compared with budget. A margin analysis is likely to provide the most useful information and this should be as detailed as possible, subject to system and cost constraints.

Receipt of goods

The correct delivery of food and drinks to retailers can be difficult to police as quantities are difficult to verify. For instance, in the pub trade barrels or other containers are not specific legal measures of volume so it is difficult to identify any shortfall, and breweries are reluctant to compensate for any perceived discrepancies. The experienced manager will be able to recognise under-deliveries by testing the weight. The problems should not deter the manager from implementing controls which reduce the risk of under-deliveries.

When goods are received, the storeman should check the delivery against the quantities recorded on the delivery note and the original order. Any discrepancies should be noted and only if the amounts agree should the delivery and order be evidenced as such. Copies should then be passed to accounts so that they can be matched against the invoice when it is received. In a pub or restaurant it may not be practical to employ a storeman, however, where possible, the verification of stock deliveries and the raising of the order should be performed by different members of staff. There is a ready market for food and drink which makes them attractive to the fraudster, therefore, it is important that the controls are tight to ensure that stock cannot be misappropriated.

Example

Alberto, the manager of Luigi's, a pizza restaurant, puts in an order for more food than is required. On delivery the van stops at a pre-arranged address agreed with Alberto and unloads a proportion of the stock. When the delivery is made to Luigi's, Alberto checks it and although it is short confirms that the order is received in full. The actual amount received is adequate to meet the business requirements so initially there is no evidence of a short order. In the meantime, Alberto and his accomplice use the stolen food in their own restaurant.

Subsequently, Alberto explains to head office that the fall in margins is due to an increased level of wastage resulting from lower than expected demand for particular menu choices. Prima facie there is no evidence of the theft.

> ***Tip***
>
> Where possible ensure that the duties of the storeman, purchaser and payments clerk are segregated.

In checking stock, particularly if it is perishable, care should be taken to ensure that it meets the quality requirements stated in the order. It is very important that the quality and specification are clearly defined on the order and that a staff member who has the necessary expertise checks receipt of the goods. In many cases the chef will be the most appropriate person to check the quality, although if the chef also raised the purchase order another responsible member of staff should be present. If the food is not of the quality expected it should be rejected and consideration given to finding an alternative source of supply.

Payment of the invoice

After the goods have been received the suppliers will raise an invoice. The invoice should be matched to the original order and the delivery note. To make sure that payment is only made for goods received, the order and delivery note should be attached to the invoice and only then authorised for payment by an appropriate member of staff.

The payment for goods is potentially the riskiest area in the purchase cycle as there is the opportunity for a person to divert money into a personal bank account. This type of fraud is common in many companies and may, for example, be perpetrated by using dummy suppliers or by colluding with a supplier. The importance of segregating the payment of invoices from the original order and receipt of goods cannot be over-emphasised. In a smaller operation where this is not possible management should exert control over the process.

> ***Example***
>
> John, an employee at the Seven Stars pub restaurant noticed that food was purchased from a particular supplier on a daily basis and, due to the number of deliveries, payment was made without matching the invoice to the delivery notes. Subsequently, John started to introduce bogus invoices into the system for the same supplier and was able to obtain payment without providing supporting documentation. He then altered the cheques and paid them into an account opened for the purpose.

When an invoice has been authorised for payment and paid, it should be evidenced as such so that it cannot be paid twice. Also, payment should never be authorised based on a photocopied invoice. Where an invoice has been mislaid, a proper copy should be obtained from the supplier.

Example

French's restaurant is jointly run by John and Louise who are the only cheque signatories, one of whom is always on site. Mary, the bookkeeper, always attaches the delivery note and order to the invoice having drafted a cheque ready for signature. John is often in a hurry and forgets to mark the invoice as paid. Recently, Mary, who is having financial problems, has fraudulently drafted two cheques in respect of the same invoice asking John (who fails to mark the invoice as 'paid') to sign the first and Louise to sign the second. The first Mary directs to her own bank account, the second is sent to the supplier in the normal way.

Tip

Be aware of changes in the circumstances of your employees particularly where they have responsibility over the bank account or have access to cash. If an employee is apparently spending beyond their means, it may be worth carrying out some discreet investigations.

Storage and stock movements

The saleability of pubs' and restaurants' stock and the ease with which it can be pilfered increase the need for good stock control. Due to the short lead times and the perishable nature of some stock, it is normal for low volumes to be held which turn over very frequently. The regular deliveries and constant movement of stock make control more difficult. It is usual for specialist stocktakers to count stock regularly, often on a quarterly basis. The frequency of counts will depend on the number of stock lines, the type of stock, the stock turnover and the cost but, as a general rule, the more frequently checks are undertaken, the better. Where it is not cost-effective to carry out full checks regularly it may be beneficial to carry out checks on randomly selected stock lines on an ad hoc basis.

Stocktakers are specialists in their field and should be used to their full potential. They should be able to provide an analysis of the information available and asked to prepare an analysis of all stock movements, including:

- opening stock;
- closing stock;
- sales volumes and prices;
- purchase volumes and costs;
- sales mix;
- gross profit by stock line.

The movements in sales should be reconciled to actual takings. If there is an EPOS system installed with the appropriate stock module, much of this information will already be available, nevertheless the information provided by the stocktaker provides a double-check ensuring that the physical stockcount can be reconciled to the stock movement shown on the EPOS system.

Any significant differences between the EPOS stock and the physical count can be investigated and, where appropriate, further action taken to minimise discrepancies in future. If the manager is reliant on the information provided by the stocktaker then ensuring the appropriate analysis is given will be of prime importance. Using this information the publican will be able to check for:

- over or under-stocking of lines;
- unusual fluctuations in gross margins;
- the effect of a different sales mix on profitability;
- evidence of theft;
- significant differences between actual and implied takings.

There should also be physical security over stock to prevent access by the general public and to allow restricted access to authorised staff only. This can be achieved by limiting the number of keyholders.

The security of stock is not the only storage consideration. Much of the stock necessary to run a restaurant, and to a lesser extent a pub, is perishable and the method of storage has hygiene and food safety implications. Therefore, perishable stock needs to be stored separately and usually refrigerated. There should be procedures to ensure that such stock is moved to a refrigerated area immediately after receipt. By necessity, smaller quantities of this stock will be held but will require more frequent orders.

For restaurants and pubs which serve food, hygiene and food safety regulations are an important consideration and should not be taken lightly. The situation can change regularly with new EC directives forcing changes in the UK. Environmental Health Officers have strong powers and sanctions which could result in the closure of an outlet in extreme circumstances. It is beyond the scope of this book to cover the regulations in detail, but managers should ensure that they are aware of the most up-to-date regulations to avoid potential problems when an Environmental Health Officer makes a surprise visit.

It is also important to keep beer at the right temperature and in the right environment to stop it spoiling. Care should be taken to ensure that the pipes are properly maintained and cleaned to avoid any contamination. The reputation of a pub may depend on the quality of the beer it serves, so every effort should be made to provide beer to the customer in prime condition.

Other stock should be kept in locked storage and only moved to the bar or kitchen when the need arises with movements recorded on a stock requisition.

Food preparation
In order to maximise gross profit margins not only must the cost of the raw materials ordered be minimised but the amount of food used in a particular recipe must be properly controlled to reduce wastage. This can be achieved by controlling the ingredients used in a dish and the portions served.

The techniques which can be used include volume forecasting, the use of standard recipes and portion control. The use of standard recipes is widespread and particularly beneficial in outlets which provide a menu that rarely changes. For example, a pizza restaurant will experiment with different recipes to ensure that the yield from the ingredients is maximised while not compromising the taste. From the results a standard cost per portion should be calculated. Variations from that standard can subsequently be investigated. Mix, yield and volume variances can all be calculated so that an unexpected fall in margins can be analysed into its component parts. Where a restaurant is reliant on providing a varied menu, standard recipes will be of limited benefit.

Volume forecasting techniques are covered in Chapter 2. The principal objective is to forecast as accurately as possible the demand for different dishes so that the optimum level of ingredients can be ordered and the staff resourcing is as efficient as possible.

Portion control is a basic concept to introduce formal controls over the size of portions served. If there are no controls over portion sizes the benefits from accurate volume forecasting and standard recipes will be undermined.

5.6 Overhead costs

Other overheads include the normal running costs of the business outlined in Chapter 2. A well-run business will be able to budget for overheads to within an acceptable margin and would not expect significant variances. However, these costs should be subject to proper controls in the same way as direct costs.

Controls should include segregation of duties between ordering, goods received and payment. There should also be proper evidenced authorisation at each stage from the order through to the payment. The invoice should only be passed for payment if the purchase order, goods received note/delivery note are authorised. Provided the systems controls are in place and working as prescribed the risk of material error or fraud is reduced.

Even with the appropriate controls, overhead costs may still spiral if they are not closely monitored. As part of the month-end procedures, costs incurred to date should be compared to budget and significant variances analysed. Problems can occur when management accounts include budgeted rather than actual costs with a view to making an adjustment at the year end. This approach can result in unwelcome surprises which could have been avoided if action had been taken earlier in the year. Another useful check is to look at costs as a percentage of turnover. This will be of limited benefit during periods of rapid turnover increases or decreases, but is a useful benchmark when turnover remains relatively static.

5.7 Physical and other controls

Tangible assets, stock and cash can all be physically removed by the opportunist thief. Therefore, as well as the internal and accounting controls there should be physical and other controls to reduce this risk.

5.7.1 Fixed assets

A degree of control can be exerted over fixed assets by maintaining a register of all the assets purchased by an operation. The register should include details of the asset and its location. Any movements between locations should be reflected in the register. From time to time a physical check should be performed and compared with the register.

5.7.2 Stock

Pub or restaurant stock is a high risk area. There should be limited access to the cellar or storeroom which should be kept locked. It should be a practical impossibility to remove stock from the premises without passing through a common area to reach the outside.

5.7.3 Cash

Both pubs and restaurants take significant amounts of cash during each session or sitting. Cash is easily pilfered and should be on site for the shortest period which is practically possible. After every shift, till reconciliations should be carried out and floats monitored. Care needs to be taken to ensure that the bankings agree to the till readings and that the float is maintained – any discrepancies should be made up by the relevant staff. Daily bankings should subsequently be agreed to bank statements and, for multi-site operations, to the returns made by each outlet.

Creating the right culture in a small cash-based business should be a key objective. Management have an important role to play in establishing this culture. By making themselves visible to all staff and ensuring that controls are properly operated, the manager will discourage dishonesty or carelessness. However, he will need to temper this with the need to avoid creating an air of distrust which could demotivate staff. The correct balance will depend on the individual circumstances.

5.8 Other specific issues

5.8.1 Accommodation

Many pubs and some restaurants also provide limited accommodation. It is beyond the scope of this book to cover this area in detail but there are some key controls which should be borne in mind.

Reservations
To avoid the risk of undercharging customers, fees agreed at the registration stage should be based on a fixed tariff although this should not preclude commercial decisions to offer, for example, special weekend rates.

Supply of goods and services
It is unlikely that a small pub or restaurant with accommodation will have a fully integrated EPOS system which allows for all services, meals, etc. to be automatically added to a particular customer's invoice.

The recording of meals, drinks and services provided should be actioned as soon as possible after the event and passed to a central point for inclusion on a customer's accommodation bill. The risk is greater for goods/services provided shortly before the customer leaves.

To reduce the risk of customers not paying for breakfast the cost can be included in the price of the accommodation, i.e., 'bed and breakfast'. Many hotels rely on an 'honesty' system for drinks consumed from a minibar, however, the easiest control is not to provide a minibar facility. Wherever possible, customers should be encouraged to pay for goods or services provided at the point of sale so that only accommodation is paid for on leaving.

Payment
It is common practice nowadays to take an imprint of a credit card to carry out a vetting procedure at the time a customer checks in. This is a sensible control which should be encouraged. Where practical all clients should be asked to settle their accounts on leaving with credit only being given in exceptional circumstances. This reduces the risk of bad debts and the possibilities for 'teeming and lading'.

5.8.2 Functions

Many pubs and restaurants will have function rooms which can be hired out for private parties. In some cases a charge will be made for the hire of the room, in others the room will be complimentary provided a set volume of business is achieved. Whatever the arrangements there are risks involved due to the large amounts of food and drinks usually involved and the difficulty the customer has in verifying the costs.

Where the function's host provides for a float to be spent after which drinks will be paid for individually, there is a risk that the barman will account for non-existent sales to increase the outlet's profits. Alternatively, he may falsely declare that the float has been spent and pocket the remaining funds. The latter will be more difficult if an EPOS system is in operation and the amounts keyed in are visible.

A restaurant with banqueting facilities can also create problems. It is common for a host to order a standard menu for his guests plus a set number of bottles of wine and other drinks. In a large party it is unlikely that the host will be able to keep track of the number of bottles opened. The temptation for the banqueting manager will be to provide fewer bottles than allowed for. Subsequently, he will be able to sell the remaining bottles again.

The nature of private functions or parties makes them difficult to control. Management should make sure that functions are separately accounted for so that the profit margins can be reviewed. However, where the customer has been defrauded the margins will not be affected. If there are concerns, stock checks can be carried out before and after a function to ensure that the stock movements agree to the total bottles invoiced to the customer.

5.8.3 AWP and entertainment

Controls over AWP and other gaming machines should be relatively straightforward. In most cases AWP machines will be rented on a fixed rental or based on a percentage of profits or a combination of both. Usually, machines are emptied once a week by the suppliers. This is the key risk area as there is scope for the supplier's employee to under-record the takings. It is important, therefore, that the manager of the outlet verifies the amounts taken from the machine at the time that it is emptied. In general, the takings will be apportioned between the parties, who should sign a two-part document as evidence.

Nowadays, with the demand for entertainment in pubs increasing many offer live acts, often based on a particular theme. The purpose of such events is to increase trade, and therefore profitability, so it is important that the costs of staging the event are compared with the increased revenue generated as a result. If this sort of analysis is not carried out, management will not be aware whether costs are being needlessly incurred.

Care should be taken in paying entertainers as there may be tax implications. These are discussed in Chapter 8 below.

The manager must ensure that the outlet has the appropriate gaming permit for the number of AWP machines in the establishment and that it has a public entertainment licence to cover any entertainment where more than two performers are involved. There is also a requirement to pay licence fees to the Performing Rights Society, which collects money on behalf of music composers, if the outlet has a jukebox or plays any form of music under copyright. There may be other potential liabilities which an outlet can incur without the manager's knowledge. It is important that the appropriate enquiries are made when any new form of entertainment is introduced to the pub. The manager needs to be aware of these obligations as substantial penalties can be imposed where an outlet neglects to make the appropriate payments.

5.9 Information technology

The use of a computer system, including EPOS, can save valuable management time and improve controls over stock and other areas. However, it is important that any system works in conjunction with internal controls. It will also be necessary to limit the access to different parts of the system using passwords or other forms of protection. For instance, it would be inappropriate if bar staff were able to access and adjust the stock records. All relevant staff should be properly trained in the use of computers to minimise the risk of keying errors and inefficiency. The detailed considerations for choosing and implementing a computer system are discussed in Chapter 4.

5.10 Disability Discrimination Act

The Disability Discrimination Act has brought in new laws aimed at ending discrimination faced by disabled people. It will have a direct effect on pubs and restaurants for two reasons, firstly, in their capacity as employers and, secondly, as providers of goods and services.

Every pub and restaurant will have to take reasonable steps to ensure that they do not discriminate against disabled people. It will be illegal to treat a disabled person less favourably than an able-bodied person because of their disability, unless there is good reason. However, importantly for many pubs and restaurants, the Act does not apply to businesses with fewer than 20 staff.

Under the Act it will be illegal to:

(a) refuse to serve someone on the grounds of their disability;
(b) offer a lower standard of service to a disabled person compared with an able-bodied person;
(c) provide a service to a disabled person on different terms from those offered to an able-bodied person.

As a result, pubs and restaurants may have to make changes to the way they operate. A pub or restaurant will not be able to run their outlet in such a way that it makes it impossible or unreasonably difficult for a disabled person to use them, unless it is fundamental to the business, e.g., dim lighting. Pubs and restaurants will also have to provide equipment, etc. which will make it easier for a disabled person to use their services, provided it is reasonable to do so. Physical obstructions must be removed where relevant or alternative access arranged. None of the costs of implementing these changes can be recovered by charging disabled people more than able-bodied people.

The provisions of the Act are being implemented in stages, such that by 2005 pubs and restaurants will be required to ensure that all disabled people have access to their premises.

The Disability Discrimination Act has wide-ranging implications for the trade and should be taken seriously.

Chapter 6 – Financial reporting

6.1 Introduction

Much of the accounting for pubs and restaurants is identical to that for any other business. However, there are areas which are of particular concern to the pub or restaurant manager. Some of the issues discussed in this chapter relate specifically to regulatory requirements governing particular accounting matters, others may have no statutory or regulatory implications but, nevertheless, are issues which are of concern on a day-to-day basis to the owner/manager of a pub or restaurant.

For multiple site operations, the accounting policies adopted by different organisations can have a significant impact on the results reported. Understanding the issues addressed in this chapter will help the manager to assess the true profitability of his operation compared with those of his competitors. From a financial reporting viewpoint, his first concern should be to ensure that the accounting bases and policies adopted conform with the regulatory and statutory requirements. For the unincorporated business there is no requirement to follow the accounting practices set out in the regulatory framework, however, for comparative purposes management may consider that it would be worthwhile to follow some, if not all, of the requirements. The points to be covered in this chapter include:

(a) the regulatory framework and how it impinges on the pub and restaurant trade;
(b) the importance of maintaining proper books and records;
(c) the compilation of financial statements from management accounts; and
(d) significant financial reporting issues for the pub and restaurant industry.

6.2 The regulatory framework and how it impinges on the pub and restaurant trade

It is the directors' responsibility to prepare financial statements for each accounting period. The balance sheet must give a true and fair view of the state of affairs of the company as at the accounting reference date, and the profit and loss account must give a true and fair view of the profit or loss of the company for the period ending on the accounting reference date.

In preparing the financial statements the directors must follow the regulatory framework, including:

(a) the Companies Act 1985 – relevant to all companies;

(b) Statements of Standard Accounting Practice (SSAPs) and, since 1 August 1990, Financial Reporting Standards (FRSs).

A listed company also has to comply with the Listing Rules of the London Stock Exchange.

Before a new FRS is published, it is preceded by a Financial Reporting Exposure Draft (FRED) on which comments are invited. Until it becomes an FRS a company is not obliged to follow the practice recommended within it, however, some entities may wish to do so particularly if informed opinion expects the FRED to proceed to full FRS status. However, care should be taken to ensure that any information so provided does not conflict with standards already in place.

Since 1991 a sub-committee of the Accounting Standards Board (ASB), known as the Urgent Issues Task Force (UITF), has looked into issues where different interpretations have been placed on the same statutory or regulatory requirements. Its objective is to respond quickly to such conflicts and issue 'abstracts' setting out its interpretation of the relevant accounting matters. A company is obliged to follow the UITF's recommendations unless there are good reasons not to.

In the late 1980s and early 1990s a number of high profile companies collapsed shortly after filing apparently healthy accounts, giving rise to concerns about the standard of reporting in financial statements. The problem achieved more notoriety when Terry Smith, an analyst, published his book entitled *Accounting for Growth* in which he identified a number of companies whose accounts he believed to be misleading. Given this background it is not surprising that the ASB has set its stall out to tighten reporting standards and to encourage a more consistent interpretation of them.

Whilst all incorporated businesses are required to work within this regulatory framework, there are some FRSs and SSAPs which are more relevant than others to the restaurant and pub trade. The accounting policies adopted can have a significant effect on the results reported, for instance, the non-depreciation of freehold property is widely believed to increase profits by up to 10 per cent for the major players. Suggested changes to make depreciation of freehold properties compulsory will result in lower reported earnings per share throughout the industry. These and other issues are discussed in detail below.

6.3 The importance of maintaining proper books and records

The pub and restaurant trade is notorious for poor record-keeping. However, the importance of keeping adequate records are twofold:

(a) to provide adequate management information on which to make business decisions; and
(b) as a base from which to prepare financial accounts.

Under section 221 of the Companies Act 1985, a company is obliged to keep proper accounting records. These should be sufficient to show and explain the company's transactions and should be such as to:

(a) disclose with reasonable accuracy, at any time, the financial position of the company at that time; and
(b) enable the directors to ensure that any balance sheet and profit and loss account complies with the requirements of the Companies Act 1985.

Record-keeping is important not only to meet Companies Act requirements but also in order to satisfy Customs & Excise and the Inland Revenue.

The restaurant and pub trade is a cash-based industry and as such is susceptible to fraud. The Inland Revenue and Customs & Excise will expect certain margins depending upon the type of operation. If those margins are not within expected parameters, the Inspectors will carry out further work to ascertain the reasons why. If they are not satisfied or if the records are inadequate to provide the relevant information, they will calculate the liability based on an assumed gross margin which is highly unlikely to be in the restaurateur or publican's favour. For the same reasons, the keeping of proper records is just as important for the unincorporated business as it is for a limited company.

For the multiple site operation adequate records should be kept by each outlet. These must be sufficient to support returns made to head office. The returns should fulfil two functions:

(a) providing head office with up-to-date trading information;
(b) providing head office with sufficient information from which to prepare accounts.

It would be usual for daily sales returns to be made to head office, with more detailed payments and receipts information returned weekly. Using this information, head office will be able to prepare monthly management accounts. Comparisons can then be made between branches and trends against budget can be analysed.

6.4 Filing of accounts

A private company has a duty to file accounts with the Registrar of Companies within 10 months of the accounting year end. A public company is required to file them within seven months of the year end. However, whilst full accounts must be made available to the shareholders, a company which meets the small or medium-sized company criteria under section 247 of the Companies Act 1985 may file an abridged version known as abbreviated accounts. This can be useful where a company wishes to keep certain information from its competitors.

Under section 248 of the Companies Act 1985 a group qualifying as a small or medium-sized group (section 249) need not prepare group accounts for a financial year provided it is not an ineligible group. The exemption does not apply unless the auditors provide a report stating that in their opinion the group is entitled to the exemption. The report must be attached to the individual accounts of the company.

For accounting periods ending on or after 25 March 1997 the special auditor's report will no longer be required. Instead, under a new section 248A the directors must state on the group balance sheet that the accounts are prepared in accordance with the special provisions of Part VII of the Companies Act relating to small companies.

6.5 The compilation of financial statements from management accounts – monthly and quarterly procedures

In order to ensure that proper books and records are maintained, in accordance with the Companies Act 1985, a publican or restaurateur will need to prepare the books in a timely fashion. Even where the business is unincorporated the records must be adequate to satisfy Revenue and Customs authorities.

The complexity of the book-keeping system will depend on the size of the business. In small pubs or restaurants it may be possible to maintain manual records, whereas the larger enterprises are likely to be computerised.

Formal monthly and quarterly procedures should be introduced to ensure that the results processed are meaningful. For example, it is important to ensure that cut-off procedures are adequate. Whilst ensuring that sales are recorded in the correct period will be straightforward, costs are likely to cause more of a problem. If income and costs are not matched it will provide management with misleading information on which to base business decisions. For example, most pubs and restaurants will receive retrospective volume rebates from major suppliers. If no account is taken of the rebates until they are received, it will have the effect of understating the gross margins in the accounts before receipt of the rebate and inflating the gross margin in the month of receipt. Other costs may also need to be prepaid or accrued if the date of payment does not reflect the period over which the costs should be accrued.

The sophistication of the procedures will be dependent on the size and type of operation. In many cases the benefits of making full provision for accruals and prepayments would outweigh the costs in management time. For items which are reasonably fixed in nature a budgeted monthly cost will be adequate for monthly accounts purposes.

Management will principally be concerned with the trading results and so should endeavour to ensure that the margin analysis is as accurate as possible. The use of EPOS systems will allow a line-by-line analysis but may not be cost-effective in a smaller operation. A similar sales analysis can be provided by an independent stocktaker and the margin then compared by period.

At the year end, the disciplines will need to be more rigid to ensure that all income and costs are included in the correct period so that financial accounts can be drawn up which show a true and fair view.

6.6 Significant financial reporting issues in the pub and restaurant industry

There are a number of financial reporting issues which are of great significance to the pub and restaurant sector. Most pub companies have expanding estates with rolling programmes for new outlets. As a result the treatment of fixed assets, including their non-depreciation and valuation, and the treatment of pre-opening expenses have a significant impact on reported results. The following issues are covered in the paragraphs below:

- revaluation of fixed assets;
- accounting for permanent or temporary diminutions in value;
- accounting for a profit or loss on disposal of a pub or restaurant;
- non-depreciation of freehold and long leasehold property;
- other property-related matters;
- pre-opening costs;
- goodwill.

The contrasting treatment by different pub companies is illustrated by research carried out on a number of pub companies, most of which serve food or own restaurant chains. The results of the research are attached at Appendix 6.

6.6.1 Revaluation of fixed assets

The alternative accounting rules set out in the Companies Act allow fixed assets to be included at their market value or current cost, although generally, fixed assets should be recorded at production cost or purchase price less depreciation. Not surprisingly, most pub companies and restaurants choose to revalue their assets. However, the issue is complicated as a company has a choice over the assets which it revalues and the frequency of those revaluations. As a result, making a meaningful comparison between different pub companies or restaurant groups is very difficult.

Most pub companies opt for periodic revaluations usually of three or five-year intervals, although some revalue a proportion of their estate on an annual basis. In some instances, a premium will be attached to the sum of the individual pubs within an estate to reflect the economies of scale which may result from the purchase of a portfolio. There is a concern amongst industry commentators that companies have been keen to revalue properties when values are rising but are more reluctant to reflect a fall in value, preferring instead to treat any decrease in value as a temporary rather than a permanent diminution.

Even if the basis of valuation is the same, empirical evidence suggests that valuations carried out for two different companies will not necessarily be comparable. Queens Moat House Hotels were valued at 31 December 1992 by two different firms of chartered surveyors using the same basis. Controversially, the valuations differed by £500 million.

This flexibility in accounting for revaluations and the fact that most pub and restaurant companies do not depreciate freehold or long leasehold properties (see **6.6.4**) has made analysts suspicious of the sector, which is reflected in the relative performance of the sector *vis-à-vis* the stock market as a whole.

The valuation of fixed assets and the practice of non-depreciation continues to excite industry comment and is an area for which the ASB is aiming to impose a more consistent approach. In March 1993, the ASB issued a Discussion Paper *The Role of Valuation in Financial Reporting* in which it proposed that there should be a continuation of the present modified historical cost system, but that it should be amended to remove existing anomalies. In April 1996 the ASB issued a Discussion Paper entitled *Impairment of Tangible Fixed Assets* to address the lack of authoritative guidance surrounding the issue of diminution in value. Subsequently, in October 1996 it issued a further Discussion Paper covering issues such as the depreciation and revaluation of fixed assets entitled *Measurement of Tangible Fixed Assets* building on the responses received from the March 1993 Discussion Paper. The ASB's recommendations arising from these recent Discussion Papers are referred to below.

Should a company revalue its portfolio of pubs or restaurants?
The majority of pub and restaurant companies revalue their portfolios for the following reasons:

(a) Companies with large estates (particularly tenanted estates) are effectively property companies and can argue that revaluing their portfolios will present the reader of the accounts with a more meaningful net current asset value per share.

(b) An asset valuation may be required by a potential lender assessing the security for a loan. A lower valuation recorded in the accounts may lead to misunderstanding.

(c) It is standard practice in the industry and may result in unnecessary focus on an individual company's accounts if such a policy were not adopted.

(d) It creates a more meaningful figure for calculations and analysis to be carried out, such as return on capital employed. However, business ratios are only meaningful if the figures from which they are calculated are derived on a consistent basis. Comparing the return on capital of one company which has not revalued its properties with that of another which has will be misleading.

Since revaluing the property portfolios of pub and restaurant companies normally creates a stronger looking and, it can be argued, more meaningful balance sheet, it is unlikely that any company with a significant portfolio would choose not to revalue, particularly as most companies do not depreciate their freehold and long leasehold property. If they did, the profit and loss account would reflect higher depreciation as the charge would be based on the revalued amount. In this situation companies would report a lower earnings per share.

In general, pub and restaurant chains should revalue their properties on an outlet-by-outlet basis. However, it is becoming increasingly common for estates to be valued on a portfolio basis, which raises the concern that a diminution in value on one may be set off against a revaluation profit on another.

How often should valuations be carried out and what basis of valuation should be used?

The present modified historical cost system of valuing fixed assets allows for periodic revaluations to be reflected in the carrying value of the asset in the balance sheet. As discussed, this has caused inconsistencies between different companies, particularly in industries where property makes up a significant portion of the balance sheet assets such as the pub or restaurant sector. Of the 15 pub companies' annual accounts reviewed, 13 included revaluations but only three of these contained a detailed note explaining their policy. Of these three, two revalued a proportion annually (either one-fifth or one-third) and the other undertook valuations 'if considered appropriate' based on a regular review.

In the Discussion Paper *Measurement of Tangible Fixed Assets* the ASB proposes that professional valuations should be carried out at least every five years and that interim valuations should be carried out in the intervening years. This is considered in more detail below.

> ***Example***
>
> Whitbread
>
> Fixed assets include properties professionally valued by Chartered Surveyors employed by the Group and by external valuers. 20% of the Group's UK properties are valued each year under a programme which ensures that every property is valued at least once every five years.

It is generally accepted that the most appropriate method of valuation for pubs and restaurants is open market value for existing use taking into account the trading potential of the business. Pubs and restaurants are normally sold as fully operational businesses and the prices are based on their trading potential. The value attached to the trading potential will take account of previous years' trading, any growth potential and the state of the market as a whole.

The Royal Institution of Chartered Surveyors (RICS) provides guidance on the valuation of properties for the purpose of inclusion in financial accounts which is incorporated in its 'Approval and Valuation Manual'. RICS defines open market value as:

> 'The best price at which the sale of an interest in a property would have been completed unconditionally for cash consideration at the date of valuation.'

The definition is subject to a number of assumptions which are reproduced at Appendix 7.

When a property is valued on the basis of its existing use, two additional assumptions are made:

> '(a) the property can be used for the foreseeable future only for its existing use; and
> (b) that vacant possession is provided on completion of the sale of all parts of the property occupied by the business.'

The Discussion Paper *Measurement of Tangible Fixed Assets* is proposing the continuation of the modified historical cost system subject to the following requirements for non-specialised properties such as pubs and restaurants:

(a) the carrying value should be the current value of the asset at the balance sheet date;
(b) pubs and restaurants should be valued by adopting the existing use value, but where open market value is materially different, the relevant information should be given in notes to the financial statements.

The valuation should be of the property and not of the business

The aim of any valuation should be to value a property excluding any internally generated goodwill and to exclude any intangible assets (such as a liquor licence) which would not pass with the property. Internally generated goodwill should therefore be separated out from a valuation as should intangible assets. The problem for a valuer will be in distinguishing between the value of the trading potential which runs with the property and the value of the goodwill created by the present owner. The principle is set out in SSAP 22:

> 'Some property assets are valued on a basis which has regard to the trading potential which attaches to the property. This trading potential is sometimes thought of as goodwill but such a basis of valuation should normally exclude any goodwill which is personal to the present owner or management and which would not pass with the property on a sale with vacant possession . . .'

Where the practice is followed:

> 'the assets concerned should be disclosed separately and the notes to the accounts should make clear that this practice has been followed and that the amount at which the assets concerned are stated does not exceed their open market value having regard to the trading potential of the business.'

In other words, a valuer should endeavour to differentiate between the value of a property taking into account its trading potential and the value of the business *per se*.

The valuation should not include fixtures and fittings already capitalised

A further difficulty arises in respect of fixtures and fittings. A pub valuation based on trading potential will inevitably include fixtures and fittings such as chairs, tables and other furnishings which are necessary for the business to function. However, some if not all of these assets are likely to have been capitalised in the accounts as a separate category of fixed assets. If these items are not deducted from the valuation they will be double counted.

Who should carry out a revaluation?

The Companies Act recognises that obtaining regular external valuations is expensive and may be impractical, and therefore allows directors, who are part of the business on a day-to-day basis, to carry out revaluations of properties and include their valuations in the financial statement provided they are disclosed as such.

The ASB's Discussion Paper *Measurement of Tangible Fixed Assets* attempts to clarify the position further to ensure greater consistency of treatment between companies, particularly those in the same industry. It recommends that:

(a) where an entity elects to revalue its pubs or restaurants, a full external valuation for all properties of the same class should be carried out every five years; and

(b) interim valuations should be undertaken in the intervening years.

The interim valuation should either be carried out by external professional valuers or, in certain circumstances, undertaken by the directors. In the case of a directors' interim valuation, the directors must take advice from a valuer holding a recognised professional qualification with recent experience in the location and category of properties concerned. That person could be an employee or officer of the company. However, it is recommended that interim valuations should be carried out by professional valuers in specific circumstances (see Appendix 7).

Accounting for revaluations
A surplus will arise if an asset is revalued at an amount higher than the net book value at the date of the valuation. The Companies Act 1985 states that any such surplus must be taken to a revaluation reserve in the balance sheet and not through the profit and loss account. In accordance with FRS 3 the surplus should be dealt with in the statement of total recognised gains and losses. The effect is to make any surplus a non-distributable reserve. Even where the asset has been previously depreciated, cumulative depreciation charged cannot be credited to the profit and loss account. It is a Companies Act requirement to depreciate assets over their estimated useful economic lives.

The suggested treatment set out in the ASB's Discussion Paper *Measurement of Tangible Fixed Assets* is consistent with the present approach prescribed by FRS 3.

6.6.2 Accounting for permanent or temporary diminutions in value

Where a revaluation of a pub or restaurant results in a decrease in its carrying value, the reduction will need to be reflected in the accounts. It is important that a diminution in value of one outlet should not be set against a revaluation surplus in another. In this respect the implication of revaluing an estate as a whole as opposed to individual outlets needs to be considered carefully.

Whilst it is a requirement under FRS 3 to write down the value of assets to reflect a permanent diminution in value, there is no detailed guidance on what constitutes permanent diminution as distinct from a temporary diminution. There is also uncertainty as to the most appropriate method of calculating the charge to the profit and loss where a permanent diminution has reduced the value of a fixed asset to below its carrying value.

FRS 3 dictates that where there has been a revaluation, any permanent diminution in value below carrying value should be charged to the profit and loss account, however, it is less clear on the treatment of the associated revaluation reserve. There are two alternatives:

(a) the related balance on the revaluation reserve is taken as a movement in profit and loss reserves; or
(b) the related balance in the revaluation reserve is taken directly to the profit and loss account in accordance with paragraph 3(7)(a) of Schedule 4 to the Companies Act.

Both these methods are acceptable at present. In practice, the first will usually result in a higher profit and loss charge in the period as the effect is to take the whole of the difference (i.e., the diminution in value) between the carrying value of the asset and its revalued amount to the profit and loss account. In contrast, the second method has the effect of recognising in the profit and loss account that proportion of the loss which takes the carrying value below the depreciated historical cost. Under para 3(7)(a) of Schedule 4 to the Companies Act, the charge for the permanent diminution in value and the release of the credit on the revaluation reserve should be shown separately with the latter shown below profit after taxation. However, industry lobbyists would like to see the two amounts netted off. In practice the first method is normally adopted.

More recently, the Discussion Paper *Measurement of Tangible Fixed Assets* recommends that, to the extent that a loss arises which reduces the carrying value down to the depreciated historical cost, it is permissible to take the loss to the revaluation reserve reported in the statement of total recognised gains and losses. However, if the carrying value falls below the depreciated historical cost, to the extent that there has been an impairment to the income-generating outlet, the proportion of the loss which takes the carrying value below the depreciated historical cost should be recognised in the profit and loss account. However, if it can be demonstrated that there is no impairment, the entire loss can be passed through the statement of total recognised gains and losses. One implication is that any reduction in the value following a revaluation based on the trading potential of an outlet must, by definition, except in rare circumstances, be an impairment and therefore reflected through the profit and loss account.

In a separate Discussion Paper entitled *Impairment of Tangible Fixed Assets* the ASB acknowledges that there is a lack of guidance in recognising and measuring the impairment of fixed assets (whether through a permanent or temporary diminution) and seeks to redress the situation by recommending that fluctuations in net realisable value below carrying value need only be regarded as impairments if the present value of cash flows expected from continuing use and ultimate sale has also fallen below the carrying value. As a result, a fall in market value (whether considered to be permanent or temporary) would not necessarily be treated as an impairment.

Further, the Discussion Paper moves away from the use of the word temporary or permanent diminution, instead focusing on an impairment resulting from a reduction in the future earning potential of an outlet *vis-à-vis* an impairment which results from general changes in price. It is suggested that the former should be recognised in the profit and loss account and the latter in the statement of total recognised gains and losses, to the extent that the impairment takes the carrying value down to the depreciated historical cost, after which the impairment should be recognised in the profit and loss account.

Until such a time that the Discussion Paper becomes an accepted standard, companies should continue to recognise the whole of a permanent diminution in value through the profit and loss account.

6.6.3 Accounting for a profit or loss on disposal of a pub or restaurant

In the paragraphs above we have discussed the treatment of unrealised gains or losses on the revaluation of fixed assets. But what should the treatment be when a property is sold? Any revaluation surpluses will have been passed through the statement of total recognised gains and losses and so, to avoid recognising a gain more than once, the gain or loss to be taken through the profit and loss account will be calculated by reference to the carrying value of the asset. The balance on the revaluation reserve should be passed through as a movement on profit and loss reserves.

Under FRS 3, material profits or losses on the disposal of fixed assets must be included on the face of the profit and loss account as a separate 'non-operating' item.

6.6.4 Non-depreciation of freehold and long leasehold property

It is common practice in the pub and restaurant sector not to depreciate freehold and long leasehold properties. If inconsistencies in the policies adopted by companies in revaluing property portfolios have made comparisons between companies within the sector very difficult, the practice of non-depreciation has made comparisons with companies in other sectors equally problematic.

The practice of non-depreciation of freehold and long leasehold properties is well established. However, the Companies Act stipulates that any fixed asset that has a limited useful economic life must be depreciated over its economic life on a systematic basis down to its residual value. SSAP 12 revised defines depreciation as:

> 'the measure of the wearing out, consumption, or other reduction in the useful life of a fixed asset whether arising from use, effluxion of time or obsolescence through technological or market changes.'

It also states that:

> 'provision for depreciation of fixed assets having a finite useful economic life should be made by allocating the cost (or revalued amount) less stated residual value of the assets as fairly as possible to the periods expected to benefit from their use.'

Given these definitions and requirements, how have pub and restaurant companies justified the non-depreciation of their long leasehold and freehold estates?

Generally speaking, most pub and restaurant companies do not depreciate leasehold property with an unexpired term of more than 20 years. Under SSAP 19, investment properties with more than 20 years to run are not required to be depreciated. However, pubs and restaurants are an integral part of the trade, and therefore held for consumption in the business, and should not be considered as investment properties. In any event, even allowing for the non-depreciation of long leasehold properties, the Companies Act implies a short-term lease is anything less than 50 years, in which case it would be more appropriate to depreciate all leases with a unexpired term of 50 years or less.

Additional arguments for the non-depreciation of long leasehold and freehold properties include:

(a) it would be inappropriate to depreciate a pub or restaurant which is not declining in value;
(b) the value of the pub or restaurant exceeds its cost;
(c) the pub or restaurant has an unlimited life;
(d) the residual value is so high and life so long that any depreciation charge would be immaterial;
(e) the pub or restaurant is maintained to an appropriately high standard in order to continue to attract customers.

The first two of these arguments do not stand up to scrutiny since they imply that the act of depreciating is a measure of the loss of value of an asset or a provision for a replacement rather than a measure of consumption, arrived at by allocating the cost (less residual value) over the useful economic life of the asset concerned.

The remaining arguments are to an extent linked. The logic is that if a pub or restaurant is maintained to a very high standard its useful economic life will necessarily be elongated and its residual value sustained. In essence, the argument is that the level of expenditure on maintaining the property to its present standard approximates to any depreciation charge made to reflect the 'wearing out' of the property. In these circumstances the level of any depreciation would be immaterial. Whilst there is some sympathy with this view it has not been formally recognised in a standard as it is felt it would be subject to abuse.

The counter-argument is that maintenance costs should be capitalised and depreciated over their estimated useful life as a separate category of fixed assets.

> ***Example***
>
> Harry Ramsden's 1995 annual report and accounts
>
> No depreciation is provided on freehold properties as it is the group's policy to maintain these assets in a continual state of sound repair. The useful economic lives of these assets are thus so long and the residual value so high that any depreciation would not be material. The residual values are based on prices prevailing at the date of acquisition or subsequent revaluation. Provision is made in the profit and loss account for any permanent diminution in value.

Harry Ramsden's accounting policy note reporting the non-depreciation of freehold properties is typical of the industry and reflects the need, following the FRRP's recommendations, to state that:

(a) the appraisal of residual values was based on prices prevailing at the time of acquisition or subsequent valuations; and
(b) the company has a policy to provide for any permanent diminution in value in the profit and loss account.

The issue remains controversial due to the inconsistencies in the methods adopted, partly as a result of the lack of guidance relating to the estimation and reassessment of residual values and useful economic lives. The ASB has tried to address the situation in its Discussion Paper *Measurement of Tangible Fixed Assets* in which it makes a number of recommendations (details attached at Appendix 8), the effect of which is to require all properties to be depreciated to their residual values provided those residual values are based on prices prevailing at the date of acquisition or revaluation. Furthermore, it re-emphasises that 'depreciation should be viewed as a measure of the cost of the economic benefits of the tangible fixed assets that have been consumed during the period'. Given the concern expressed by interested parties it is likely that the ASB's recommendations will be introduced in some form in the foreseeable future.

6.7 Other property-related matters

6.7.1 Sale and leaseback

Sale and leaseback of an outlet may be used by a company to improve a short-term cash flow problem or to meet a particular cash need.

Under SSAP 21 *Accounting for Leases and Hire Purchase Contracts* the treatment will depend on whether the lease agreement is in the nature of a finance or operating lease. If the leaseback arrangements are a finance lease, the property will remain on balance sheet and the proceeds for the sale of the outlet treated as a secured loan repayable over the period of the lease. The balance of the total lease payments over and above the proceeds of the sale represent the finance costs to be taken to the profit and loss account over the period of the lease in accordance with SSAP 21.

On the other hand, if the leaseback is in the form of an operating lease, the property would be treated as a sale in the normal way with any profit or loss shown on the face of the profit and loss account in accordance with paragraph 20 of FRS 3.

Under FRS 5 the substance of the transaction needs to be carefully examined to decide whether any leaseback – particularly where the lessee is granted an option to repurchase – is more in the nature of a financing transaction than an operating lease, in which case it should be brought on balance sheet as a finance lease. This will involve reviewing the terms to see whether the lessor is being compensated for exposure to losses or is simply receiving a normal 'lenders' return'. Clearly, if no compensation is included, the lease is more in the nature of a financing operation and should be recognised as a finance lease.

6.7.2 Capitalisation of interest costs

The Companies Act allows any interest on the capital cost of financing the construction of a pub or restaurant to be capitalised as part of the production cost. The amount capitalised will depend firstly on how the project concerned is financed and secondly on the company's overall borrowings. Even if the company has not had to borrow specifically to finance the project, it can deem part of its overall borrowings to be the incremental costs of financing the project and capitalise an appropriate portion of the interest. However, notional interest cannot be charged where a project is financed through equity or a new issue of shares and not through borrowings.

The problem with the capitalising of interest is that it is optional and so, again, leads to inconsistencies in accounts. The ASB has recognised this in its Discussion Paper *Measurement of Tangible Fixed Assets* and proposes that the capitalisation of interest should be either mandatory or totally prohibited, but has no preference at present.

In any event the interest should only be capitalised during the period of 'production' of the asset. In the case of a pub or restaurant, it seems logical to continue to capitalise interest up to the date when trading commences, i.e., when the asset is ready for use. None of the companies we reviewed defined the period over which interest was capitalised. Subsequently, the interest costs should be charged to the profit and loss account to be matched against the income.

> ***Example***
>
> The Greenalls Group – 1995 Report and Accounts
>
> The cost of tangible fixed assets represents the actual purchase price paid. Cost includes gross interest on capital invested in major property development, and attributable overheads.

The total amount of interest costs incurred, together with the amount capitalised, must be disclosed. The amount of interest capitalised should normally be shown as a deduction from gross interest payable.

6.8 Pre-opening expenses

Pre-opening costs are those costs (other than construction and related costs) incurred by the pub or restaurant prior to it becoming available for use after its construction or major refurbishment. Typically, pre-opening expenses will include rent and rates, marketing, advertising and promotional costs, staff training and staff employment costs.

Pre-opening costs are normally deferred on the grounds that they should properly be matched against income from the operation when it comes into use. This is acceptable providing it can be argued that the costs incurred now will help to generate increased income in the future. It should normally be possible to justify such treatment by referring to forecast trading results for the operation concerned. If this is not the case the costs should be written off to profit and loss account immediately.

The problem a pub or restaurant company has is in deciding what comprises pre-opening costs, over what period to defer costs and over what period to write off the costs subsequently.

The period over which costs may be deferred is intuitively straightforward in that there seems little room for doubt that costs should be deferred from the date of commencement of work to the date of opening of the outlet concerned. However, many companies have found ways to extend the period by interpreting the date of an outlet's 'opening' in different ways. Often the accounting policy note in the account is unclear and leaves the date after which deferred expenditure is written off open to misinterpretation.

> ***Example***
>
> The Greenalls Group – 1995 Report and Accounts
>
> In the case of contractors and major development of hotels, pre-opening costs and related start up expenses incurred in the period up to commencement of full trading are deferred and amortised over five years.

The period of time over which these costs are written off can also vary and will depend to an extent on the type and size of operation. However, there appears to be little consistency in approach with some companies not including a policy note regarding pre-opening expenses and others capitalising costs as part of the costs of construction or as part of leasehold improvements.

> ***Example***
>
> My Kinda Town plc – 1995 Annual Account
>
> Leasehold improvements include pre-opening expenses. The carrying value of these costs is reviewed annually by the directors in the light of the trading experience of the restaurants and a write-off is made, if necessary.

Ideally, the policy on pre-opening costs should be as transparent as possible by stating the precise period over which pre-opening costs are deferred and the period over which they are written off. The note should also state exactly which costs are being deferred.

6.9 Accounting for acquisitions – goodwill

In recent years, partly as a result of the Beer Orders there has been constant activity in the pub and restaurant market.

Where a group has made an acquisition, the assets brought into the group will have to be stated at fair value in accordance with FRS 7, which sets out for the first time what constitutes fair value.

FRS 7 has reduced the opportunity for the costs of reorganisation, additional provisions and future operating losses to be included as part of the fair value of the liabilities of an acquired company. In particular, it sets out the general principle that the following be treated as post-acquisition items:

(a) charges resulting from the acquirer's intentions or future actions;
(b) impairments, or other charges, resulting from events subsequent to the acquisition;
(c) provisions or accruals for future operating losses or for reorganisation and integration costs expected to be incurred as a result of the acquisition, whether they relate to the acquired entity or to the acquirer.

Only if the acquiree can demonstrate that it was independently committed to the changes requiring the provisions prior to entering into negotiations for the takeover should the provisions be allowed as a fair value adjustment. If the acquiree undertook the changes at the behest of the acquirer, this implies it became a subsidiary at an earlier date.

Purchased goodwill is the difference between the fair value of the net assets acquired and the fair value of the consideration given. Under present practice SSAP 22 allows purchased goodwill to be treated as an asset (rather than a consolidation difference) and amortised on a systematic basis over its useful economic life, but the preferred practice is to eliminate purchased goodwill immediately against reserves. In FRED 12 *Goodwill and Intangible Assets* issued in June 1996 the ASB proposed that goodwill should be capitalised and:

(a) amortised over a period which normally should not exceed 20 years;
(b) carried at cost less provisions for permanent diminution in value assessed annually.

6.10 Other accounting matters

6.10.1 Base stocks

Pubs and restaurants alike have a need for minor fixed assets including glasses, cutlery and tablecloths. By their nature these items need to be replaced as they are subject to vigorous use. It would therefore be impractical to record each item separately as fixed asset or to apply a depreciation policy to them. How should these items be accounted for? One method would be to write them off to profit and loss account as and when the costs are incurred.

Alternatively, and more usually, a base stock can be established, which represents the likely level of requirement at any one point in time. A fixed amount equal to the base stock should be capitalised and not subject to change either by additional purchases or by depreciation unless there is a permanent change in the level of activity of the company. Any new expenditure is written off to profit and loss account as incurred. Such a treatment is permitted under the Companies Act provided the base stock is not material to an assessment of the company's state of affairs and is not subject to material variations.

6.10.2 Accounting for tronc

The accounting for tronc, i.e., tips and gratuities, is important only to the extent that the method used will dictate whether or not NICs are payable. Provided that any tips and gratuities are collected into a central pool or tronc prior to being distributed amongst the staff by a 'troncmaster' no NIC will be payable. This is considered in more detail in **8.4** below.

6.10.3 Brewery loans

It is fairly common for a publican to accept lump sums or periodic payments from a brewer in return for agreeing to purchase beer exclusively from that brewer. The payment received may be potentially repayable, but the agreement may provide for periodic waiver of the liability provided the terms of the exclusivity agreement are adhered to. If the agreement runs its full course, more of the lump sum will be repayable.

In these circumstances, the right to the income is contingent on the publican continuing to operate within the terms of the agreement. Therefore, the amounts received should only be credited to the profit and loss account when, in accordance with the agreement, they are no longer repayable. Over time, provided the conditions of the agreement are met, the entire lump sum will be credited to the profit and loss account.

In these circumstances the requirement under the Companies Act and accounting standards to disclose the repayment periods between amounts repayable (within one year, between one and two years, between two and five years, and over five years) can only be based on forecast barrelage for the relevant periods. In subsequent years the amounts disclosed in the accounts may not be directly related to the previous year's estimates.

6.10.4 Franchising

Franchising is a method which allows a business to expand with minimum risk where capital outlay is a limiting factor. It will normally involve the franchiser charging the franchisee an initial fee for training staff and setting up the business and a recurring fee usually based on turnover, but may also include a mark-up on purchases. Effectively, the recurring fee is a charge for the use of the brand name in an established business and may include a recharge for the use of central services such as marketing and purchasing. The franchisee, on the other hand, has the benefit of investing in an established business with the added advantages associated with a centralised marketing department.

For accounting purposes, the principal concern will be how to treat the initial fees in the books of the franchisee and the franchiser. In the case of the franchisee it would be normal to capitalise the initial payment and amortise over the duration of the franchise contract. The recurring fee should be written off as incurred. In the books of the franchiser the income from the initial fee may be taken directly to profit and loss or deferred and spread over the duration of the franchise contract. As a separate issue the franchiser will need to consider whether any goodwill which arose on the purchase of the brand by the franchiser should be amortised and set against the income taken.

6.11 Summary

This chapter has covered the major financial reporting issues affecting the pub and restaurant industry. Most of the significant matters relate to fixed assets which form an integral part of a restaurant or pub company's balance sheet. At present, there are inconsistencies in the manner in which properties are accounted for which makes comparisons within the sector and with other sectors difficult. The ASB has recognised the problem and has issued Discussion Papers which attempt to resolve these inconsistencies. It is likely that many of the accounting treatment options available now will not be available in the foreseeable future. In particular, it seems likely that all companies will be obliged to depreciate their freehold and long leasehold properties.

Chapter 7 – Taxation

7.1 Introduction

This chapter focuses on the areas of taxation that are of particular relevance to pubs and restaurants and assumes some familiarity with the UK tax system. It deals primarily with the taxation of pubs and restaurants owned and/or operated by companies; it also refers briefly to the tax treatment of sole traders and family partnerships, particularly in the light of the new self-assessment tax regime. Statutory references are to the Income and Corporation Taxes Act (ICTA) 1988 unless otherwise stated.

7.2 Trading income

The main sources of income for pubs and restaurants are set out in Figure 7.1 below.

Figure 7.1

Income source	*Pubs*	*Restaurants*
Alcohol	✓	✓
Food	✓	✓
Catering and functions	✓	✓
Room sales	✓ (Those with accommodation also)	
Games machines	✓	
Snooker/pool and darts	✓	
Gratuities/service charge		✓
Sundry income, e.g., telephones	✓	✓
advertising	✓	

All these sources of income will normally be taxed as income of the same trade under Schedule D Case I. A licensed victualler running a tied house is treated as carrying on a trade at the public house of which he is a tenant.

7.3 Other income

Apart from its trading income, a pub or restaurant may have some other sources of income, examples of which are as follows:

(a) There may be a flat or flats above or attached to the pub or restaurant in respect of which the company or other owner receives rent which would be taxable under Schedule A.

(b) It is possible for a property investment company to own a public house or restaurant and let it to a tenant or manager. Rent paid to the company would be subject to corporation tax under the Schedule A rules.
(c) Income from pub catering will usually form part of the ordinary Schedule D Case I profits of the tenant or owner of the pub. However, it may be a business on the side run independently by a manager.
(d) In the case of the licensee, any cash gratuities he receives are taxable, whereas drinks bought for him by customers are treated as not being taxable as the nature of the gratuities are such that they are not normally convertible into cash.
(e) Receipts under exclusivity agreements. Under the terms of these agreements the amount received from the brewery may not be repayable if certain conditions are met (see **6.10.3** above).

    The possibility that in certain circumstances, a receipt under an exclusivity agreement may have to be repaid does not cause it to be characterised as a loan (see *Smart* v *Lincolnshire Sugar Co Ltd*, 20 TC 643). The two issues to consider are:

    (i) whether the receipt is on capital or on revenue account; and
    (ii) if revenue, the time at which it should be recognised.

    Whether a receipt under an exclusivity agreement is revenue or capital, or mixed, depends upon the purpose for which it is paid. Where the trader is free to spend the lump sum as he chooses, the lump sum should be treated as part of the ordinary Schedule D Case I taxable profits, even if the sum was in fact used to meet capital expenditure. If, however, the sum was received specifically to meet capital expenditure, and was in fact used for that purpose, it should be treated as a capital receipt. It will reduce the quantity of capital allowances claimable in respect of the expenditure in question (see **7.9**).

    In practice, the tax treatment will follow the accountancy treatment (see **6.10.3**), with the result that the lump sum will be spread over the period of the agreement.

If trading losses are incurred, they can be set against any profits (income from other sources and capital gains) taxable in the same accounting period and, if there are insufficient profits available, profits of the three preceding years.

7.4 Expenses

The rules for deductible expenditure will largely follow the Schedule D Case I rules, i.e., costs charged to the profit and loss account will be allowable provided they are not of a capital nature and they are incurred 'wholly and exclusively' for the purposes of the trade (s74(1)).

7.4.1 Repairs

Repairs and maintenance expenses, provided they are not of a capital nature, are deductible under s74(1)(d) if they are wholly and exclusively expended for the purposes of the trade. It is not always clear, however, whether expenditure is allowable as a repair or disallowable as capital although the courts have frequently addressed the issue.

Repairs are considered further at **7.12** below.

The legislation prevents accounting provisions for future expenditure being deductible as repairs. Repair expenditure must be actually incurred for it to be allowable, therefore tax relief cannot be obtained for costs exceeding the costs of repairs carried out.

If a publican or restaurateur carries out works to a newly acquired building, to convert it for use as a pub or restaurant, or to convert an existing pub or restaurant to his particular style, it is probable that the great majority of the cost would be treated as capital for tax purposes, regardless of the accounting treatment. This would be true even of work such as painting or decorating. The case of *Odeon Associated Theatres Ltd* v *Jones* (1971) 48 TC 257 has, however, established that if all the following criteria are satisfied the cost of repairs and other works of a revenue nature, e.g., painting and decorating, are tax deductible:

(a) the property was fit to use for the purpose it was acquired before the repair or other revenue works were carried out;
(b) the price paid for the property was unaffected by the state of repair;
(c) the cost of the work is treated as revenue for accounting purposes.

It would normally be much less difficult to persuade the Inland Revenue that revenue works carried out to a newly acquired building were tax deductible, if the building could be opened for trade before the works were carried out.

7.4.2 Dilapidations

The publican or restaurateur may be required to make good any dilapidations which the tenancy requires. If the expenditure relates to deferred repairs which would have been allowed if the repairs had been executed during the life of the lease, the expenditure is deductible. Such expenditure is not allowable, however, if it is of a capital nature.

7.4.3 Private purposes

Expenditure for the maintenance of the individual owners' or their families' accommodation, or any sums that are expended for private purposes as opposed to trading purposes, are disallowed under s74(1)(b).

The case of *Sharkey* v *Wernher* (1959) 36 TC 275 established the principle that where stock was taken for own consumption it had to be credited in the books at market value and not at cost. However, this is not so in the case of eating establishments, based on the premise that meals are not trading stock. The cost of such meals will be disallowed under s74(1)(b).

Where a company owns the pub or restaurant, the *cost* of meals would be tax deductible with a taxable benefit accruing to the director which would be equivalent to the cost of the meals to the company. Meals for staff generally are considered in section **8.6** below.

Any alcoholic beverages and cigarettes, etc. that are consumed by the individual owner, his spouse or family, will need to be reflected as profit in the accounts at market value. Items consumed by a company director or employee and other benefits in kind are dealt with in Chapter 8 on PAYE.

Planning point

A restaurateur or publican should ensure that any personal benefit obtained from his expenditure is kept to a minimum. Alternatively, such expenditure should be clearly distinguishable from expenditure incurred wholly for business purposes so as to ensure that the latter is deductible.

7.4.4 Private occupation

Where the licensee or restaurateur lives on the premises, expenditure may be incurred both for business purposes and for personal benefit. If the private benefit is merely incidental, the whole expense will be allowable following *Bentleys, Stokes and Lowless* v *Beeson* (1952) 33 TC 491. In other cases, it may be necessary to make an apportionment of the expenditure, but if this is not possible, the expenditure will not be deductible (see **7.4.3** above).

The running costs of the accommodation itself will need to be apportioned to determine how much relates to the private living accommodation. In *McLaren* v *Mumford* (1996) STC 1134, the tenant of a public house was required by the brewery to reside on the premises. He failed in his claim that the whole of his expenditure on rent, rates, lighting, heating and insurance should be allowed as a deduction in computing his taxable profits. Only five-sixths of the expenditure in question was allowable as a deduction.

In arriving at a suitable proportion of costs to claim as a business expense, two related issues must be considered:

(a) The same allocation will need to be applied to claims for tax relief in respect of interest on loans to acquire the property. A high allocation to the business rather than to the private living accommodation will be beneficial, as tax relief in respect of the business loan interest is available at the trader's marginal rate. Relief for mortgage interest paid in respect of private accommodation is restricted to 15 per cent.

(b) It will impact on the extent to which the capital gains tax exemption for a main residence is available at such time as the property is sold.

Where it is an employee who occupies any private living accommodation owned by the business, say, above the pub, this is potentially a taxable benefit on the employee (see **8.8** below). The full running costs of the property would, however, be deductible expenditure in arriving at the taxable profits of the business.

7.4.5 Business entertainment

A business is not allowed to deduct business entertainment expenses from its taxable Case I profits (s577), except insofar as the expenditure is incurred on staff entertainment (s577(5)). However, s577(10) may be of use to publicans and restaurateurs as it allows the deduction of expenses incurred for the provision of anything which it is their trade to provide (such as food and drink) and which is provided in the ordinary course of that trade for payment, or with the object of advertising to the public generally, gratuitously. If, for example, a restaurateur provides free samples of his food at a promotional event, such as a stand at a fair, the cost of providing the food would be tax deductible.

7.4.6 Legal expenses

Legal and professional expenses relating to capital and non-trading items will be disallowable. Legal expenses incurred in connection with a first application to the licensing justice to grant a new licence, e.g., for a licensed house, are disallowable (*Kneeshaw* v *Albertolli* (1940) 23 TC 462). The legal expenses incurred relating to the obtaining of a renewal of an existing licence are allowable.

If the licence relating to particular premises is transferred from one trader to another the relevant expenses are not allowable, whereas if the transfer is from one employed manager to another then they are allowable. The legal expenses relating to the 'removal' of a licence from one set of premises to another are disallowable (*Morse* v *Stedeford* (1934) 18 TC 457).

Costs incurred in the drawing-up of a new tenancy or lease are not allowed, as being of a capital nature, although they are allowable where the lease does not exceed 21 years. In practice, where there is a re-letting of an existing lease, the expenses will be allowable where the new lease cannot exceed 50 years.

Expenditure incurred in negotiating rent reviews is deductible.

7.5 Pre-trading expenditure

The tax treatment of pre-opening expenses depends on the nature of the expenditure. Typical types of expenditure include promotional expenses, refitting and extension costs, interest charges and general set-up expenses.

Revenue expenditure incurred before the publican or restaurateur starts to trade is treated as if it had been incurred on the day the trade commences and is allowable, provided it is incurred not more than seven years prior to the date of commencement of trade and would have been allowable if incurred after commencement (s401). Expenditure of a revenue nature incurred on a recently acquired building to enable it to be used for trade purposes is, however, not normally deductible for tax purposes (see **7.4.1** above).

Capital expenditure eligible for capital allowances incurred prior to commencement of the trade is deemed to have been incurred on the day trading commences. Such expenditure is dealt with more fully at **7.9.**

7.6 Special considerations

There are a few areas where problems may arise in practice. These are as follows.

7.6.1 More than one trade

In the case of pubs providing accommodation, the Inland Revenue may seek to argue that the publican is carrying on an additional separate trade, i.e., that of providing accommodation, which is distinct from the main public house trade. A similar situation could occur in respect of the catering and functions activities of both pubs and restaurants. If this were the case, a problem could arise in respect of losses. Losses of one trade can be set against profits from a *different* trade in the same accounting period and, if there are insufficient profits available, the losses can be carried back for up to three years and set against prior year profits. Losses brought forward in respect of one trade would be 'ring-fenced' and unavailable for set-off against profits from the other trade. This could result in surplus trading losses being unrelieved unless sufficient profits were generated in the future from the trade with the losses.

Planning point

It is advisable for publicans and restaurateurs to take care as far as possible that all the activities fall within the same trade. If this is not possible, and losses from one trade are likely to exceed other profits, they could be minimised, for instance by disclaiming capital allowances and setting them against future profits.

7.6.2 Termination payments

Certain breweries and pub companies have ceased using tenants to run their public houses and instead have appointed managers. As the tenancies tended to have little or no provision for compensation on termination, the breweries have been making substantial *ex gratia* payments to the tenants to induce them to leave, which take into account the business that the tenants have built up. The Brewers and Licensed Retailers Association, which is the breweries' trade body, has agreed a scale of compensation payable to tenants which is based upon the rateable value of the public house and the length of service of the tenants.

Such payments are likely to be exempt from income tax only if the facts are similar to those within the case of *Murray* v *Goodhews* (1977) 52 TC 86. Watneys made payments to one of its tenants which were held not to be liable to income tax as they were entirely voluntary and unsolicited and were in recognition of the long association between the parties. Further, they were not made by virtue of any right of compensation and nor were they made in return for any services rendered. There had been no negotiation of the payments between the parties and there was no link to any future trading relationship between them. See further *Simpson* v *John Reynolds & Co (Insurances) Limited* (1975) 49 TC 693.

It is unlikely that such a payment would be liable to capital gains tax, as the payment could not be said to derive from an asset. There are two cases, *Davis* v *Powell* (1976) 51 TC 492 and *Drummond* v *Austin Brown* (1984) 58 TC 67, where compensation payments were made by landlords to tenants under statute and these payments were held not to be liable to capital gains tax as they did not derive from the particular leases. Compensation payments should be distinguished from a capital sum paid which relates to the early surrender of a lease; the latter payment could be subject to capital gains tax.

7.6.3 Moving pubs

As mentioned above, a licensed victualler is treated as carrying on a trade at the particular public house of which he is a tenant. The effect of this is that if the tenant wishes to leave that pub and move to a new one, albeit tied to the same brewery, for tax purposes there will be a cessation of the existing trade and a commencement of another one at the new pub.

Planning point

A licensed victualler who is considering taking a tenancy at another pub should consider the tax consequences before the move, in particular whether unrealised trading losses incurred in respect of the existing tenancy would be wasted as a result of the move. See **7.6.1** above.

7.7 Interest

Legislation was introduced in 1996 at s337A, which changed the basis of taxing loan interest, both receivable and payable. The new legislation provides that interest receivable or payable by a company will be taxable or deductible respectively under Case I, on an accruals basis. The new rules apply from the start of the company's first accounting period ending on or after 1 April 1996. Previously, interest receivable was taxable on a receipts basis and loan interest payable deductible as a charge on a paid basis.

7.7.1 Capitalised interest

Paragraph 14 of Schedule 9, Finance Act 1996 provides for the treatment of interest ('debit or credit') which is capitalised in valuing a 'fixed capital asset or project' under normal accountancy practice. The interest is to be brought into account for corporation tax purposes for the accounting period for which it is 'given', in the same way as a debit or credit is brought into account in the company's profit and loss account for that period.

Although this would imply that capitalised interest is deductible on an accruals basis, there is no definition of the word 'given' and so the position is not crystal clear.

7.8 Lease-related payments

The rules relating to the taxation of leases are complex and are outside the scope of this book. Some specific points are, however, worth mentioning here.

7.8.1 Premiums

There are special rules relating to premiums contained within s34. Basically, where a lease is granted (not assigned) at a premium and the lease does not exceed 50 years then the landlord is treated as receiving an additional amount of rent which is taxable to corporation tax (or income tax) under Schedule A. The proportion taxable under Schedule A is equal to:

$$\text{Premium less } \left(\text{premium} \times \frac{\text{length of lease in complete years} - 1}{50}\right)$$

Example

Premium £100,000, length of the lease 21 years. The proportion taxable under Schedule A is as follows:

$$£100{,}000 - \left(£100{,}000 \times \frac{21 - 1}{50}\right) = £60{,}000$$

The balance which is not taxable under Schedule A (£40,000 in the above example), is dealt with under the capital gains tax regime.

The tenant receives a Case I deduction that corresponds to the amount chargeable on the landlord, except that the deduction is spread over the period of the lease (21 years in the example).

7.8.2 Overseas issues

Where a tenant pays rent directly to a non-UK resident landlord, he must deduct income tax at the basic rate (24 per cent in 1996/97) from the rental payments. The tax must be accounted for to the Inland Revenue on a quarterly basis. If rental payments are made to a UK agent acting on behalf of a non-resident landlord, they should be made gross and it is the agent's responsibility to deduct tax when accounting to the landlord. Application can be made to the Inland Revenue's Financial Intermediaries and Claims Office for approval to receive the income of the rental business without tax deducted, provided:

- the landlord's UK tax affairs are up to date; or
- it has never had any UK tax obligations; or
- it does not expect to be liable to UK income tax.

7.9 Capital allowances

Depreciation charged in the accounts in respect of fixed assets is specifically disallowed for tax purposes. Instead, UK tax relief is given on some categories of capital expenditure by means of capital allowances. For most pubs and restaurants, the only category of capital expenditure that will qualify for capital allowances will be plant and machinery. It should be noted that the accounts classification of capital expenditure does not determine the tax category for capital allowances purposes.

Capital allowances are available in respect of only certain categories of buildings. Pub and restaurant buildings do not qualify for capital allowances unless they form parts of hotels, in which case hotel buildings allowance (HBA) would be available, or they are located in an enterprise zone when enterprise zone allowance (EZA) may be available. HBA and EZA are dealt with below in sections **7.10** and **7.11** respectively.

7.9.1 Rate of allowance

Capital allowances are currently available at the rate of 25 per cent per annum on a reducing balance basis.

Example

	£
Year ended 31 December 1996:	
Qualifying expenditure	1,000
Writing-down allowance 25%	250
	750
Year ended 31 December 1997:	
Writing-down allowance 25%	187
	563
Year ended 31 December 1998:	
Writing-down allowance 25%	141
Tax written down value	422

Notes:

In each year, the writing-down allowance is deducted from taxable profit and tax relief is obtained at the taxpayer's rate of tax

The tax written down value at 31 December 1998 is available for writing-down allowances in future years on the same basis, i.e., 25 per cent per annum, subject to any future change in tax legislation.

7.9.2 The meaning of plant and machinery

Capital allowances can be claimed on capital expenditure on plant and machinery. Neither plant nor machinery are defined in the tax legislation, although the Finance Act 1994 introduced provisions specifying what does not qualify for capital allowances (see below).

It is not normally difficult to recognise machinery. Any item with moving parts would be expected to qualify. There is uncertainty, however, over items such as mechanically operated doors, where the Inland Revenue view is that the mechanism and its associated electrical supply qualifies, but the door fails to qualify. This apparently strange view is reinforced by the Finance Act 1994 legislation.

The meaning of plant has been considered by the courts in numerous cases. The rules formulated by the courts are frequently misinterpreted, but can be summarised as follows:

(a) the primary rule is that an item is plant if it constitutes a part of the means with which the trade of the taxpayer is carried on;
(b) in order to apply this rule, it is essential to establish what the trade of the taxpayer is and the function of the item in the conduct of the trade;

(c) the item must be held as a fixed asset; it cannot be plant if it is trading stock;
(d) The item cannot be plant if it functions as premises.

The test of whether an item is plant is a functional test and not a physical test. If an item which is physically part of the premises functions as part of the means with which the trade of the taxpayer is carried on, it is plant. If, on the other hand, an item functions to accommodate or shelter the trade, it functions as premises.

Capital allowances are normally available for chattels, that is, items treated as fixed assets in the accounts which are not fixed to the premises. Tables and chairs are typical examples of chattels found in pubs and restaurants that qualify for capital allowances.

Items attached or fixed to buildings are fixtures. It is necessary to apply case law to determine whether or not a fixture qualifies for capital allowances and, as indicated above, it is the way in which the fixture is used for the purposes of the particular trade, i.e., pub or restaurant trade, that determines whether it qualifies.

Although all capital allowances cases are important because they establish rules which have to be applied in all situations, there are four cases of particular importance to pubs and restaurants, because they concern, respectively, an hotel/pub, a restaurant, a fast food restaurant and a floating restaurant.

In *CIR* v *Scottish and Newcastle Breweries Limited* (1982) 55 TC 252, the company claimed capital allowances on a number of features installed in its hotels, comprising light fittings, murals, wall decor, pictures and metal sculptures. The Inland Revenue argued that the decor and murals performed much the same function as attractive wallpaper or mural paintings, that is to say, enhancing the setting. The House of Lords decided, however, that the decor and other items qualified as plant for two reasons:

(a) they embellished the premises rather than becoming part of the premises;
(b) they functioned to produce an atmosphere attractive to customers, i.e., atmosphere was part of what was being sold to customers.

To put it another way, the items constituted part of the means with which the trade of the hotel was carried on and hence they functioned as plant and not as premises.

The *Scottish and Newcastle Breweries* decision provides authority for pubs and restaurants to obtain capital allowances on decorative items attractive to customers.

In *Hampton* v *Fortes Autogrill Limited* (1979) 53 TC 691, false ceilings in a restaurant were held not to qualify as plant because they merely provided cladding, and concealed services and pipes for water, beer and Coca Cola. False ceilings can qualify as plant, however, if they function as part of a heating or ventilation system.

The 1988 case of *Wimpy International Ltd* v *Warland* 61 TC 51, is probably the most important of all recent capital allowances cases and Hoffmann J's decision in the High Court is regarded as a landmark judgment. This judgment was upheld in the Court of Appeal and Hoffmann J's subsequent elevation to the House of Lords adds, perhaps, even more importance to his decision.

Wimpy refurbished its fast food restaurants, incurring significant amounts of capital expenditure, with the object of attracting customers. They claimed capital allowances on a substantial number of items which were disputed by the Inland Revenue including the following:

- replacement shopfronts;
- wall and floor tiling;
- restaurant area light fittings;
- two types of false ceiling;
- cold water tanks;
- external, roof-mounted, plant housing.

The shopfronts, wall and floor tiling and one type of false ceiling were regarded as merely part of the premises. All the other above items were held to qualify as plant.

The Special Commissioners had found, on the evidence, that the light fittings were intended to attract customers and did not function as premises (similar to the *Scottish and Newcastle* light fittings), but in spite of this finding they held that the light fittings did not qualify. This was overturned in the High Court on the basis that the decision was at variance with the findings of fact.

The Special Commissioners had held that the external, roof-mounted, plant housing was plant and this was not challenged by the Inland Revenue in the High Court. The housing was required because air cooling and extraction plant was located on the roof of one of the restaurants and the local authority insisted that it should not stand in the open. The housing qualified as plant on the basis that the plant and housing formed a single unit, even though the housing was not required to enable the plant to operate. It is worth pointing out that the Inland Revenue normally refuse similar claims because, they say, a Special Commissioners' decision does not provide binding authority. This is in spite of the fact that the Court of Appeal in *Wimpy* specifically approved the entire Special Commissioners' decision, except of course to the extent that it related to the lighting.

Wimpy installed additional cold water tanks to provide the cold water capacity required for their restaurant. The Special Commissioners held, and the Courts agreed, that these tanks, together with the cold water piping serving them, qualified as plant because they were required for specific trade reasons and hence they were part of the means with which the trade was carried on. Prior to *Wimpy*, the Inland Revenue had normally refused capital allowances claims for cold water tanks and pipes, although hot water tanks and pipes were allowed. All cold water tanks and pipes will now qualify if they meet the same criteria as those in *Wimpy*.

Perhaps the most confusing part of the *Wimpy* decision related to false ceilings. One type failed to qualify because (as mentioned above) it merely formed part of the premises. The other type was held to qualify because it was intended to form a feature which would attract customers.

Hoffmann J's decision is regarded as particularly important because he restated the tests which determine whether an item qualifies as plant. Essentially, according to Hoffmann J, an item qualifies as plant if the following tests are all satisfied:

- it is used for business purposes (the 'business use' test);
- it is not used as stock in trade, i.e., it is a fixed asset;
- its use is not as part of the premises (the 'premises' test).

The final case, *Benson* v *Yard Arm Club Ltd* (1979) 53 TC 67, concerns floating restaurants. A boat was converted into a floating restaurant on the River Thames. It was held that the boat comprised the premises within which the trade was carried on, rather than functioning as part of the means with which the trade was carried on. In one sense this was a curious decision because it is a rare instance of a chattel failing to qualify as plant. It is important to note that the view was expressed, in another tax case, that if the boat had had an engine and had cruised up and down the river whilst diners were eating in the restaurant, it would have qualified as plant because then it would have functioned as part of the means with which the trade (providing cruises and restaurant facilities) was carried on.

Readers should note that the Inland Revenue allow a number of items for capital allowances as part of their general practice. Among items normally found in pubs and restaurants that are allowed by the Revenue are the following:

(a) heating and ventilation systems, including pipes and ducts;

(b) hot water tanks and pipes;
(c) washbasins, sinks, WCs and other plumbing fixtures;
(d) spotlights and other lighting, including associated wiring, provided to meet the particular requirements of the pub/restaurant (but not general lighting);
(e) curtains and blinds for windows.

7.9.3 Finance Act 1994 provisions

The Finance Act 1994 introduced legislation, the purpose of which was summarised by the Financial Secretary to the Treasury as follows:

> 'It introduces a schedule containing new rules which provide that buildings, structures or land, with certain exceptions, cannot qualify for capital allowances as plant or machinery. These new rules are not intended to change the treatment of assets that qualify as plant at present, as a result of court rulings. The intention is to clarify and strengthen the boundary between buildings and structures on the one hand, and plant on the other.'

The schedule he referred to became Schedule AA1 to the Capital Allowances Act 1990 (CAA 1990) and it applies to expenditure contracted after Budget day 30 November 1993. Broadly speaking, Schedule AA1 operates as follows:

(a) it lists parts of buildings such as walls, floors, doors and windows, and structures such as roads and vehicle parks, that are disqualified from being plant;
(b) it lists items that are deemed to be 'unaffected' by the Schedule, even though they may be parts of buildings or structures.

Items of a type that have been held to qualify as plant in tax cases are deemed to be 'unaffected' by the Schedule, as are items allowed as plant by the Inland Revenue under Revenue practice.

The effect of Schedule AA1 on pubs and restaurants can be summarised by saying that fixtures, i.e., items fixed to the building, will qualify for capital allowances only if they are included in column two of Table 1 in Schedule AA1. Table 1 is reproduced at Appendix 9. All items must still satisfy existing case law, i.e., the rules explained at **7.9.2**, to qualify.

The following items, frequently found in pubs and restaurants, will qualify for capital allowances under current law:

(a) items allowed by Revenue practice (see above);
(b) electrical, cold water and gas systems provided to meet specific trade requirements;
(c) storage equipment, including cold rooms, display equipment, counters and similar items;

(d) cookers, dishwashers, refrigerators, washing machines, etc.;
(e) lifts and hoists (but not lift shafts);
(f) computer systems, TV and surveillance systems, including wiring;
(g) sprinkler systems and fire alarm systems;
(h) burglar alarm systems;
(i) decorative assets provided for the enjoyment of the public;
(j) advertising hoardings and signs;
(k) any machinery.

The Finance Act 1994 introduced provisions imposing time limits for making capital allowances claims on plant and machinery (s118). Under s118, a claim for capital allowances must be made within two years after the end of the accounting period in which the expenditure is incurred. If the two-year time limit is not complied with, however, all is not necessarily lost. It may be possible to make a claim in a current year for prior year expenditure in certain circumstances (which are outside the scope of this book).

7.9.4 The meaning of 'expenditure' – which costs can be claimed?

The capital allowances claim is not restricted exclusively to the purchase price of the item of plant or machinery. The legislation refers to the 'provision' of plant or machinery and the courts have held that this includes any cost that is a 'necessary preliminary' to the provision of plant or machinery.

The following types of expenditure may qualify for capital allowances, as part of the cost of provision of plant or machinery:

- installation costs;
- transport costs;
- preliminaries;
- professional fees.

This meaning is extended by s66 CAA 1990 where plant or machinery is installed in an existing building. Section 66 specifies that alterations to an existing building, incidental to the installation of plant or machinery, qualify for capital allowances. For example, this would cover a lift shaft (otherwise specifically disqualified under Schedule AA1) where it is incidental to the installation of a lift in an existing building.

7.9.5 New build, extension and refurbishment projects

A significant proportion of expenditure on new build, extension and refurbishment projects will relate to plant and machinery and qualify for capital allowances. As mentioned in **7.12.1** below, the higher this proportion, the higher the tax relief available and the lower the net, after-tax, cost of the works as a whole.

> ***Planning point***
>
> Steps should be taken, wherever possible, to maximise the plant and machinery content and identify the costs qualifying for capital allowances. It is often possible to design buildings and their contents so that more of the total cost qualifies for capital allowances than would otherwise be the case. It is sensible for a tax adviser to become involved at the planning stage by examining draft specifications. It is also important for the tax adviser to arrange with the project manager or quantity surveyor that appropriate cost analyses of the works will be prepared. This may mean providing him with a pro forma analysis. A cost analysis will be required of the total project cost, although it may be helpful if stage payments are analysed, especially if the project straddles the end of an accounting period.

The date when expenditure on plant or machinery is deemed to be incurred, for capital allowances purposes, is the date when the obligation to pay becomes unconditional. There are special rules for long-term contracts which are outside the scope of this book. These rules are of particular importance when a project straddles the end of an accounting period.

7.9.6 Buying existing buildings

The purchase of an existing building will include the fixed plant content and capital allowances can be claimed on the amount of the purchase price allocated to plant.

Where a property is purchased for use as a pub or restaurant, the purchaser or, in practice, his tax adviser, should take whatever steps are necessary to maximise his capital allowances claim on the purchase price. It will be important to make a detailed inspection of the property to identify the fixed plant content and to investigate what claims were made by the vendor, since the purchaser's capital allowances claim on fixed plant items will be restricted to the cost claimed by the vendor.

The purchaser and vendor can make a joint election to the Inland Revenue that will determine how much of the purchase/sale price is allocated to fixed plant. However, the purchase/sale price allocated to fixed plant cannot exceed the vendor's original cost. The election can be made in respect of purchases/sales taking place on or after 19 March 1997 under provisions contained in the 1997 Finance Act.

7.9.7 Selling existing buildings

When plant or machinery items are sold, the sale proceeds are deducted from the 'pool' of qualifying expenditure which restricts future writing-down allowances. If the sale proceeds exceed the pool value, a balancing charge arises.

Example

Year ended 31 December 1998:	£
Tax written down value at 31.12.97	563
Sale proceeds	100
	463
Writing-down allowance 25%	116
Tax written down value at 31.12.98	347

When a property is sold, the fixed plant content is treated for capital allowances purposes as being sold for a disposal value equal to the sale proceeds apportioned to the plant. Following the passing of the 1997 Finance Act, a vendor of a property who has claimed capital allowances on the fixed plant content can make a joint election with the purchaser that will determine the disposal value (see **7.9.6** above).

Planning point

The vendor of a property who has claimed capital allowances on the fixed plant content should join with the purchaser in making an election to the Inland Revenue (see **7.9.6** above). This will determine the disposal value and prevent any higher figure from being taken into account for capital allowances purposes.

Companies owning chains of pubs or restaurants may finance the purchase and/or development of new pubs or restaurants by the sale and leaseback of existing properties. Such transactions would give rise to a disposal of fixed plant for capital allowances purposes. There would in fact be two capital allowances problems because, before the disposal value could be determined, it would be necessary to identify which plant items were contained in the sale. This problem is, however, outside the scope of this book. It is possible to avoid a capital allowances clawback in such circumstances by restructuring the deal as a lease and leaseback, i.e., granting a long (over 50 years) lease for a premium and taking an underlease.

7.10 Hotel buildings allowances

There is a possibility that pubs which provide accommodation may be eligible for hotel buildings allowances (HBA). The allowance is given at

4 per cent per annum on a straight line basis on qualifying expenditure. In order to qualify the following conditions must be met:

(a) the building must be of a permanent nature;
(b) it must be open for at least four months of the season. The season is comprised of the seven months from April to October, inclusive;
(c) while it is open in the season:
    (i) it has at least 10 bedrooms to let;
    (ii) the accommodation consists wholly or mainly of letting bedrooms; and
    (iii) the services provided for the guests normally include the provision of breakfast and evening meals, making beds and cleaning rooms.

It is unlikely that a pub, which has sufficient bedrooms, etc. to qualify for HBA, will be able to bring the building comprising its main trade, i.e., the provision of drinks, etc., within the allowance. Consequently, an apportionment will be required.

Hotels that qualify for HBA can arrange matters such that a restaurant building which is part of the hotel or attached to it can also qualify.

If a building is used primarily as a qualifying hotel, but also as a restaurant or pub, HBA can be given on the whole cost of the building if the construction cost of the non-qualifying part does not exceed 25 per cent of the construction cost of the whole.

If HBA is available on part of a building and the owner or partner or their family uses one or more rooms for personal accommodation, the area used will not be regarded as part of the hotel under s19(5)(b).

7.11 Enterprise zones

If a pub or restaurant is constructed within a designated enterprise zone, enterprise zone allowance (EZA) of 100 per cent, i.e., an allowance equal to the whole of the building expenditure, will be available.

EZA is available in respect of any commercial building or structure situated in an enterprise zone.

7.12 Refurbishment projects

There are two significant tax issues to consider in relation to a refurbishment project, which are as follows:

(a) identify and maximise tax-allowable costs, i.e., costs qualifying as revenue expenditure and costs qualifying for capital allowances;

(b) the sub-contractor's tax deduction scheme.

7.12.1 Identify and maximise tax-allowable costs

Consideration should be given to the tax status of refurbishment projects at planning stage. It is frequently the case that work can be carried out in different ways, all of which achieve the same objective, but one of which has more favourable tax treatment which may reduce the net (after-tax) cost of the work.

Example

The existing windows in a building are badly fitting and draughty. A choice exists between fitting secondary double glazing to the existing windows at a cost of £40,000 and fitting replacement windows (the modern equivalent of the existing windows) at a cost of £50,000 – on the face of it, it would be cheaper to fit secondary double glazing. However, the £50,000 cost of replacement windows would be treated as repairs for tax purposes and would be tax deductible. The double glazing cost would be capital and no tax relief would be available.

The comparative costs would be as follows:

	£
Replacement windows	50,000
Tax relief at 33%*	16,500
Net cost	33,000
Double glazing, no tax relief	40,000

*Corporation tax rate

The correct decision, taking tax relief into account, would be to fit replacement windows.

Planning point

It is important to maximise and identify both the revenue and capital allowances content of a refurbishment project at the planning stage, since the higher the tax relief available, the lower the net, after-tax, cost.

Revenue expenditure is dealt with in **7.4.1.** Capital allowances are dealt with at **7.9.**

7.12.2 Replacements

A main problem area for tax purposes is the treatment of replacements. In order to qualify as revenue for tax purposes, the courts have provided two rules, both of which must be satisfied and these are as follows:

(a) the replacement must be made because of the need for repair of the item replaced;
(b) the replacement must comprise like for like or the modern equivalent of the item replaced; and
(c) the replacement must relate to a component part of an entity.

On the other hand, if expenditure meets either or both of the following criteria, it cannot be treated as revenue for tax purposes and must be treated as capital:

(a) the replacement constitutes an improvement; or
(b) an entire item, i.e., an entity, is replaced.

If improvements are carried out which make a repair unnecessary, there is no tax deduction allowed for notional repairs.

Accounting treatment is also an important factor in determining tax treatment. If expenditure can be charged to the profit and loss account in accordance with standard accounting practice, this will be of considerable assistance in persuading the Inland Revenue that it is tax deductible.

It can frequently be difficult to determine whether something being replaced is the modern equivalent rather than an improvement, or a component part rather than an entity. Both these questions were considered in the 1980 tax case, *Brown* v *Burnley Football & Athletic Co Ltd* 53 TC 357. Burnley replaced one of the stands at Turf Moor, their football ground, because they were advised that the previous stand was no longer safe. The replacement stand was built in the same place as the previous stand and it had substantially the same capacity for spectators. It was accepted that the replacement stand was the modern equivalent of its predecessor. It was held, however, that the premises occupied by the club did not comprise an entity (as claimed by the club), but a number of distinct parts of which the stand was one. As the stand was an entity, its replacement could not be treated as revenue for tax purposes.

An alternative claim that the replacement stand was plant also failed, because it was held that the stand did not perform any function in the processes which constituted the club's trade (see **7.9.2** above).

Worse still, Burnley were relegated in the season that the replacement stand was built, the players blaming their poor home performances on lack of atmosphere because one end of the ground was empty of spectators!

7.12.3 Sub-contractors' tax deduction scheme

A special tax withholding scheme operates in the construction industry. Whenever a *contractor* pays a *sub-contractor* for a *construction operation*, a statutory deduction, equivalent to basic rate tax, must be made from the payment unless the sub-contractor holds a valid tax exemption certificate (form 714). This system is commonly referred to as the Construction Industry Tax Deduction Scheme (or CITDS)

The £250,000 threshold

Although CITDS appears to have nothing to do with pubs or restaurants, in fact the tax legislation is widely drawn. Any kind of business may find it has to operate the scheme if it regularly spends more than £250,000 a year on 'construction operations'. These include any work undertaken on a building in the course of construction, demolition, alteration or repair. In practice, this means that a business outside of the construction industry may find itself within the scheme simply as a result of commissioning a new building, or carrying out repairs on a number of properties over the course of a year.

The threshold is applied using a three-year running average on the basis of the normal financial year of the business. From the end of the financial year in which the running average exceeds £250,000 or expenditure in the year exceeds £750,000, the business becomes a 'contractor' for the purposes of the scheme. It cannot then get out of the scheme until the end of the financial year in which the running average drops below £250,000.

How the exemption scheme works

When a sub-contractor holds a valid tax exemption certificate, the contractor can make payments to him without deductions, but only if the payment is for a construction operation. It is not possible, for example, to make tax-free payments to a casual evening barman on the strength of a 714, even though he may be working quite legitimately on a building site during the day.

Tax exemption certificates

The certificates, which are made of plastic and resemble a credit card, fall into three main types:

- 714C – for larger limited companies;
- 714P – for smaller limited companies and partnerships;
- 714I – for sole traders.

Before making a payment without deduction, the contractor has to satisfy himself that the certificate is valid and that the person presenting it is the authorised user. The 714P and 714I certificates carry the sub-contractor's photograph, and all three carry a signature. Because there tends to be a lot of fraud in this area, contractors are strongly advised to check the original certificate in each case and never to accept just a photocopy.

The exception to this concerns larger sub-contracting companies who use the 'certifying document' method, that is to say, they present all their exemption details in the form of a letter, which also gives details of a nominated bank account. Payment can then be made into that account, provided it is due under the terms of a written contract.

Holders of 714P and 714I certificates are not entitled to use the certifying document method. On receiving a payment, they are required to give the contractor a voucher (form 715) showing the total payment received (net of VAT), which the contractor then has to send off to the Inland Revenue at regular intervals.

The deduction scheme

Whenever a sub-contractor has no exemption certificate, the contractor has to make statutory deductions at the basic rate of income tax. The deduction is not based on the whole payment – VAT and the direct cost of any materials purchased by the sub-contractor are first discounted. The contractor then has to add the deductions to his normal PAYE payments which he makes monthly to the Collector of Taxes. The sub-contractor is entitled to a deduction certificate (form SC60) at least once at the end of each tax year and more often if requested.

Annual returns

Details of all payments to holders of exemption certificates must be returned annually to the Inspector of Taxes on form 704. For sub-contractors paid under deduction the correct form is SC35.

Failure to deduct

Any 'contractor' who fails to make the necessary deductions may be held liable for all the amounts he should have deducted unless it can be shown that the sub-contractors have already been assessed on the income in question. Underpayments or late returns will attract penalties and interest in much the same way as for PAYE and NICs.

Planning point

A point sometimes overlooked by non-construction businesses is that once you are within CITDS, the scheme applies not just to major projects but also to every little repair job on your properties. Consider applying to your tax office for the *small works exemption*. If it is granted, you will not need to operate the scheme on jobs costing £250 or less.

Proposed changes to CITDS

A number of changes to the scheme are due to come into effect on 1 August 1998. These include raising the £250,000 threshold to £1,000,000 and the introduction of mandatory registration cards for non-exempt sub-contractors. A turnover test will be applied to sub-contractors seeking exemption certificates, so it is likely that the number of exempt sub-contractors will decrease significantly.

7.13 Disposal of pub or restaurant

7.13.1 Case I implications

Where a business owns only one pub or restaurant, the sale of that venue would result in a cessation of trade and the end of an accounting period. If losses have been incurred, one of the reliefs summarised at **7.15** may be available.

7.13.2 Capital gains tax implications

On a sale of a pub or restaurant the sale proceeds received will be subject to capital gains tax or, where the property is held by a company, corporation tax on capital gains. If the pub or restaurant is sold as a going concern, part of the sale proceeds may relate to goodwill and there may be a sizeable gain involved if the business has been doing well.

If the vendor reinvests the sale proceeds in another pub or restaurant, rollover relief may be available to defer the capital gain (s152 TCGA 1992). The new pub/restaurant must be acquired within 12 months before or 36 months after the disposal of the old pub/restaurant. The Revenue may be prepared to extend this period where there is a firm intention to acquire a new asset within the time limit but circumstances beyond the control of the trader prevent him from doing so.

The old and the new pub/restaurant need to be actually used for the purposes of a trade, but *not* necessarily the *same* trade. Furthermore, the new pub or restaurant must be taken into immediate use in the trade, although the relief will otherwise be available where the reason for non-immediate use falls within Extra-statutory Concession D24, for example, the owner proposes to incur capital expenditure on enhancing the value of the property.

The sale of goodwill also qualifies for rollover relief (s155 TCGA 1992).

Example

Tipsy Ltd operates both a pub and a restaurant trade. It purchased a pub in February 1990 for £80,000 which it sold for £150,000 in June 1996, having used it throughout its period of ownership for the purposes of its trade. An extension to the pub had been built in April 1992, costing £10,000. In June 1997 Tipsy Ltd purchased a new restaurant for £200,000 which was immediately used in its restaurant trade.

(a) Disposal of pub – capital gains computation

	£	£
Proceeds of sale of pub		150,000
Less: acquisition cost	80,000	
Indexation allowance (0.273)	21,840	
		(101,840)
Enhancement expenditure	10,000	
Indexation allowance (0.102)	1,020	
		(11,020)
Capital gain		37,140

(b) Rollover relief claim

	£
Acquisition cost of restaurant	200,000
Less: capital gain rolled over	(37,140)
Base cost of restaurant	162,860

7.13.3 Capital allowances implications

The capital allowances section above (**7.9**) includes coverage of the capital allowances consequences of a sale of a pub or restaurant.

7.14 Self-assessment

Self-assessment is the term used to describe the new Inland Revenue system which requires new style annual tax returns to be completed by sole traders and partnerships and which introduces a strict regime of potential penalties. The system involves new compliance responsibilities and paperwork, new tax payment dates, new Inland Revenue enquiry powers and a number of related changes.

7.14.1 Standard accounts information (SAI)

The new tax returns are more detailed than the previous style and include specific pages relating to the self-employed. Similar pages exist in the new partnership tax return.

The pages include a mandatory profit and loss account format into which all of the figures from a trader's accounts have to be entered in a specified manner, including the expenses which are disallowable for tax relief. Only those businesses whose turnover is less than £15,000 or more than £15 million in the relevant year are exempt from the obligation to provide standard accounts information. In some cases it may be appropriate to consider changing the style of future accounts to mirror the Inland Revenue format which has been widely criticised as inflexible and insufficiently detailed.

> ***Planning point***
>
> The Inland Revenue plan to extract statistical information from comparisons of the SAI information available from traders' tax returns. They will also compare the figures from one year to another in respect of each taxpayer. They will inevitably commence enquiries where there are significant fluctuations from one year to another. It would be wise, therefore, to identify carefully how the expenses from a trader's business accounts will be allocated between the SAI headings and to ensure that the same allocations are used in future years.

7.14.2 Record-keeping

The concept of keeping records is not new. Under the self-assessment tax system, however, the requirements for record-keeping have become more onerous as there is now a legal obligation to both make and retain suitable records in respect of income and expenditure relating to the business. The importance of maintaining proper books and records has already been addressed at **6.3** above.

With effect from 6 April 1996, sole traders and partners have been obliged to retain records to substantiate any receipts and expenses figures that relate to entries on tax returns covering income and capital gains. The new tax legislation states that the papers must be kept until 70 months (almost six years) from the end of the tax year. This equates with the fifth anniversary of the deadline for submitting the relevant tax return.

The legislation allows for a penalty of up to £3,000 to be charged for each tax year where there has been a failure to maintain or retain adequate records to substantiate entries on a tax return or claim.

The Inland Revenue state that they only intend to charge the full penalty 'in the most serious cases, for example where records have been deliberately destroyed . . . or where there is a continuing failure to keep records after the taxpayer has been advised of future record-keeping requirements'.

Once self-assessment is fully operational, if a trader cannot produce the required records, the Inspector may well extend his enquiries further. Thus, the potential £3,000 penalty may not be the only disadvantage of inadequate record-keeping. No one can afford to ignore the time, effort and cost of dealing with Inland Revenue enquiries. Proper record-keeping will help to minimise the damage generated by such enquiries.

7.14.3 Estimates and private use adjustments

The supporting guidance notes explaining how to complete the new tax return contain specific reference to the use of estimated figures. The notes highlight a new obligation to identify on the return any figures 'which may not be very reliable' and to explain how such figures have been arrived at. The Inland Revenue anticipate that such disclosure will enable them to identify incorrect returns. Separate penalties may then be charged for negligence and for a lack of adequate record-keeping.

The notes also state that there is no need to make specific reference to an estimate 'which while not a precise figure, is sufficiently reliable to enable you to make an accurate tax return'.

Clearly, it is important to minimise the need for estimates either in the underlying accounts or in making any adjustments to arrive at the taxable profits of the business.

The calculations of any estimates which are used, will form part of the records to be retained. The guidance notes specifically confirm that estimates calculated on the basis 'of detailed records of a representative sample period' should be sufficiently reliable to enable accurate tax returns to be completed.

The first self-assessment tax returns were issued at the start of April 1997 in respect of the tax year ended 5 April 1997. As yet, there is no practical experience to which anyone can refer to determine precisely how the Inland Revenue will apply their new powers in respect of unsupportable estimates or where inadequate records have been retained.

The kind of estimates that will commonly arise include:

(a) private consumption of stock (see **7.4.3** above);
(b) proportion of running costs relating to business/private accommodation (see **7.4.4** above); and
(c) private/business use of telephone and motor car (see **7.4.4** above).

7.14.4 Inland Revenue expectations

As discussed in **6.3** above, the Inland Revenue will carry out investigations into unusually low reported gross margins.

Under the self-assessment regime the Inland Revenue have extended powers to make enquiries aimed at identifying errors and omissions from tax returns. An Inspector no longer has to justify his selection of a particular return so it will not initially be clear whether he holds information which casts doubt on the accuracy of the return or whether the selection is genuinely random.

Business Economic Notes relating to various trades are used by Inspectors of Taxes as background information in examining accounts. Copies are available from the Reference Room, Inland Revenue Library, Mid-Basement, Somerset House, London WC2R 1LB (price £1.50 post-free). Of the 22 currently available the following may be of interest:

BEN9 – Licenced Victuallers;
BEN16 – Catering – General;
BEN17 – Catering – Restaurants;
BEN18 – Catering – Fast Foods, Cafes and Snack Bars.

7.15 Losses

The detailed rules relating to the tax reliefs available in respect of losses are complex and are outside the scope of this book. A simple comparison, however, between reliefs available to sole traders and partners compared with those of companies are worth mentioning here.

In each case a trading loss is computed in the same way as trading profits.

7.15.1 Income tax

As part of the introduction of the new self-assessment system, the basis for taxing business profits was moved from a preceding year basis to a current year basis. Tax relief may now be obtained for trading losses:

(a) by set-off against other income arising in the same year of assessment or the preceding year;
(b) by carry forward for offset against subsequent profits of the same trade;
(c) under the special rules permitting the carry back of losses arising in any of the first four years of assessment from the commencement of trading. Relief can be claimed for the loss against other income of the preceding three years, earlier years first;
(d) under the special regime allowing relief for terminal losses arising on the permanent discontinuance of the trade. Losses sustained in the 12 months up to the date of discontinuance, so far as not otherwise relieved, may be carried back and set off against profits of the same trade in the three years of assessment prior to that in which the discontinuance occurs. In this case relief is given against profits of later years first.

As indicated at **7.6.1** above, losses brought forward in respect of one trade would be 'ringfenced' and unavailable for set-off against profits from another trade.

Under the current year basis of assessment, the trading loss will be identified after deducting any available capital allowances and after adding back any balancing charges which may arise under the capital allowances regime.

7.15.2 Corporation tax

Tax relief may be obtained for trading losses as follows:

(a) by set-off against other profits (including chargeable gains) of the same accounting period;
(b) in addition (but not in place of the above claim), the company may claim that the balance of the loss not so relieved is carried back and set against the profits (including chargeable gains) of, in effect, the three previous annual accounting periods. The claim would be made against the most recent of the years first;
(c) by way of carry forward for set-off against future profits of the same trade in succeeding accounting periods;
(d) by making a claim to carry back a loss incurred in a trade in an accounting period in which the trade ceases. This enables the trading loss sustained in the final accounting period of trading to be set against any profits in the same period, or carried back for up to three years and set against profits of any description. Trade charges paid in the final accounting period may be added to the loss to be carried back with the trading loss under section 393A(i)(b).

Chapter 8 – PAYE and National Insurance

8.1 Taxation of employees

Employee taxation places a number of burdens on employers. In addition to the obvious requirement to account for PAYE and National Insurance on wages and salaries, employers also need to be aware of the potential tax implications of other payments. Then there is the obligation to file annual P9D and P11D returns of employees' expenses and benefits, a task made more onerous by the arrival of self-assessment. Numerous pitfalls lie in wait for the unwary. This section therefore looks at common problem areas, with particular attention to those prevalent in pubs, restaurants and similar businesses.

8.2 Casual and part-time staff

The nature of pubs and restaurants – not least the hours they must keep – makes it inevitable that there will be a heavy dependence on part-time and casual staff. Although the PAYE rules for this type of employee were tightened up as long ago as the early 1980s, the notion still persists in many quarters that employers are allowed a certain quota of casual labour without having to worry about PAYE or NICs. Equally, there are those who are tempted to disregard the tax and NI aspects for fear of being unable to recruit and keep staff, or because they come under pressure from staff to pay 'cash in hand'.

The Inland Revenue are well aware of these problems. Their compliance officers often target restaurants and pubs as areas where there is a strong chance of recovering arrears. When they do, it is the employer who has to meet the bill, which will almost certainly include interest and penalties as well as the tax and NICs.

8.2.1 Part-time staff

When part-timers are taken on they must be treated no differently from any other employee for tax purposes. They should be paid and taxed through the payroll using the appropriate tax code:

(a) if they bring a current P45 from their last employer, the tax code will be shown on that;

(b) if they do not, they must be asked to sign form P46;

(c) if they certify on form P46 that this is their first job since leaving full-time education they can be given the code which grants them their basic personal allowance (code 404L in 1997/98);

(d) if they certify that this is their only or main employment, they can be given the emergency code (code 404L week one/month one basis in 1997/98);

(e) if they are unable or unwilling to sign either declaration on form P46 or indicate that they are receiving a pension, they should be taxed at the basic rate of tax (23 per cent in 1997/98, code BR).

8.2.2 Casual staff

The tax treatment of casual workers, be they bar staff, waiters, kitchen assistants or whatever, depends on the length of time for which they are taken on. If they are going to be employed for more than one week, the rules are exactly the same as for part-timers. If they are engaged for one week or less, they do not need to be asked to sign form P46. Instead, the employer has to keep a record of their names and addresses and use the emergency code, unless he knows – or it is reasonable to assume – that the casual worker has other employment, in which case code BR must be used.

8.2.3 Students

Students studying in the UK who are taken on to work *during vacation periods* do not need to be taxed provided that:

(a) they do not expect to earn more than their personal allowances in the tax year (£4,045 in 1997/98); and
(b) they sign the necessary declaration on form P38(S).

A fresh form P38(S) needs to be completed each tax year, so, for example, two forms will be needed for a student whose work during the Easter vacation straddles the end of one tax year and the beginning of the next. Students who work *at other times* should be treated the same as any other casual employees and asked to sign form P46.

It is important to note that the P38(S) procedure does not apply to students studying overseas unless they have been sponsored by BUNAC (British Universities North America Club) or one of a small number of other sponsors listed in Inland Revenue booklet CWG2 (Employer's further guide to PAYE and NICs).

8.2.4 National Insurance

There are no special rules for casual or part-time employees. Class 1 NICs, employee's and employer's, have to be accounted for whenever earnings reach the lower earnings limit for the week or month (£62 per week or £269 per month in 1997/98). Note that earnings from other employments do not have to be taken into account for this purpose unless it is with the same employer.

There are no special rules for students either, although of course schoolchildren will not be liable to NICs until they reach their sixteenth birthday.

> ***Planning points***
>
> Never be tempted to pay casual staff without deduction and simply return the details on form P38A at the end of the tax year. If you do, the Tax Inspector will pass the form straight to the Inland Revenue auditors who will then call to find out why PAYE was not operated.
>
> If you sometimes have to pay casuals at the end of an evening, so that there is no time to put payments through the payroll first, you may find it easier to treat each payment as being net of tax. It can later be grossed up through the payroll and the tax accounted for as appropriate. For example, if the employee received £30, this is the equivalent of £38.96 gross on which basic rate tax of £8.96 is payable.

8.3 Self-employed or employee?

From time to time it will happen that newly engaged workers claim not to be liable to PAYE because they are self-employed and look after their own tax affairs. (This is especially common with 'resting' actors who may be seeking casual work to fill in between engagements.) They may even be registered for VAT and present invoices for payment. There are obvious financial advantages to both sides – on the one hand the worker will have less tax to pay because the self-employed can claim more allowances and deductions than employees and on the other hand the employer avoids having to pay secondary NICs. However, great care is needed in such situations. If untaxed payments are made to a worker who is in reality an employee, it is always the employer who is left with the tax bill.

There are two important principles to keep in mind. The first is that in law there is actually no such thing as a self-employed person – the same individual may be simultaneously employed in one situation and self-employed in another. The second is that whether or not a person may be treated as self-employed is a question of fact and not personal choice.

8.3.1 Tests to be applied

There are no legal definitions of employment or self-employment, but over the years the courts have built up a series of tests which they then apply to individual cases. Broadly, these fall into four categories as follows:

(a) *Mutuality* – is there a continuing obligation on the part of the worker to offer his or her services, and on the part of the employer to find work for the worker to do? If so, this points towards employee status. However, lack of mutuality does not automatically establish self-employment. For example, there may be a lack of mutuality in respect of casual workers but they would still be regarded as employees for tax purposes.

(b) *Integration* – is the worker integrated into the employer's business, part and parcel of the organisation? Or is he or she an independent outside contractor engaged on an arm's-length basis? For example, most businesses would rightly regard their window cleaner as self-employed, but not if the business was that of a window cleaning contractor. Conversely, it is reasonable to assume that bar staff will be employees because their work is integrated into the pub's principal activity of selling drinks.

(c) *Control* – is the worker subject to any degree of management, direction, supervision or control as to where, when and how they perform their duties? (This can be actual or potential – for example, hospital consultants have a great deal of autonomy in the way they go about their work, but ultimately they are answerable to the hospital management and so are classed as employees.) Evidence of control is always taken as a strong indicator of employee status.

(d) *Economic reality* – or, put more simply, is the worker genuinely in business on his or her own account? If they are, there is a good chance that they are self-employed. If not, they are almost certainly an employee. Various sub-tests can be applied to build up a picture under this heading, such as:

  (i) does the worker have to carry out the duties in person, or are they free to hire and fire helpers or supply the services of a substitute?
  (ii) does the worker work mainly or exclusively for one 'customer'?
  (iii) has the worker invested any capital in his or her 'business'?
  (iv) if the work requires any major items of equipment, are they supplied by the worker or by the 'customer'?
  (v) if work is not up to standard, does the worker have to put it right at his or her own expense?

In recent years the courts have given increasing importance to the economic reality test, but none of the tests is conclusive in itself. It is the overall impression which counts, and that is often something of a grey area. If in doubt, it is always better to err on the side of caution and operate PAYE.

8.3.2 Performers and entertainers

Licensees and restaurateurs need to exercise care when engaging artistes and performers to entertain customers. Although the majority of entertainers can safely be treated as self-employed, the Inland Revenue and DSS are constantly looking for opportunities to reclassify them as employees, particularly where an engagement is permanent or regular, or the performer uses equipment provided by the employer. For example, a disc jockey who provided all his own records, turntables and lighting would almost certainly be self-employed, but if they were provided by the licensee or restaurateur, this would point towards employment.

8.4 Tips and gratuities

Tips, gratuities and service charges are an accepted fact of life in restaurants and pubs, but the tax and National Insurance consequences are less well understood. Such payments always count as pay for tax purposes because they arise from the employee's job. However, the way the tax is collected – and the National Insurance consequences – varies according to how the tips, etc. are distributed.

(a) If cash tips are collected from tables and retained by individual waiters and waitresses, there is no requirement for anyone to operate PAYE. Nevertheless, the tips are taxable. The onus is on individual employees to declare the tips on their personal tax return. Where this is not done, as is often the case, the Inspector of Taxes may estimate the level of tips and adjust the employee's tax code accordingly.

(b) If tips are collected into a central pool, or 'tronc', before being shared out by a member of staff, the Inland Revenue will require the distributor, or 'troncmaster', to operate PAYE.

(c) If tips and service charges are collected and distributed by the employer, they should be aggregated with each employee's pay and taxed through the payroll.

8.4.1 National Insurance

The position with regard to NICs is different. Class 1 NICs will not be payable on tips or gratuities unless the employer both decides how the tips and service charges are to be allocated among the staff and is involved in the payment process in some way. If the tips and gratuities are allocated or distributed by someone acting independently of the employer, NICs will not be due, even though PAYE may be payable.

Service charges will normally fall within the scope of Class 1 NICs because, unlike tips and gratuities, they are not a voluntary payment by the customer but a charge which, if passed on to staff, is viewed by the Contributions Agency as earnings.

> ***Planning point***
>
> To avoid NIC liability on tips and gratuities, make sure that the payments to staff are shared out by someone, such as a 'troncmaster', acting independently of the employer.

8.5 Travel between home and work

In normal circumstances, travel between an employee's home and usual workplace is treated as a private expense. If the employer provides transport, or meets the employee's travel costs in any way, a taxable benefit will result. There are two Inland Revenue concessions in this area which may be relevant to the catering industry.

8.5.1 Late night taxis

It is not uncommon in pubs and restaurants for staff to be taken home by taxi late at night either because public transport is inadequate, or because it is not considered safe for the employee to travel by any other means. Extra-statutory Concession A66 gives tax relief for such journeys provided three main criteria are met:

(a) the employee works until 9.00pm or later;
(b) late working is not frequent, i.e., the employee does not work late on more than 60 occasions in the year; and
(c) the journeys are not regular, i.e., they do not follow a predictable pattern such as every Friday night.

Where these conditions are not met, a taxable benefit will nearly always result. Also, experience has shown that some Tax Inspectors try to withhold the concession where late working is part of the normal pattern for a particular business.

Planning point

Where the taxi journey is potentially taxable, any reimbursement by the employer should be treated as pay for tax and National Insurance purposes. Use of a taxi account in the employer's name avoids NICs. There will still be a taxable benefit, reportable on form P11D, for employees earning over £8,500 a year (inclusive of expenses and benefits) but for others earning below this rate, for example, many part-time staff, there will be no tax liability.

8.5.2 Disruption to public transport

A further concession, ESC A58, exempts the excess cost of home to work travel and overnight accommodation near the workplace incurred when public transport is disrupted. However, the disruption must be due to strikes or other industrial action. The concession does not extend, for example, to disruption due to adverse weather conditions, public holidays or terrorist activity.

8.5.3 National Insurance

Where either of the two Inland Revenue concessions applies, no National Insurance liability arises. In all other cases NICs will be due on any reimbursement by the employer. If the employer meets the cost directly, for example through an account with a taxi firm, there will be no National Insurance liability.

8.5.4 Employees with no fixed base

Where an employee does not work permanently at one location, but works for relatively short periods at a time at a series of locations in succession, the Inland Revenue take the view that each location is the employee's normal workplace for the duration of his stay there. The effect of this is to make all the employee's journeys to and from that location into private travel. Consequently, any payments made to the employee in respect of his travel costs will be regarded as taxable. Within the catering industry this could affect, for example, relief managers who may be viewed by their employers as having a travelling appointment and being entitled to all their travel expenses. If necessary, professional advice should be sought where the tax treatment of travel expenses is in any doubt.

With effect from 6 April 1998, the position will change. From then on, the cost of travel to and from any place of work which a site-based employee attends in the performance of their duties can be paid free of tax. Other employees will be able to claim tax relief on the cost of business journeys to somewhere other than their normal place of work, but only to the extent that it exceeds the cost of the employee's normal commuting. It remains to be seen how these proposals will work out in practice.

8.6 Meals for staff

As a general rule, providing staff with meals at their normal place of work can result in a taxable benefit. However, the tax legislation specifically excludes the benefit of a canteen in which meals are provided for the staff generally, and a further concession, Extra-statutory Concession A74, extends the exemption to meals provided on the employer's premises, provided the meals are reasonable in scale and either they are available to all employees or meal vouchers are provided to those employees for whom meals are not available.

Sometimes employers with multiple locations are unable to provide the same facilities at all sites. When this happens Concession A74 does not strictly apply, but experience suggests that most Tax Inspectors are willing to apply the concession on a site-by-site basis.

Where meals are provided for selected groups of employees only, those employees will be in receipt of a taxable benefit. Similarly, meals taken by senior staff in any kind of executive dining room will also be taxable unless the purpose is to entertain third parties.

8.6.1 Special provisions affecting pubs and restaurants

It is not uncommon for pub or restaurant staff to take their meals in the same dining areas as the general public. Where this occurs, Concession A74 may not apply and the meals could be taxable. To get the benefit of the concession staff must take their meals either at a different time from the general public, or in a section of the dining area designated for the use of staff only. The Inland Revenue are more likely to grant the concession in respect of a 'staff only' area if it is cordoned off in some way.

8.6.2 Meal allowances

Any cash allowances or reimbursements made to staff in respect of meals at their normal workplace should be treated as pay and put through the payroll. PAYE and NICs should be deducted as appropriate.

8.6.3 Meal vouchers

Provided they are given to all staff, meal vouchers may be given tax-free to employees but only up to the value of 15 pence per day. (This figure was in fact set many years ago when three shillings was the price of a reasonable meal – it has never been increased in line with inflation!) Where vouchers are given at a rate which exceeds 15 pence a day, the excess will be a taxable benefit for all staff, regardless of their level of earnings. The taxable excess must be reported on form P11D or P9D as appropriate.

8.6.4 National Insurance

As mentioned above, NICs are payable on cash allowances and reimbursements in respect of workplace meals. However, no liability attaches to vouchers (provided they are not exchangeable for cash) or to meals which constitute genuine 'payments in kind'.

8.6.5 Staff entertaining generally

Where an annual Christmas party or alternative annual function of a similar nature is open to the staff generally, the Inland Revenue will not seek tax on the relevant benefit arising to each employee where the expenditure is less than £75 per head. This relates to the total cost of the function, including VAT and any transport or accommodation provided by the employer, divided by the number of people attending.

Where the cost of the entertainment is more than £75 per head, tax will be payable on the full amount of the deemed benefit in kind. Where there is more than one annual function and their total cost per head exceeds £75, the functions that total £75 or less will not be taxed. Any other functions will be taxed in full.

For the avoidance of doubt, the Inland Revenue do not regard casual hospitality as constituting an annual party or function of a similar nature.

8.7 Uniforms and clothing

The provision of any kind of clothing for staff is likely to be a taxable benefit unless the clothing falls into one of two categories:

- protective clothing; or
- uniform.

8.7.1 Protective clothing

Protective clothing, if the Inland Revenue accept it as such, does not give rise to a tax liability. So, for example, items such as aprons, overalls, chef's hats, gloves, footwear with steel toe caps, etc. are generally accepted as being tax-free.

Jeans provided by an employer would normally be viewed as a taxable benefit, but occasionally there will be situations where protective leg wear is called for and jeans are the most suitable form.

8.7.2 Uniforms

If the Tax Inspector accepts certain items of clothing as being uniform, they will not be taxable. However, the Inspector has a narrower definition of uniform than the public at large. Formal waiters' uniforms will normally be accepted as non-taxable. However, the fact that staff are all dressed in a corporate style will not in itself remove the taxable benefit. The inspector looks at each component of the uniform – shirt, trousers, jacket, tie or whatever – and any item which is capable of being worn as everyday clothing will be taxed. He will not be impressed by arguments that the items are left behind at work each night or that the style is not to the employee's taste.

To avoid a tax liability, the article must either be unsuitable for ordinary everyday wear, or carry a distinguishing insignia or logo identifying the wearer as an employee of the organisation. Moreover, the logo must be permanently attached – pins, clips or Velcro will not do!

Some items may be less clear-cut, for example tee-shirts or sweatshirts bearing the insignia of the pub or restaurant which are also offered for sale to customers. Whilst it could no doubt be argued that the clothing was simply a kind of uniform which identified the wearer as an employee, the Inland Revenue might wish to run a counter-argument that the clothing was everyday wear since it was being sold as such to the public. In such cases there may be no obvious answer and employers may need to negotiate the tax treatment with their local tax office.

8.7.3 Calculating the taxable benefit

The value of the benefit depends on whether the employee is paid at a rate equivalent to £8,500 a year or more. If they are, they can be taxed on the full cost of the uniform if it is given to them outright. If it remains the employer's property, they will be taxed on 20 per cent of the value of the uniform when it was first provided as a benefit.

Employees paid at a rate equivalent to less than £8,500 a year will be taxed on the second-hand value of the clothing if it is given outright. If the clothing remains the employer's property, there will be no tax liability at all.

8.7.4 National Insurance

There will be no NIC liability if the clothing is non-taxable, or taxable but remains the employer's property. If the clothing is given outright, NIC liabilities will arise where the employee purchases the clothing and is reimbursed by the employer, or where the employer settles an invoice made out to the employee.

> ***Planning point***
>
> Always attach a logo or insignia if at all possible, as this removes the liability altogether. Failing that, ensure that the clothing remains the property of the employer. 'Lower paid' employees, i.e., those earning at a rate of less than £8,500 per year, will then have no liability at all.
>
> Avoid NIC liabilities by 'loaning' the clothing or by ensuring that it is purchased by the employer.

8.7.5 Laundry

The rules for tax and NICs on laundry and dry cleaning costs are broadly similar. If the clothing is accepted as being protective or uniform, any laundry and dry cleaning costs met by the employer will not be liable to tax or NICs. Conversely, laundry and dry cleaning costs in respect of everyday clothing will be taxable and, if the employer has reimbursed the employee, also liable to NICs.

8.8 Living accommodation

When an employee occupies living accommodation provided by his or her employer, a potentially taxable benefit results, unless the accommodation falls into one of three very narrow categories of exemption. Briefly these are where:

(a) the accommodation is necessary for the *proper* performance of the employee's duties – in other words the employee could not do his or her job properly if they lived anywhere else;
(b) it is provided for the *better* performance of their duties and theirs is the kind of job where it is *customary* to provide living accommodation; or
(c) there is a special threat to the employee's security and the accommodation is provided as part of special security arrangements.

The exemptions are not available for company directors unless they are full-time working directors with no *material interest* in the company. (A material interest is taken as more than 5 per cent of the ordinary share capital.)

Where a taxable benefit arises, the value of the benefit is reduced by the amount of any rent which the employee pays.

8.8.1 Exempt accommodation

Category (c) listed at **8.8** above is unlikely to be of use to restaurateurs and licensees, but the other two may be.

With regard to category (a), the courts have ruled that, to qualify for it, an employee must show that it is necessary for him or her to live in that property and no other. This sounds very restrictive, but the Inland Revenue readily accept that it applies to managers of public houses residing on the premises.

As for the second test, the Inland Revenue will first consider the *customary* aspect. The simplest way to do this is by turning the question around and asking whether *not* providing accommodation for a particular class of employee would be considered exceptional. The test is tougher than it sounds – in the case of *Vertigan* v *Brady* (1988) the court held that the fact that two-thirds of all nursery foremen were provided with free accommodation by their employers was not enough to establish a custom! The *better performance* aspect takes into account whether the employee works unsocial hours or is required to be on call. The Inland Revenue accept that this exemption can apply to managers of traditional off-licences which keep public house hours.

8.8.2 The tax charge

Where the benefit is taxable, the charge is based on the higher of:

- the rateable value of the property; or
- the annual rent paid by the employer.

Newer premises, built after the introduction of the Community Charge, may not have a rateable value, so an estimate may have to be agreed with the Tax Inspector. In Scotland, gross annual values are higher than in the rest of the UK because they are taken from the 1985 revaluation. To compensate for this anomaly, Scottish values are multiplied by 100/270 to get back to the pre-1985 figure.

Where the accommodation cost more than £75,000, there will be an additional tax charge. This is calculated by multiplying the excess over £75,000 by the 'official' Inland Revenue interest rate in force at the beginning of the tax year.

In certain limited circumstances the current market value of the property must be substituted for the cost. This happens where:

(a) the cost of the property exceeds £75,000;
(b) the employee first occupied the property after 31 March 1983; and
(c) the property had been owned, or partly owned, for at least six years by the provider.

8.8.3 Connected benefits and expenses

If the accommodation is tax-exempt, there is no further benefit in respect of any rates or council tax paid by the employer. There will still be a tax charge on other associated benefits and expenses, but this is limited to 10 per cent of the employee's *net taxable emoluments* (these are, roughly, the total amount of pay on which the employee pays tax under PAYE) where the associated benefits and expenses come under any of these headings:

- heating, lighting and cleaning;
- repairs, maintenance and decoration; and
- furniture, etc. for normal domestic occupation.

If the accommodation is not exempt, all connected benefits and expenses will be taxable in the normal way, except that no benefit arises for structural alterations and repairs or any other expenditure which would normally be the landlord's responsibility.

8.8.4 National Insurance

Normally, no NICs are payable on accommodation provided by an employer, unless exceptionally the property is leased in the employee's name, when the rent paid by the employer will attract a liability. With other benefits and expenses, the liability depends on the contractual position. Where bills are issued to the employee, NICs will be due if the employer makes the payment. Where bills are issued to the employer, i.e., the contract exists between the employer and the supplier of the services, etc., no NICs will be payable because the employer will be settling his own liability and not the employee's.

> ***Planning points***
>
> As far as possible, try to ensure that all bills – electricity, gas, telephone, etc. – are in the name of the employer. This will not affect the tax position – a report on form P11D is still needed – but avoids liability to Class 1 NICs.
>
> Similarly, if a property is leased, it should be leased in the name of the employer, not the employee

8.9 Staff suggestion schemes

Tax-free cash awards can be made to employees under the terms of a staff suggestion scheme if the scheme meets the criteria of an Inland Revenue concession (Extra-statutory Concession A57). Broadly these are as follows:

- the scheme is formally constituted with set rules;
- it is open to all employees;
- the suggestion is outside the scope of the employee's normal duties;
- except for encouragement awards, awards are only made if the suggestion is to be implemented;
- the amount of the award is geared to the expected saving; and
- there is an overriding maximum of £5,000.

Where a meritorious suggestion is not implemented, it is still possible to make 'encouragement awards' of up to £25.

8.10 P9Ds, P11Ds and dispensations

All employers are required to make annual returns to the Inland Revenue on forms P11D and P9D of the benefits and expenses they pay or provide to their staff.

8.10.1 Form P9D

The use of form P9D is limited to employees whose total remuneration – including all benefits and expenses – is paid at a rate of less than £8,500 a year. Many part-time staff potentially fall into this category. The employer must report any:

(a) accommodation;
(b) vouchers (including luncheon vouchers over 15 pence a day) or credit cards;
(c) personal bills of the employee which the employer has paid;
(d) gifts in kind and other benefits in the form of 'money's worth', i.e., something which the employee can convert to cash by selling it or disposing of it.

Genuine business expenses do not have to be reported at all.

8.10.2 Form P11D

For directors and all other employees earning over the £8,500 threshold for form P9D, form P11D is required. Employers are required to report all benefits in kind, and all expenses. Both business and personal expenses have to be returned, whatever the method by which they were paid. Some employers mistakenly suppose that only reimbursed expenses have to be reported. In fact all expenses are reportable, whether reimbursed, paid by company credit card, charged to a company account, paid direct by the employer or whatever. The only expenses which can legitimately be omitted are those covered by a formal Inland Revenue dispensation.

8.10.3 Dispensation

A dispensation is a formal notice from an Inspector of Taxes to an employer advising that certain specific payments and allowances need not be reported on P11D or P9D returns. Most commonly, a dispensation will cover such items as business travel and subsistence, third party entertaining and business calls made from employees' home telephones. Dispensations are granted when the Inspector is satisfied that the items to be covered are non-taxable and reasonable in amount, and that the payments are properly recorded and adequately controlled. An employer who wants a dispensation has to write to the tax office setting out the items to be covered and providing details of the authorisation and control systems which operate.

Planning point

An Inland Revenue leaflet, IR69, gives information on dispensations, including an application form. However, a note of caution is necessary – applying for a dispensation can trigger a full Inland Revenue P11D compliance review. It is therefore strongly recommended that you consult your professional advisers before applying and, if necessary, ask them to carry out a P11D 'health check' before proceeding.

8.11 National Insurance

Class 1 NICs are payable on the full amount of all earnings paid to an employee when those earnings exceed the lower earnings limit applicable to the payment. The limit is normally changed each tax year. For 1997/98 the limit for weekly paid staff is £62 per week, and for monthly paid staff is £269 per month.

'Earnings' includes wages or salary and almost all other payments taxable under PAYE. However, in addition it includes payments 'for the benefit' of the employee. Thus, a benefit or facility provided for an employee can become 'earnings' for NIC purposes if it involves the settlement of the employee's personal liability by the employer. Common examples of this include employee's home telephone rentals, or other domestic utilities.

8.11.1 Staff with other employment

Many part-time workers in pubs and restaurants have their main employment elsewhere. However, their other earnings will not usually affect their NIC position and the normal NIC rules will apply. The exceptions to this will be where:

(a) their main employment is with the same employer, in which case their earnings should be aggregated for NIC purposes; or
(b) they are already paying maximum contributions in their main employment, in which case the employee should apply to the Contributions Agency Deferment Group for an exemption certificate CA 2700 (known as a 'deferment'). A copy of form CA 2700 will then be sent to the employer, who must still account for employer's contributions but not employee's.

8.11.2 Dispensations

Where the Inspector of Taxes has granted a dispensation in respect of a certain type of payment, the Contributions Agency now accepts that no Class 1 NIC liability arises, provided that the terms of the dispensation are strictly adhered to. This follows the government's general policy of trying to bring PAYE and National Insurance into line.

8.11.3 Long-term unemployed

With effect from 6 April 1996, employers are entitled to a full rebate of employer's NICs in respect of new employees who were previously unemployed. The worker must have been out of work for at least two years immediately prior to being taken on, and the rebate is available for 12 months.

8.12 PAYE settlement agreements

Often employees are provided with modest benefits or incentives, on which their employer would prefer them not to have to pay tax. Common examples of this are in-house meals and uniforms without an insignia. In these cases it is possible for the employer to make an annual settlement with the Inspector of Taxes, whereby the employer pays a lump sum to the Inland Revenue and the Inspector agrees not to assess the employees. No details are then required, either on forms P9D and P11D or on the employee's personal tax return. These arrangements are known as PAYE settlement arrangements (PSAs).

The sum paid by the employer is in effect an additional benefit to the employee, so the employer's liability is calculated on a grossed-up basis. For example, a £77 benefit for an employee who normally pays tax at 23 per cent is worth £100 when grossed up and the employer will have to pay £23 to the Inland Revenue, whilst a £60 benefit for a 40 per cent taxpayer will be grossed up to £100 and the employer will have to pay £40.

8.12.1 The scope of PSAs

To qualify for inclusion in a PSA, the expense or benefit must be:

(a) minor, relative to the employee's total remuneration; or
(b) irregular, not following any predictable pattern; or
(c) on items to which it is impracticable to apply PAYE, or to identify the amount of the benefit to an individual (such as staff parties)

PSAs cannot be used for cash payments, round sum allowances or major benefits such as cars, living accommodation and beneficial loans.

8.12.2 National Insurance

At the time of writing, there is no provision for including Class 1 NICs in a PSA. As a result, when a PSA is used to settle tax on a benefit which attracts Class 1 NICs (for example, an employee's home telephone bill or other personal expenses), the NICs must still be accounted for through the payroll in the normal way. However, the DSS has issued a consultative document outlining its proposals for a new class of NICs to be called Class 1B.

Once introduced, these will be payable at a rate equivalent to the standard employer's contribution (currently 10 per cent), both on any benefit which would normally attract Class 1 NICs, and on the tax borne by the employer under the PSA arrangement.

8.13 Returns, due dates and penalties

The table in Figure 8.1 below sets out details of the main PAYE returns and notifications which employers are required to submit to the Inland Revenue:

Figure 8.1

Return	*Description*	*Due date*
P46	Notification to the tax office of a new employee without a P45 from their previous employer.	No statutory deadline.
P14	Year-end return for each employee showing pay, tax and NIC details.	19 May following the end of the tax year.
P35	Employer's annual statement, declaration and certificate listing all employees paid during the year with their tax and NIC details.	19 May following the end of the tax year.
P60	Employee's annual certificate of pay, tax and NICs.	From 1996/97 must be handed to the employee by 31 May following the end of the tax year.
P38A	Employer's supplementary return of employees not listed on form P35 and who received more than £100 in the tax year.	As for form P35.
P9D	Annual return of certain benefits and expenses over £25 to employees earning at a rate of less than £8,500 a year. With effect from 1996/97 a copy must be given to the employee.	6 July following the end of the tax year (with effect from 1996/97 onwards – previously 6 June).
P11D	Annual return of all benefits and expenses paid to employees earning at a rate of £8,500 a year or more, and to directors. With effect from 1996/97 a copy must be given to the employee.	As for P9D.
P46(Car)	Quarterly notification to the tax office of changes in the allocation or specification of company cars.	Within 28 days of the end of each quarter, i.e., 2 August, 2 November, 2 February and 3 May.

8.13.1 Penalties

The next table (Figure 8.2) gives details of the penalties which employers can incur in respect of late, incorrect or fraudulent returns. Except where the penalties are automatic, the amounts shown are the maximum penalties permitted by the tax legislation. Non-automatic penalties are usually open to negotiation with the Inland Revenue, who take account of such things as the employer's co-operation (up to 40 per cent discount), the degree of disclosure (up to 20 per cent discount, plus a further 10 per cent if the disclosure is voluntary) and the seriousness of any irregularities involved (up to 40 per cent discount).

Figure 8.2

Return	*Penalty*	*Note*
Late P35/ P14s	Automatic penalty of £100 per month per 50 employees or part thereof.	The P35 and its accompanying P14s count as a single return.
P35/P14s over 12 months late.	Additional non-automatic penalty of up to 100 per cent of any tax and NICs outstanding on 19 April following the tax year concerned.	Mitigable penalty.
Other late returns	Up to £300 for each return, plus a further £60 per day per return if the failure continues after the award of the initial penalty.	Mitigable penalty.
Incorrect returns	Up to £3,000 per return.	Mitigable penalty.

8.13.2 Interest

Interest has been charged on late payments of PAYE and NICs since the 1992/93 tax year. The interest runs from 19 April following the end of the tax year in question. Interest may also be due in respect of late payment of tax relating to 1991/92 and earlier tax years where the Inspector of Taxes raises a formal Schedule E assessment on the employer, termed a 'Regulation 49 determination'.

8.13.3 Inland Revenue and Contributions Agency compliance activity

Both the Inland Revenue and the Contributions Agency operate teams of compliance officers who carry out routine spot checks on employers to ensure that PAYE and National Insurance are being operated correctly and that all expenses and benefits are fully reported on P11D returns.

Visits by the Contributions Agency will concentrate primarily on NICs but any evidence of PAYE or P11D failures is automatically passed to the Inland Revenue who then carry out their own inspection. The Inland Revenue's PAYE auditors concentrate mainly on PAYE and National Insurance matters but will also look at benefits and expenses. Likewise, their counterparts in the P11D compliance teams will also look at payroll matters if necessary. It should be assumed, therefore, that a visit by any of these three types of compliance team will eventually lead to the whole area of employee taxation coming under scrutiny.

When irregularities are discovered, tax and NICs may be recovered for the current tax year and up to six closed years. In exceptional circumstances the Inland Revenue and DSS have the right to go back even further. In addition to recovering the arrears, they will also impose penalties and interest as described above.

Pubs and restaurants should always take seriously the possibility of a compliance visit happening at very short notice. Rightly or wrongly, the industry is viewed by the Inland Revenue and DSS as being 'accident prone' and therefore receives high priority when cases are being selected for inspection. It is always advisable to seek professional assistance with an inspection and, as a preventive measure, it is worth asking your advisers to carry out periodic PAYE/P11D 'health checks' to ensure that any problems are rectified well in advance of any official compliance visit.

8.14 Self-assessment

The new self-assessment tax regime which came into effect on 6 April 1996 has a number of implications for employers which need to be noted.

8.14.1 Form P45

This is now a four-part form, since it includes an extra copy of the form to be retained by the employee. In addition, employers now have to show the total pay in 'this employment' if this differs from total pay in the tax year to date.

8.14.2 Form P60

There is now a deadline for giving employees a copy of their year-end tax certificate, form P60. The deadline is 31 May following the end of the tax year. The first year this applies to is 1996/97, so employees will be entitled to a copy of their 1996/97 P60 by 31 May 1997. The Inland Revenue have the power to impose penalties on employers if this deadline is not met.

8.14.3 Form P11D

From 1996/97 onwards employers do not just have to report their employees' benefits on P11D returns – they also have to calculate the 'cash equivalent', or taxable value, of a number of benefits, principally cars, vans, cheap loans, living accommodation and relocation assistance. The form now includes a number of extra working sheets specially for this purpose. In recognition of the extra burden this places on employers, the deadline for submitting P11Ds has been extended to 6 July from 1997 onwards.

In addition, employers now have a legal responsibility to let employees have a copy of their P11D and to supply details of any dispensations held. The deadline for this is again 6 July. If an employee has left between 5 April and 6 July, the employer has to forward the information to the employee's last known address. There is no immediate obligation to supply the information to employees who leave before that. However, if the employee makes a written request within three years of the end of the relevant tax year, the employer then has 30 days to supply the information or face a penalty.

8.14.4 Benefits provided by third parties

Employers now also have a duty to report details of any benefits or expenses given to their staff by a third party, but only where the employer has been involved in 'arranging' the benefit or expense. Employers will be regarded as having 'arranged' a benefit or expense where they have played any part in guaranteeing or facilitating it or had any kind of active involvement. Otherwise, it is the responsibility of the third party to provide the employee with the necessary information in writing by 6 July following the end of the tax year.

8.14.5 Taxed Award Schemes

Some organisations which run incentive schemes also take care of the employee's tax liability under a formal arrangement with the Inland Revenue known as a Taxed Award Scheme. In these cases, the organisation responsible will let the employee have details on a designated Inland Revenue form and no action is needed on the part of the employee's own employer.

Note that if a retailer gives a small discount to someone else's employees, this is not treated as a taxable benefit unless goods or services are being provided at less than cost price.

8.14.6 Further guidance

More detailed guides to self-assessment are available from the Inland Revenue and can be ordered on their special telephone helpline number (0345 161514) or viewed on the Internet at http://www.open.gov.uk/inrev/irleaf.htm.

8.15 Profit-related pay (PRP)

What exactly is PRP? Profit-related pay (PRP) is a government-sponsored scheme which links employees' pay with their employer's profits in return for a measure of tax relief. With careful planning, a business can use PRP to control staff costs and enhance employees' take-home pay without seriously eroding pre-tax profits.

8.15.1 The tax relief

To qualify for relief, a PRP scheme has to comply with the tax legislation and be registered with the Inland Revenue. It has to apply to at least 80 per cent of the employees in a business. There is, theoretically, no limit on the amount of PRP which can be paid to individuals, but the tax relief is finite. At present, it is restricted to the lowest of three figures:

- 20 per cent of the employee's pay inclusive of PRP; or
- the actual amount of PRP received; or
- £4,000.

Thus, PRP currently makes it possible to increase take-home pay by up to £920 for an employee who pays tax at the basic rate of 23 per cent, and £1,600 in the case of a 40 per cent taxpayer.

Following an announcement in the November 1996 Budget, PRP tax relief is being phased out over four years. For 'profit periods' starting on or after 1 January 1998, the £4,000 tax-free ceiling will be reduced as follows:

(a) ceiling £2,000 for profit periods beginning between 1 January and 31 December 1998;
(b) ceiling £1,000 for profit periods beginning between 1 January and 31 December 1999;
(c) no relief for profit periods beginning on or after 1 January 2000.

8.15.2 Conditions necessary for a PRP scheme

To qualify for tax relief, a PRP scheme must be formally registered with the Inland Revenue. To obtain registration, the scheme must satisfy the following conditions:

(a) it is governed by formal written rules which comply with the tax regulations;
(b) it relates to a clearly defined employment unit which operates with a view to profit and is capable of producing a profit and loss account to Companies Act standards;
(c) anyone able to control, directly or indirectly, more than 25 per cent of the ordinary share capital of the company is excluded;
(d) at least 80 per cent of the workforce participate;
(e) employees participate on similar terms, i.e., the basis of distribution of PRP must be objective and not discriminate against particular individuals or groups of employees.

8.15.3 What can go wrong?

By its very nature PRP has to involve an element of risk. Profits cannot always be forecast with as much accuracy as one would like, but the PRP legislation provides safety mechanisms which go some way towards smoothing out the peaks and troughs. The main causes of 'accidents' are lack of foresight at the planning stage and inadequate training of the staff who operate the scheme.

The worst that can happen to a PRP scheme is complete cancellation. The employer may wish to cancel if profits are significantly below – or above – forecasts. Equally, the Inland Revenue may do this if there have been irregularities in the way the scheme is operated. In practice, the Revenue's PRP Unit uses cancellation only as a last resort and will try to help employers to put mistakes right whenever possible.

If a scheme is cancelled, any tax relief which has already been given is clawed back from the employer. In practice, there can still be an overall saving to the employer, as the tax may come to less than the cost of the pay rise that would have been given if PRP had not been introduced.

Overall, the risks of a PRP scheme are calculable, manageable and far outweighed by the advantages.

Chapter 9 – Value added tax (VAT)

9.1 General principles

VAT is primarily a tax on consumer spending and is based upon the business supply of goods and services. The basic principle is to charge VAT at each stage in the transaction chain. If the customer is himself VAT-registered then the VAT charged will be recoverable where it relates to an onward business transaction. It is only when the transaction involves the general public or a businessperson who cannot recover all of his VAT that the tax sticks as a charge on the supply.

9.2 Services supplied and VAT rates

9.2.1 Standard rated supplies

The main supplies that publicans and restaurateurs are likely to make, which are subject to VAT at the standard rate, include the following:

(a) the provision of catering, e.g., meals, snacks and similar supplies;
(b) the supply of alcohol, soft drinks and other related bar sales;
(c) sleeping and related overnight accommodation, e.g., B&B;
(d) the supply of sleeping accommodation to an individual where the let exceeds four weeks. From the 29th day, VAT is only due on the supply of facilities and services but this must be at least 20 per cent of the total charge;
(e) income from gaming, amusement and similarly related games equipment, e.g., bar billiards;
(f) income from cigarette, contraceptive and similar related vending machines;
(g) income from pay phones;
(h) the letting of rooms for the purpose of a supply of catering;
(i) the supply of camping and caravan facilities;
(j) car parking (if a charge is made).

9.2.2 Zero rated supplies

Typically, a publican's or restaurateur's zero rated supplies would include cold take-away food.

The standard rated and zero rated goods and services are known as 'taxable supplies' and will lead to VAT registration (see **9.3** below).

9.2.3 Exempt services

The following exempt services may be supplied by a pub or restaurant:

(a) the letting of rooms other than for a catering or sleeping purpose;
(b) income from the let of space, e.g., the right to site a cigarette machine on a wall where the income is retained by the operator.

These exempt services do not lead to a VAT charge and do not count towards VAT registration.

9.3 Registration for VAT

A publican or restaurateur making or intending to make any taxable supplies is required to be registered for VAT if either of two limits are breached. The limits are:

(a) total taxable turnover in excess of £48,000 within the last 12 months (on a rolling 12-month cumulative basis); or
(b) total taxable turnover expected to exceed £48,000 within the next 30 days.

The registration limit is subject to an annual budgetary increase in November. The above limits have been in force since 27 November 1996

The registered person in these circumstances can be a sole proprietor, a partnership, a limited company or even an association of individuals, such as a club.

> ***Tip***
>
> Check your annual taxable turnover at the end of each month. If your turnover is over the registration limit complete the VAT registration application and send it to the VAT office within 30 days of the month end.

9.3.1 Buying a business as a going concern

There are special rules where a person buys a pub or restaurant as 'a going concern'. If a business is regarded as a transfer of a going concern for VAT purposes, no VAT must be charged on the transfer. However, the purchaser is required to become VAT-registered if the current owner is already VAT-registered because his supplies have gone over the limit or if, following the purchase, the new owner expects to go over the threshold limit within the next 30 days. The purchaser must take into account the supplies of the vendor in the 12 months beforehand when considering whether VAT registration is mandatory.

9.3.2 Registration procedure

Where a person becomes liable to be VAT-registered he must notify his local VAT office or, if within the London area, the Registration Centre in Newry, Northern Ireland, of his liability within 30 days of the end of the relevant month. For example, if a small restaurant's takings exceeded £48,000 in the seven months ending July it would have to notify its VAT office by the end of August and become registered for VAT from 1 September. Registration for VAT is always made on form VAT 1 or form VAT 20 (Welsh version) and must be signed by the sole proprietor, partner or director of the applicant. If the registration is for partnership, it must also be accompanied by form VAT 2 listing all the names and addresses of the partners.

9.4 VAT return

Once a person has become registered for VAT he is obliged to make periodic VAT returns to Customs on form VAT 100. These forms will be sent direct to the taxable person by Customs from the Central Computer Centre at Southend.

Most publicans or restaurateurs can expect to be on quarterly returns. The taxable person can request any quarter which suits his own preference, i.e., a calendar year end or one which coincides with his financial year, i.e., ending 30 April. All VAT due during the current quarter must be accounted for in box 1 of the VAT return and transferred to box 3. Box 2 is related to EC purchases and is unlikely to be relevant. VAT which has been paid over in respect of purchases for resale or overhead expenses can be reclaimed in box 4 of the VAT return and the net figure, usually a payment, is shown in box 5 and must be paid over to Customs within 30 days of the end of the VAT return period. For example, a return for the three months ending 31 August must be sent with a remittance for the net amount of VAT due to the VAT Central office at Southend to arrive by 30 September. There are penalties for sending a return or payment in late or for sending in incorrect or inaccurate returns.

> ***Tip***
>
> Choose your VAT return period to fit in with your financial year end. This makes it easier to reconcile your annual turnover with your VAT return.

The VAT return also has four additional boxes for turnover values (box 6), purchase values (box 7) and for EC trade (boxes 8 and 9). Boxes 6 and 7 must be completed but boxes 8 and 9 are unlikely to be relevant. The values in boxes 6 and 7 reflect the values of supplies and purchases excluding VAT.

9.4.1 Annual returns

For businesses with a turnover less than £300,000 there is a special scheme which allows VAT to be returned on an annual basis. Applicants must have been VAT-registered for at least 12 months. Application is made on form VAT 600. Under this scheme the applicant then makes nine monthly payments based on 10 per cent of the previous year's net VAT, with the tenth and final balancing payment two months after the end of the accounting year. In practice, the publican is able to send in one VAT return with a balancing payment 14 months after his accounting year began. There are further reliefs and concessions for very small businesses where the turnover does not exceed £100,000 per annum, which in some circumstances only need to make quarterly payments or even no interim payment at all. The balance of tax will be collected with the submission of the VAT return.

9.4.2 Time of supply

The time of supply of goods or services or the time when VAT becomes due is always the earlier of one of the following points:

(a) the time when the supply of goods or services is made;
(b) the time when cash or other consideration is received;
(c) the date when a VAT invoice is issued, which must be within 14 days of the basic supply of goods or services (see (a) above).

A retailer is not obliged to raise a VAT invoice and, therefore, in reality, for most pubs and restaurants the time of supply will be the collection or receipt of money and the retailer will use an appropriate retail scheme to determine the VAT payable.

> ***Tip***
>
> Generally, VAT is due when either:
>
> - cash is received; or
> - invoices are sent out;
>
> whichever is the earlier.

9.4.3 Accounting for VAT

Except where a pub or restaurant supplies zero rated take-away food or receives exempt rents, all income received will be subject to VAT on a cash received, VAT-inclusive basis. This is the simplest of schemes specifically designed for retailers, known as retail scheme A, and VAT is charged according to the VAT fraction. Currently, with the standard rate of $17\frac{1}{2}$ per cent the VAT fraction is 7/47.

> ***Example***
>
> What is the VAT element of £100 of receipts?
>
> $$£100 \times \frac{7}{47} = £14.89 \text{ VAT and therefore } £85.11 \text{ of net income.}$$

Where a restaurant is supplying cold take-away food, the income for this food should be identified separately, perhaps with a separate till button from the standard rated takings. VAT is then only accounted for on the standard rated element. This is known as retail scheme F. There are a number of retail schemes but only the two mentioned above can be applied to the pub or restaurant trade.

9.5 VAT recoverable

Any restaurateur or publican who is registered for VAT will be able to recover the VAT incurred on goods and services supplied to him, provided they are used for business activities. This VAT is known as input tax. Any taxable person claiming input tax on his VAT return must be aware of the evidence that is required to support the claim and areas where input VAT is either blocked or not recovered in full.

9.5.1 Evidence and records

Any person claiming credit for input tax must be in possession of what is known as a tax invoice. There are other special rules relating to importations and acquisitions of goods from outside of the UK, but they are not considered relevant in this context. A tax invoice must be obtained from the supplier of goods and services and it must contain the following information:

- the name, address and VAT registration number of the supplier;
- the name and address of the pub or restaurant;
- an identifying number and date of issue;
- a description of the goods or services supplied;
- a value of the goods supplied plus VAT where appropriate;
- the gross amount payable less any discounts offered;
- the rate of VAT charged.

The invoices should then be listed and aggregated for the VAT quarter to which they relate using the tax point on the original invoice and securely filed and retained for at least six years, unless authorisation from Customs for a lesser period is obtained.

> ***Tip***
>
> If VAT is charged to you always ensure you receive a proper VAT invoice before you pay for your supply, otherwise you may find that the VAT authorities refuse to repay the VAT, in which case the purchase has cost 17.5 per cent more than it should.

9.5.2 Non-deductible items

There are certain goods and services which, although purchased by the business, are not eligible for VAT recovery under any circumstances or where there are special rules. Most commonly in this sector these will be:

- the purchase of motor cars unless used wholly or exclusively for business purposes;
- business entertainment;
- domestic accommodation for directors or proprietors;
- goods or services not used for business purposes; and
- road fuel.

Motor cars

VAT incurred on the purchase of a new motor vehicle cannot be recovered unless the car is used wholly and exclusively for some business purpose. However, a motor car which is leased, where the publican or restaurateur is never the legal owner, is not caught by this restriction, but only 50 per cent of the VAT on the leasing charge can be recovered providing the vehicle is used for some business purposes. This rule was introduced on 1 August 1995, and cars where the 50 per cent restriction applies, i.e., 'N' registration and after, should carry a clear endorsement on the invoice. Prior to that date the recovery of VAT on leased cars could be made in full providing the vehicle was used in part for business purposes. This full recovery relates to 'M' registration and earlier models and remains fully recoverable even after 1 August 1995.

Repairs and maintenance of a car are not covered by this restriction and VAT can be recovered in full regardless of whether or not there is private use of the vehicle. Vans and similar commercial vehicles are also not subject to the restriction and VAT can be recovered in full on the purchase and maintenance of such vehicles, but a private use VAT charge would have to be made. Consequently, when a car is sold, no VAT becomes due unless a profit above the original purchase price is made, when VAT is due on the margin of profit. However, when a commercial vehicle is sold, VAT is due on the full second-hand selling price.

> ***Tip***
>
> Where a car is leased post-1 August 1995, i.e., 'N' registration and after, and it is supplied with a maintenance agreement, make sure the maintenance part of the agreement is shown separately or in a separate contract. In this way VAT can be recovered in full on the maintenance element. If the maintenance part is included in the contract to lease, then it becomes subject to the 50 per cent restriction.

Business entertainment

Business entertainment is defined as the provision of hospitality or entertainment for anyone who is not an employee of the business. In this sector it will include the provision of free drinks and meals to customers on which the VAT recoverable will be restricted. In respect of meals, the amount of VAT incurred is likely to be negligible, but in respect of drinks the publican or restaurateur will need to keep a record of free drinks given. This does not include free drinks and meals to staff where VAT incurred can be recovered. (This is covered in more detail in **9.6** below.)

Accommodation

Any VAT incurred on accommodation for employees can be recovered as input tax, providing a charge for rent is not made. If a charge is made, VAT can be recovered, but VAT must be accounted for on the receipts on a VAT-inclusive basis.

The Wages Order for the industry prescribes set minimum rates of pay for most hotel and allied workers and provides for differences in remuneration for those employees receiving accommodation and/or meals and those who do not. Where new employees elect to receive these benefits and receive a lower scale of pay in accordance with the Wages Order, there is no payment for the accommodation or meals and therefore no tax due on the difference between the two rates of pay.

Where costs are incurred on accommodation provided in a business establishment, such as a flat above a pub for the directors or proprietors, the VAT element is not seen as business input tax and cannot be recovered. Where, however, part of the accommodation is set aside for business use, such as for an office, then the VAT for that part of the accommodation or on items of furniture is treated as recoverable for VAT purposes.

Non-business use

Where VAT is incurred on goods or services which are not used for business purposes or are diverted from a business use then VAT cannot be recovered on those items. Examples of supplies which may fall into this area are:

(a) drinks for private use (in practice VAT is recovered initially but paid over quarterly on private use);
(b) own residential accommodation;
(c) goods supplied to the business but not for a business purpose, e.g., private television set; or
(d) goods for another person's business, e.g., a subsidiary business.

Road fuel

Special rules apply to the purchase of petrol and diesel used in either a car or a commercial van which are used at least in part for non-business purposes. Basically, the VAT can be recovered in full but a scale charge, based on the Inland Revenue road fuel scale charge has to be applied on a quarterly basis. Broadly, if the value of the input tax recovered is greater than the charge it is worthwhile adopting this scheme. If it is not, and the value of the charge exceeds the amount of input tax to be recovered, then it is better not to recover any VAT at all. As mentioned earlier this does not affect the right to recover VAT on repair and maintenance which can be recovered in full even if the vehicle is only used partly for business purposes.

> ***Tip***
>
> Work out over a representative period, say six months, the amount of VAT that can be recovered on fuel bills. If this is more than the scale charge, then it is worth recovering the VAT and paying the charge, otherwise do not claim any VAT on fuel bills, thereby avoiding the scale charge.

9.6 Supplies of drinks

The retail sale of drinks and related items over a bar will be the main VAT supply of a pub and to a lesser extent, a restaurant. Whilst the supply of all drinks will bear VAT at the standard rate (zero rate cannot apply in these circumstances) there are certain anomalies which arise. These are listed below.

9.6.1 Free drinks to customers

Free drinks to customers for whatever purpose are seen as a supply of business entertainment. Strictly speaking, VAT should not be recovered on goods used for business entertainment but, in practice, as they are supplied from a common stock, publicans and restaurateurs should keep a list of such free drinks given and charge VAT on the deemed cost price. This VAT is then aggregated with all the other output tax (VAT on sales) and accounted for on the quarterly VAT return.

9.6.2 Staff drinks

Where staff are given free drinks, this is not a supply for VAT purposes and no VAT becomes due. Input VAT can, however, still be recovered. If staff pay for the drinks, whether at full or reduced prices, then VAT becomes due in the normal way on the price paid.

9.6.3 Own drinks

Where the proprietor or employer consumes or takes drinks from business stock, it is considered to be a supply for private use. Input VAT remains recoverable, but VAT becomes due on the cost price of the drinks or items taken from stock. In practice this can be recorded with the free drinks to customers.

> ***Tip***
>
> Keep a book handy next to the bar in which free drinks given to customers or consumed by yourself can be recorded. The cost price should also be shown. The VAT on the cost of the drinks should be added back to the VAT return each quarter. In this way, any visiting VAT officer can see that free drinks are being accounted for.

9.6.4 Off-sales and special promotions

Goods sold for consumption off premises are liable to VAT on their sales price. Goods which are sold as a promotion, such as during a 'happy hour' or special event, are subject to VAT in the normal way. However, it is important to keep a record of these items as, especially in respect of off-sales and promotional events, they will have an effect on the mark-up which the publican will be achieving during a given period. This may be important if a visiting VAT officer queries why profits are not as high as he would have expected (see **9.13** below).

9.6.5 Other points

The pub and bar trade is accepted as one which suffers stock wastage. In respect of a pub for instance with long cellar lines, the wastage could easily be anything between 1 and 4 per cent of its draft beer purchases. Proprietors in this business are advised to keep records of wastage, or at least have a good idea of the amount wasted, in case they are challenged by Customs. Examples of such wastage are:

- pipe cleaning and drawing off;
- waste from drip trays, fobbing, ullage and cask tops and bottoms;
- breakages and other wasted stock;
- returned drinks; and
- thefts of stock.

Thefts of stock should not be confused with theft of money. Loss of stock prior to sale carries no VAT implications while theft of takings by staff still carries a VAT liability.

9.7 Supplies of catering

Catering is defined as any supply of food and drink for consumption on the premises or the supply of hot food or drink for consumption off premises. When catering is supplied it is subject to VAT at the standard rate. Cold food supplied for consumption off premises is zero rated for VAT purposes. In this respect, the goods must be consumed away from the premises at which they are sold. Often the guidelines are blurred as to where premises begin and end and there have been many VAT Tribunal cases on this point, but generally speaking the following principles can be applied. Premises include:

(a) the curtilage of an office block or factory where a catering outlet is situated;
(b) the grounds surrounding any area where a catering point is situated, providing that does not include a public road or thoroughfare;
(c) the forecourt or garden of a public house, café or restaurant; and any other enclosed area where either access is restricted or admission is by payment, such as a sports meeting or entertainment event.

Foods sold through stalls, mobile restaurants, and other outlets in public spaces, will normally satisfy the take-away rules for cold food, providing it is clearly not for consumption at the outlet or at tables provided by the outlet.

9.7.1 Free meals for customers

Free meals for customers are supplies of business entertainment and VAT should be restricted to the standard rated cost of providing the meal. However, as the meal is likely to consist basically of zero rated purchases of food, providing no additional taxable overhead has been incurred in providing that meal, the VAT in such cases is generally likely to be nil.

9.7.2 Staff meals

No VAT is due on free meals to employees, providing they make no payment for those meals or there is no reduction in their salary specifically to take account of meals consumed. (See under accommodation at **9.5.2**.)

9.7.3 Own meals

Meals taken by a publican or restaurateur for himself and his family are clearly not in the course and furtherance of the business, and so any VAT incurred in providing these meals is irrecoverable and must be adjusted for. Conversely, there is no VAT due on the supply of those meals.

9.7.4 Other points

Although not subject to VAT in their own right, supplies of food which have been prepared for catering and which are subsequently wasted should be detailed, as it is not unknown for visiting VAT officers to try and recreate records for supplies of catering from the original purchases of food. This is particularly relevant in catering outlets such as fish and chip shops, where VAT officers try to recalculate the number of fish portions sold from purchases or the number of bags of chips which can be obtained from the initial bulk purchase of potatoes.

9.7.5 Tips and service charges

Tips and similar gratuities which are freely given are outside the scope of VAT. Service charges which are mandatory and added to the cost of the meal are subject to VAT. However, if it can be shown that the service charge is optional and still at the customer's discretion, then they are treated the same as tips or gratuities.

> ***Tip***
>
> Ensure that any tip or gratuity given is at the customer's discretion, i.e., make it clear on all documentation that it is not compulsory, to avoid an additional charge to VAT.

9.8 Other related points

9.8.1 Gaming machines

A gaming machine is a machine constructed or adapted for playing a game of chance which a player pays to play either by inserting a coin or a token. VAT on the takings from a gaming machine must be accounted for by the person who supplies the machine to the public. Customs accept that the tax point for income on the gaming machine is the date the cash is removed or collected from the machine. In addition, the supplier of the gaming machine would require a gaming machine licence which is obtained from the local Collector of Customs & Excise.

In respect of other equipment provided for amusement or sport, such as pool tables or bar billiard tables, VAT is due on any income at the time of collection. VAT is also due on the same principle from vending and similar machines located in a pub or restaurant.

9.8.2 Rentals and functions

The letting of rooms for catering or accommodation is always subject to VAT. The letting of a room, however, for other non-catering functions, such as a room hired to a local association for monthly meetings, will be VAT exempt. Where a business puts on entertainment for which it makes a charge, normally as an admission fee, either with or without catering, then the charge will be subject to VAT in the normal way.

> ***Tip***
>
> When letting a room with other facilities ensure that the room hire is shown separately to avoid attracting output VAT.

9.8.3 Sports and competition fees

An entry fee for a competition would normally be subject to VAT, unless it is to do with sport or physical recreation, when it is exempt providing the whole of the fee is allocated towards the provision of prizes related to entering that competition. Where a pub recharges individuals an equal amount for putting a team in a local football league, that has no implication for VAT purposes.

If a business donates a prize for a sports competition or similar event, that is a business gift. Providing the value of the prize excluding VAT is £15 or less, VAT can be recovered on the purchase without any onward VAT charge; otherwise, if VAT is recovered on the purchase of the gift, then VAT becomes due on the onward supply.

9.8.4 Other sources of income

Pubs and restaurants may get small amounts of income from a varicty of other sources. It is impossible to list all the areas in which they may arise, but examples which proprietors should be aware of, include the following:

- income from pay phones;
- commission from local taxi firms; and
- sales of business assets.

In respect of this last point, businesses should always remember that if they sell any item, either second-hand, part exchange or as scrap, VAT is due on the actual amount of consideration received. The only exceptions to this general rule are the sale of motor cars (unless a profit has been made), or private or personal items which are not part of the assets of the business.

9.9 Records

This heading will not deal with records and accounts generally, which are dealt with elsewhere, but will touch on record and accounting requirements which have a specific implication for VAT purposes. In the main,

Customs make no specific requirements as to what sort of records are kept and are usually happy to accept normal commercial records, providing they give a true and accurate record of takings and a clear audit trail.

9.9.1 Gross takings

As VAT is due on the amount of a pub or restaurant's gross takings, it is important that they are recorded accurately. The controls exerted by the business in its collection and record of daily gross takings will be one of the key indicators to Customs & Excise whether there is any money not being recorded and hence any VAT revenue at risk.

Demonstration of good control, e.g., till roll readings, computerised point of sale information, etc. will go a long way to convincing Customs that there is no under-declaration or suppression of takings.

Gross takings consist not only of all the payments as they are received, but also the full value of all credit sales at the time they are made. If credit sales are made but the cash is not received, the business still has to account for the VAT, but may be able to claim bad debt relief at a later date (see **9.9.4** below). There were previously two methods of accounting for VAT on takings but this was changed from 1 April 1997.

9.9.2 Adjustments to gross takings

As gross takings are vital to determining the amount of VAT due, there are requirements as to what must be included within the heading, and what can be excluded. Items which must always be included within gross takings are:

- cash payments from the till;
- thefts of money;
- a value for free drinks and similar gifts to customers at cost;
- a value for goods diverted to own or non-business use at cost.

Items which must be excluded from gross takings are:

- receipts for exempt supplies;
- void transactions;
- ineligible credit card transactions;
- refunds to customers;
- unsigned cheques and similar invalid cheques;
- foreign currency;
- till breakdowns and float discrepancies;
- other till errors or incorrect codings.

9.9.3 VAT account

It is a requirement that every taxable person must keep a record known as the VAT account. The object of the VAT Account is to show how, and from where, figures inserted into boxes 1, 3 and 4 of the VAT return have been determined. It is the first stage in the audit trail.

The VAT account consists of two parts:

- the VAT payable portion (entered into boxes 1 and 3);
- the VAT allowable portion (entered into box 4).

The VAT payable portion will generally include VAT from gross takings, VAT from other areas, VAT adjustments from earlier periods and the fuel scale charge. The VAT allowable portion will consist of the total amount of input tax allowed, any bad debt relief and appropriate adjustments from earlier quarters.

9.9.4 Bad debt relief

As stated earlier, businesses will find that they have to account for VAT on credit sales for which no monetary consideration is received. VAT has to be accounted for in the VAT quarter in which the credit sale is made, but there is a scheme which subsequently allows bad debt relief assuming there is no agreement for deferred payment. Broadly, if the debt still remains unpaid six months after payment is due, the VAT can be recovered on the VAT return for that quarter, providing certain conditions are met. Any business finding itself in this position should check those conditions before claiming the relief.

Any subsequent adjustments under the scheme must be dealt with outside the business retail scheme.

9.9.5 Errors from previous returns

Where a business discovers that it has made an error in accounting for VAT in previous VAT periods, it must make a voluntary adjustment in either of the following two ways, depending on the amount involved.

Error up to £2,000
Where the net value of the error does not exceed £2,000, an adjustment can be made in the current VAT account.

Error exceeds £2,000
Where the net error exceeds £2,000 the business must inform the local VAT office immediately, disclosing the net amount of the error and sending in a remittance of the amount involved. Disclosure can be made on

a special form known as form VAT 652. In any event, disclosure of sums over £2,000 cannot be made on the VAT return and, if they are made, Customs do not accept them as voluntary disclosures. Disclosures to Customs over £2,000, even if made in the prescribed manner, will attract interest at the statutory rate. Adjustments on VAT returns do not attract interest.

Since 18 July 1996, a restaurateur or publican has only been able to go back three years from the current VAT return period to seek repayment of any VAT on sales which may have been overpaid. Similarly, if VAT on purchases or expenses has been underclaimed, the three-year restriction for making a claim also applies.

9.9.6 Other points

Records have to be retained for a period of six years. If this causes storage problems, application can be made to the local VAT office to determine whether a shorter period will be permitted. Customs & Excise have extensive statutory powers. The main ones relating to this type of trade will be in the area of:

- requesting information and the production of documents;
- the removal of documents (as necessary);
- the opening of vending machines;
- the right to visit and inspect the taxable premises (but not the private premises); and
- the requirement to provide security for tax.

9.10 Property

The rules and regulations covering VAT land and property are many and complex. It would not be appropriate nor possible in this section to discuss them in any detail and any business involved in buying, selling, leasing, surrendering or assigning an interest in property should always take professional advice. However, there are a few basic points which a business should be aware of as regards public houses, restaurants and similar properties.

9.10.1 New buildings

A new pub or restaurant sold freehold within the first three years from the date of its certificate of completion will always be subject to VAT at the standard rate. A building which is sold freehold after that period will be VAT exempt. A building of this type may well contain residential or similar living accommodation. If it is a new building, and it is being sold freehold, the value will need to be apportioned as the living or residential area will always be exempt of VAT. A public house or restaurant which is the subject of a lease will be exempt from VAT whether it is a 'new' or 'old' building, and whether it contains living accommodation or not.

If a building is sold as part of the transfer of a business as a going concern then, subject to certain conditions, VAT must not be charged even if the building is 'new'.

9.10.2 The option to tax

As stated above, with the exception of a new freehold commercial building, the grant of any interest in any existing commercial building, whether freehold or leasehold, is VAT exempt. However, there is a method whereby such interests can be charged to VAT, known as the 'election to waive exemption', or more commonly the 'option to tax'. The reason a business would choose this option is to recover VAT that would otherwise be blocked because it related to an exempt supply. The election has to be made by the landlord or leaseholder of the property, who must notify the local VAT office in writing within 30 days of exercising the election. If the election is not notified, it is not valid. Once an election has been exercised, all the interests in that property will be subject to VAT. An election affects the whole of the building, not just part of it or individual rooms within it, although living accommodation occupied by the employer or employees always remains VAT exempt.

Therefore, if a pub had rooms above which it let for meetings or a restaurant had a specially constructed conference annex, both of which would normally generate exempt income, and the option to tax had been exercised, all income arising from those lets would be subject to VAT and all input VAT would be recoverable. The option, once exercised, is irrevocable for 20 years (except for a three-month cooling off period), and so should be taken only after careful consideration.

9.11 Business splitting

Not uncommon in the pub and catering industry is the splitting of a business activity into two or more parts, known as disaggregation. For example, a husband may run a pub while the wife runs the catering and/or a bed and breakfast activity. If any artificial separation of a business results in an avoidance of VAT, Customs have the power to issue a direction that the specified persons (i.e., the people running the businesses) should be treated as one single taxable person for VAT registration purposes. This direction is only effective from a current date. It is not retrospective.

In recent years Customs have indicated that such schemes fall into the area of avoidance. Publicans and restaurateurs are therefore advised to consult their professional advisers before any formal action is taken.

9.12 The VAT inspection

Unlike the Inland Revenue, the standard control procedure by which Customs check that VAT is being accurately accounted for is to physically visit the premises of taxpayers. Larger taxpayers obviously have more VAT visits than small taxpayers, but everybody can expect a visit at some time. The visit should always be by pre-arrangement and the time should be convenient to the business. If for some reason it is not, because it is a particularly busy period or the relevant staff are on holiday, then it is both appropriate and prudent to rearrange the visit for a later date. The visiting officer will always carry an identity card and it is not unreasonable to ask him to produce it at the beginning of the visit.

9.12.1 Preparation for the visit

The date and time of the visit should be arranged so that the proprietor is able to spend time with and give attention to the visiting VAT inspector. It is better for the meeting to take place away from the actual work area, i.e., not in the restaurant or near customers, though this may not always be possible. Books and records should be up-to-date and made available on the day of the visit, and whoever prepares the records should be present. It is helpful if any problems or areas of difficulty relating to VAT are addressed at the beginning of the visit, rather than left for the officer to identify at some later stage.

9.12.2 Make-up of the visit

While no two VAT visits will be the same, and it is impossible to predict exactly what will take place on a VAT visit, most follow a general format as follows:

(a) an initial interview with the proprietor to establish the basic facts about the business and details about its business activities;
(b) a variety of general credibility checks which may include:
  (i) comparisons with similar trades;
  (ii) a lifestyle examination;
  (iii) an examination of VAT return figures; and
  (iv) an inspection of premises;
(c) a check of records and documentation, including:
  (i) cash books, sales records and till rolls;
  (ii) purchase invoices;
  (iii) stocktaking sheets;
  (iv) price lists;
  (v) wastage records; and
  (vi) bank records;
(d) a check for credibility.

This is likely to occur if the visiting inspector is not satisfied with the VAT performance of the business and would include:

- an average weighted mark-up;
- a food to drinks ratio;
- a bank reconciliation; or
- an accounts reconciliation.

9.12.3 Areas of common error

A visiting VAT inspector may not be satisfied with the declaration of VAT for many reasons. Some common areas of error include the following:

(a) excluding gaming machine, video and vending machine takings;
(b) excluding income from pay phones;
(c) omitting to account for VAT on free drinks and own consumption;
(d) failing to include income from special functions or one-off events;
(e) failing to add back cash payments made from the till into the gross takings;
(f) failing to account for VAT on sale of assets;
(g) omitting to account for VAT under the fuel scale charge regulations;
(h) accounting errors, such as ignoring credit notes or retrospective discounts;
(i) claiming VAT on purchase of a motor car;
(j) claiming VAT of the full value of a leased car after 1 August 1995 ('N' registered cars and after); and
(k) failing to account for VAT on cheque or credit card payments which have gone directly into the bank and not through the till.

This list is not exhaustive, but gives examples of what a visiting VAT officer will be looking for. Should a VAT officer be unhappy with the tax which is being returned, and he is unable to find any obvious reason for it, it is likely that he will engage in one of the more sophisticated credibility checks which may lead to an assessment for tax. This is dealt with in some detail in the next section.

9.13 VAT assessments

Although a VAT officer may not be able to find anything specific, he may still consider that the tax being reported is below what is expected for the size or type of establishment, or that the margins are lower than he would expect to see, or that the accounting controls are weak. If this is the case, he may carry out credibility exercises such as:

(a) an average weighted mark-up to determine what a given value of goods purchased for resale should yield in VAT terms over a representative period; or

(b) a drinks to meals ratio, which estimates the VAT yield based on drinks purchased and consumed as part of a meal.

If an officer conducts one of these two exercises and concludes that VAT has been significantly underdeclared then, providing he has examined all the facts correctly and taken all relevant matters into consideration, he will be at liberty to issue an assessment under what is known as 'best judgement'. If this should happen, the onus is on the taxpayer to show to the VAT office, or ultimately to the VAT Tribunal, that the assessment has not been issued in 'best judgement' or is in some other way materially incorrect or wrong. This can often be a very difficult thing to do and it is much wiser to try and prevent this situation arising by ensuring that an officer is satisfied with the records he has seen.

9.13.1 Average weighted mark-up exercises

A VAT officer who is unhappy with the tax declarations of a pub, or even a restaurant with a significant bar income, may undertake an average weighted mark-up exercise.

The object of this exercise is to calculate notional gross takings by establishing a 'weighted mark-up' in a given period. Applying that mark-up to the cost of goods sold after making an allowance for wastage and goods sold below expected retail price, in theory leaves the expected gross takings for the period. The VAT can then be extracted from the notional gross takings and compared to the actual VAT declared, and if that is significantly lower, then the VAT officer will seek explanations for the discrepancy. If he considers the explanation unsatisfactory, then he will issue an assessment 'in best judgement' based on this discrepancy.

Example of a mark-up exercise

In a three-month period coinciding with a VAT return quarter, a publican has the following trading position in respect of his stock:

	£
Opening stock	7,485
Purchases	56,722
Closing stock	(6,890)
Cost of goods sold	57,317

Having obtained a gross cost of goods sold in the period, it has to be reduced for wastage and similar allowances and for any goods which have been given away or consumed at less than the retail price. For example:

	£	£
Wastage:		
Pipe cleaning	340	
Drip trays	400	
Drawing off	200	
Breakages	70	
		1,010
Drinks not sold:		
Free drinks to staff	900	
Own use	900	
		1,800
Total allowances against cost of goods sold		(2,810)

The net cost of goods sold are as follows:

Cost of goods sold	57,317
Allowances	(2,810)
Net cost of goods sold	54,507

Customs will apply their mark-up percentage to this figure having estimated the average weighted mark-up percentage from a review of the cost and selling prices. An example of a mark-up exercise is shown in Appendix 10.

Example

In this example, the average weighted mark-up is 113.79 per cent (see Appendix 10) which is then applied to the net purchases to arrive at an expected net takings figure as follows:

			£
Net cost of goods sold			54,507
× Mark-up (113.79%)			62,023
Add together for expected sales			116,530
Less takings declared (VAT exclusive)			(110,763)
Net discrepancy			5,767
For, say, 12 quarters	× 12	=	69,204
VAT thereon	× 17.5%	=	12,110

In the event that Customs are not satisfied that there is a suitable explanation for the discrepancy, they will issue an assessment for tax based on this principle. In this example the tax has been extrapolated for three years (12 quarters) which is the maximum period Customs can assess unless fraud is alleged.

As previously discussed, the onus for challenging such an assessment rests with the taxpayer who must show that the assessment has not been raised in best judgement. Not only must it be arithmetically correct, but the officer must have taken into account all the factors which will affect the projected sales figure. Some of the areas regularly overlooked are:

- wastage;
  - pipe cleaning;
  - drawing off;
  - drip trays/fobbing;
  - ullage;
  - cask tops/bottoms;
  - breakages;
  - out of date stock;
  - serving wrong drinks;
- operational factors;
  - price changes, both purchases and sales;
  - serving of over-measures;
  - promotional activities;
  - pilferage of stock;
  - staff drinks;
  - drinks for draymen;
  - off-sales;
  - changes in circumstances;
  - beers/wine/liqueurs used in food preparation;
  - till errors/non-drink items passing through till;
  - seasonality and product mix changes;
  - number of bars operated.

If, after assessing all these factors, there is still a discrepancy, VAT will be due in line with the assessment.

9.13.2 Drinks to meals ratio

The mark-up exercise is a proven tool in testing credibility where goods only are involved. Where, however, goods (drinks) are sold as part of the provisions of services (catering) then an alternative approach is required. Customs regularly check the credibility of restaurants by a method known as the 'drinks to meals' ratio. The principle of this approach is to establish the drinks element of restaurant sales as a fixed percentage of the total sales. The objective is the same as that for the average weighted mark-up test which is to establish gross takings based on a logical method over a representative period.

Basis

Customs will examine and analyse a full set of invoices over a given period. Obviously, the longer the period, the more accurate the findings; a representative period of one month is likely to be more accurate than one week.

The results of an analysis might be as shown in the following example.

> ***Example***
>
> Period analysed: month of June:

		£
Total number of bills		415
Total value of bills		20,780
Drink element of bills		4,467
Drinks to meals ratio	$\frac{4{,}467}{20{,}780}$	= 21.5%

As in the previous exercise it is also necessary to work out an average weighted mark-up on the cost of drinks purchased for resale. The principles established in the earlier exercise are the same; the mark-up (MU) is applied to a cost of drinks sold value (CODS) in a given period.

The following formula can then be applied over a representative period as follows:

$$\frac{(\text{CODS} + \text{MU}) \times 100}{\text{Drinks to meals ratio}} = \text{Net value of expected total sales}$$

An example of how this may be applied in a given period can be shown as follows.

> ***Example***

Takings from annual accounts excluding VAT	£256,000
CODS in the period (excl. VAT)	£38,870
Drinks mark-up (established by a mark-up exercise)	124.6%
Drink to meals ratio	21.5%

Substituting these figures into the formula you arrive at the following equation:

			£
Net value of expected total sales	$\frac{38{,}870 + (1.246 \times 38{,}870)}{0.215}$	=	406,055
Less declared takings			(256,000)
Discrepancy for VAT assessment			150,055
VAT assessment		× 17.5%	26,260

In the absence of a satisfactory explanation Customs may allege the figure represents underdeclared or suppressed takings and charge VAT on top of that sum (we are dealing at this stage with VAT exclusive amounts).

Mitigating factors

As in the mark-up exercise there are various factors which the restaurateur must ensure Customs are aware of before they embark on the drinks to meals ratio exercise. These are:

(a) ensure the mark-up exercise has been accurately carried out;
(b) ensure the drinks to meals period is representative, e.g., it was not over a period when free wine was being given, or drinks were on promotion;
(c) ensure the drinks to meals ratio is correct;
(d) ensure any separate bar sales are advised; and
(e) ensure any bar losses are taken into account.

9.13.3 Summary

The above are two examples of exercises which Customs regularly conduct to establish a credibility assessment of a pub or restaurant. These two approaches are not the only methods and Customs in severe cases will 'plant' officers in the restaurant to actually buy meals so that they can check later whether the receipts have gone through the books and records. This is known as an invigilation and may well lead to a larger credibility exercise should an attempt to trace the original receipt prove fruitless at an early stage.

If a taxpayer finds himself the subject of one of these exercises it is important that he takes it seriously as it is a clear indication that Customs believe some VAT is not being accounted for. The publican or restaurateur should therefore ensure at an early stage he makes available all relevant information to the VAT officer; in the long run it will benefit his case and reduce any VAT assessment which may arise.

What does a publican or restaurateur need to do? As explained, once an officer has raised an assessment based on his best judgement the onus is on the business to disprove his calculations.

Whilst, ultimately, the business may be able to demonstrate its 'innocence' and overturn the officer's assessment this will invariably involve the business in additional cost either in terms of time 'wasted' or the involvement of external advisers.

It is obviously in the business's best interests to avoid such problems in the first instance and this can be achieved by a combination of the following:

(a) *Ensuring good cash control.* Retain all till rolls, use electronic point of sale equipment where possible, keep accurate records of cash purchases made from the till. Record mis-rings, errors, etc. as they occur with explanations where necessary.

(b) *Stock control.* Regular stocktaking (monthly) which provides notional takings with a comparison to actual takings. Any adverse variances should be investigated at an early stage.

(c) *Miscellaneous.* Keep copies of previous price lists, menus and evidence of promotional events, e.g., happy hours.

Demonstrating to Customs that a business is well-run and controlled can avert potential problems. Time spent on putting the correct procedures in place early on could save both time and money in the future.

Chapter 10 – Audit

10.1 Introduction

It will be appreciated that no two audits are the same, even those of companies of similar size which are involved in the same field of business and with comparable operating procedures. This is undoubtedly true of the audits of pubs and restaurants. The whole approach to the audit in these instances depends on many factors, all of which will have an impact on the detailed audit procedures which are used.

The purpose of this chapter, however, is to outline the overall approach to the audit of a typical pub or restaurant and to consider certain techniques which may be applied in a variety of circumstances. The subject is covered under the following headings:

- audit objectives;
- planning;
- working papers;
- quality control;
- internal controls and audit risk;
- audit procedures;
- reporting.

It is assumed that the reader has a working knowledge and understanding of current Statements of Auditing Standards (SASs) issued by the Auditing Practices Board. A standard audit work programme is included in Appendix 11. This is not meant to be a prescriptive list of tests to be followed in every situation but rather an illustrative checklist of some of the more important audit procedures which are frequently applied. In all cases it is crucial that audit work on a particular assignment is specifically designed to meet individual circumstances and objectives.

10.2 Audit objectives

The overriding objective of an audit under the Companies Act 1985 is to enable the auditor to give an opinion on the financial statements of the client company taken as a whole and thereby to provide reasonable assurance that the financial statements give a true and fair view of the company's results and state of affairs, and have been properly prepared in accordance with relevant accounting and other statutory requirements.

On occasions, management may request auditors to perform certain non-statutory duties such as internal audit and review, stocktaking and providing other forms of assurance to management.

In many cases clients regard these value-added services as an essential part of the overall provision of an all-round service. However, before deciding to accept these additional responsibilities, the auditor must carefully consider any conflicts of interest. No other services may be provided to any client which in any way compromise, or could be seen to compromise, the auditor's independence.

On acceptance of a new audit client, auditors should agree the precise terms of their engagement with the client in writing in order to confirm their acceptance of the appointment, to set out the relative responsibilities of the directors and the auditors, and to agree the scope of the engagement and the form of any reports which may be required. Thereafter, the auditors should constantly keep the engagement terms under review and issue revised engagement letters as appropriate.

Contrary to popular belief, it is not the responsibility of the auditor to detect fraud. It is the responsibility of the directors of the company to take such steps as are reasonably open to them to prevent and detect fraud. The fact that an audit is carried out may, however, act as a deterrent but, in general, auditors carry out their statutory duties by planning and designing their audit procedures so as to have a reasonable expectation of detecting material misstatements in the financial statements arising from fraud or error.

Fraud may take many forms including (SAS 110):

- falsification or alteration of accounting records or other documents;
- misappropriation of assets or theft;
- suppression or omission of the effects of transactions from records or documents;
- recording of transactions without substance;
- intentional misapplication of accounting policies; or
- wilful misrepresentation of transactions or of the entity's state of affairs.

The responsibility of directors to prevent and detect fraud is primarily discharged by implementing appropriate systems of internal control and constantly reviewing the effectiveness of these systems.

In the particular case of pubs and restaurants, a large number of part-time or casual workers may be involved many of whom have access to large amounts of cash and other assets of the business such as wines and spirits, which are prone to theft. The auditor should be alert to the extent of audit risk arising from fraud and devise the audit strategy accordingly. It has often been said that it is impossible to waste time planning an audit.

Whilst this might be too sweeping a generalisation, especially in the days of cost-conscious clients, there is undoubtedly some substance to this statement.

10.3 Planning

The distinct elements of the planning process are set out below. Each in its own way is essential in devising an appropriate audit strategy so that the work can be carried out in the most efficient and cost-effective manner.

Figure 10.1

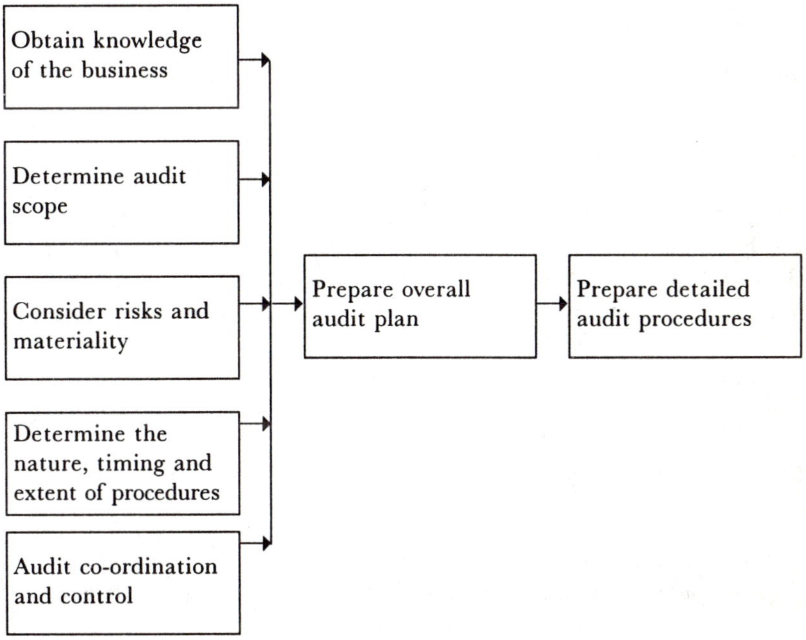

The objectives in planning an audit are firstly to establish an overall audit plan and, secondly, to use this plan to devise the detailed audit procedures which are required to achieve the audit objectives. It is usual to document the overall audit plan as a written audit planning memorandum which acts as a set of instructions to the audit team and serves as a means to control and record the execution of the audit work. The overall audit plan also sets out those important considerations which have been taken into account in arriving at the audit strategy. The task of implementing the overall audit plan is achieved by the detailed audit programme. Again, this should be a formal written statement which itemises the individual audit tests and procedures to be performed during the course of the audit process. It should also cover logistical matters like timing, audit budgets and staff planning.

The level of detail contained within the overall audit plan and the audit programme will of course vary from client to client. There are no hard and fast rules to be observed, other than the auditor satisfying himself that the audit plan and the audit programme are appropriate to the circumstances, bearing in mind such factors as the complexity of the audit, the degree of audit risk, the experience of the audit team and their familiarity with the client.

It is essential to consider certain key matters before drawing up and finalising the overall audit plan. These matters are as follows.

10.3.1 Obtain knowledge of the business

It is inconceivable that an efficient and effective audit can be carried out without at least a basic knowledge of the business. It is used by the auditors in assessing audit risks, determining the scope and nature of the audit procedures and in assessing the financial statements for credibility. As well as helping to determine and direct the audit work, a sound understanding of the business and the environment in which it operates can assist the auditor in making constructive recommendations to management for improvements in business practices.

SAS 210 includes a comprehensive list of factors to consider when planning the audit of any business. A sample of sources relevant to pubs and restaurants include:

(a) the auditor's prior experience of the client and the industry generally;
(b) visits to different pubs and restaurants operated by the client;
(c) discussions with financial and non-financial personnel (for example, pub managers, chefs and waiters);
(d) industry publications and trade journals such as *The Publican Newspaper* and *The Licensee*;
(e) internally produced documents (for example, minutes of meetings, promotional literature, budgets, management accounts, operating and policy manuals).

Some time should be devoted, especially in the first year of an audit assignment, to visiting various operating locations and taking advantage of the facilities offered. As well as providing background information it also gives the auditor first-hand experience of the environment in which the business operates and an insight into the culture of the client and its customers.

It is important to recognise that pubs and restaurants, like all businesses, are influenced to a large extent by external factors. A pub with a large, well-kept garden would be expected to dramatically increase its wet sales during a very hot summer. The same conditions would generally tend to reduce demand for food sales in the evening. A restaurant situated near to a university and catering for the student market will be required to provide menus to suit the limited budgets of student customers. Such an establishment will also suffer from a downturn in trade during the vacational months around Christmas, Easter and in the summer. In reviewing the trading performance of this kind of restaurant, the auditor should be put on alert if other trends occur, but he or she will only be aware of what to expect if the knowledge of the business has been gained in the first instance.

10.3.2 Determine audit scope

The overall audit scope will be agreed in the engagement letter and will principally require the auditor to express a true and fair opinion on the financial statements. The way this objective is to be achieved will depend upon the individual circumstances of the client. For a business operating a chain of pubs or restaurants, the results and net assets of certain locations may be totally immaterial to the business as a whole. In such cases sufficient audit evidence may be obtained by simply carrying out desk-top reviews of the results of the smaller sites, either individually or in aggregate, and concentrating in-depth audit testing on the more substantial premises within the chain.

10.3.3 Consider risks and materiality

Once the auditor has obtained a sufficient knowledge of the business he or she will be in a position to identify areas of audit risk and set materiality levels.

Audit risk areas within the pub and restaurant trade invariably revolve around the completeness of income, especially cash and equivalent sales (for example, cheques, credit cards and luncheon vouchers), and the safeguarding of drink supplies. The existence of large numbers of casual employees may also give rise to potential problems in accounting for payroll costs and in the proper settlement of employment taxes. In assessing the risk the auditor will draw upon all of the experience gained in similar businesses and in prior years. A pub or restaurant with fluctuations in trading margins which cannot readily be understood or explained should be a cause for concern and may indicate that not all transactions are being properly recorded, either through error or wilful misappropriation of sales revenue.

10.3.4 Determine the nature, timing and extent of procedures

At this stage of the planning process, the auditor should be in a position to determine the extent to which reliance is to be placed on tests of control as opposed to substantive audit procedures, including for example the extent of reliance on the work of the internal audit function.

An internal audit department is only likely to exist in larger pub and restaurant businesses and, even if one does exist, it is likely to concentrate on the detailed application of operational procedures, most of which will have no direct relevance to the work of the external auditors. As a result, the extent of reliance on the work of the internal audit department is probably restricted in most instances. However, it may be the case that some benefit can be obtained from a review of summaries of the internal audit department's work to highlight areas of concern to which the external auditor should pay particular attention. Other important considerations to be addressed include the extent to which computer-assisted audit techniques are to be employed on the audit. There are various packages available and as a general rule their usefulness is dependent upon the size and complexity of the entity being audited.

Typically, computer-assisted audit techniques can be used to:

- perform margin analysis;
- make comparisons of actual to budgets and prior years;
- test for duplicate payments;
- reperform ageing of debtors analyses.

It is also at this stage in the planning process that consideration should be given to the extent of testing that should be done before or at the year end. Depending on the audit timetable, it may be appropriate to arrange circularisations of creditors at a point before the year end to enable the responses to be received and collated in time for the audit completion. Debtors are unlikely to be material.

Stocktake attendances by the auditor should also be considered at an early stage in planning. By their nature pubs and restaurants do not normally have material levels of stocks at any one point in time. Independent stocktakers are usually employed to count and value wet and dry stocks and the auditor can usually rely upon the results of these examinations. More detailed audit procedures may be required if the entity has a history of large stock shortages or surpluses.

Most pubs and restaurants are subjected to regular stock counts throughout the year. Management will regard these as a control procedure to verify margins being reported.

10.3.5 Audit co-ordination and control

As with all other audit assignments, the auditor of a pub or restaurant must consider matters relating to the overall co-ordination and control of the work. These include:

(a) Involvement of other auditors for subsidiary companies and the need to direct their work and reporting procedures. In extreme circumstances arrangements should be made to review other auditors' working papers. However, a more common approach is to request the subsidiary auditor to complete audit questionnaires which detail the scope and results of the work undertaken.
(b) The operating locations to be visited. Most pubs and restaurants have a centralised accounting function and visits to other sites may not be required during the course of the detailed audit work.
(c) Staff planning and timings.

10.4 Working papers

Working papers are the tangible evidence of the audit process. They record:

(a) the planning and performance of the audit;
(b) the supervision and review of the audit work; and
(c) the audit evidence resulting from the audit work performed which the auditor considers necessary and on which they have relied to support their audit opinion.

Audit working papers may take many forms including computerised data. The nature and extent of working papers is a matter of professional judgement but should be based on the working papers that would be necessary to provide an experienced auditor, with no previous connection with the audit, with an understanding of the work performed and the basis of the decisions taken.

As with all audits those areas that involve difficult questions of principle or judgement may subsequently be questioned by third parties possibly with the benefit of hindsight. It is therefore important that the working papers that deal with the areas record all relevant facts known at the time of the audit and demonstrate the thought process by which any judgement was arrived at.

Working papers should be designed and organised to meet individual circumstances. Although standardised working papers tend to increase audit efficiency, it is never advisable to follow such a standardised approach without regard to the particular requirements of the entity being audited.

In general, working papers should include the following if relevant (SAS 230):

(a) information concerning the legal and organisational structure of the entity;
(b) extracts or copies of important legal documents, agreements and minutes;
(c) information concerning the industry, economic environment and legislative environment within which the entity operates;
(d) evidence of the auditor's understanding of the accounting and internal control systems;
(e) evidence of inherent and control risk assessments and any revisions thereto;
(f) evidence of the auditor's consideration of the work of internal audit and the conclusions thereon;
(g) analysis of transactions and balances;
(h) analysis of significant ratios and trends;
(i) a review of the nature, timing and extent of auditing procedures undertaken and the results of such procedures;
(j) details of procedures regarding subsidiaries whose financial statements are audited by other auditors;
(k) copies of communications with other auditors, experts and other third parties;
(l) copies of correspondence with the entity, reports to directors or management and notes of discussions with the entity's directors or management concerning audit matters;
(m) letters of representation from the entity's directors or management;
(n) a summary of the significant aspects of the audit including details of the information available, the amounts involved, management's views, the conclusions reached and how these matters are resolved or treated; and
(o) copies of the approved financial statements and auditor's report.

All working papers should contain details of when they were prepared and by whom, and they should also contain evidence of the review procedures undertaken.

10.5 Quality control

SAS 240 requires that quality control procedures should be applied to each audit which are appropriate to that particular audit and which ensure compliance with auditing standards. All work assigned to audit assistants should be directed, supervised and reviewed in a manner which provides reasonable assurance that such work is performed adequately.

The means by which these objectives are achieved will vary from audit firm to audit firm and from assignment to assignment. As a minimum, quality control will consist of the following:

(a) appropriate direction and delegation of work to assistants who are aware of their responsibilities and the objectives of the work they are asked to perform;
(b) supervision of the work of assistants by more senior audit personnel who monitor the progress of the audit to ensure that assistants understand the audit directions, are competent and that the work is being carried out in accordance with the overall audit plan and the audit programme;
(c) review procedures, whereby the work of each assistant is independently reviewed by a person of appropriate experience. In this way, all significant accounting and auditing issues should be identified and resolved appropriately and all audit objectives achieved.

The following must be reviewed on a timely basis within the framework of the overall audit process:

- the audit plan and the audit programme;
- the assessments of inherent and control risks, including the results of the tests of control and conclusions drawn therefrom;
- the results of substantive testing and the conclusions drawn from these tests;
- the financial statements, audit adjustments and the wording of the proposed audit report.

On larger, more complex audit assignments or those of entities which contain an element of public interest, for example listed companies, it may be appropriate to invite a senior auditor with no direct involvement in the work to give a second opinion by performing an additional review of particularly sensitive audit and accounting issues.

10.6 Audit risk and internal control

SAS 300 requires that auditors should obtain an understanding of the accounting and internal control systems sufficient to plan the audit and develop an effective audit approach, and to use professional judgement to assess the components of audit risk and to design audit procedures to ensure the risk is reduced to an acceptably low level.

Audit risk is the risk that the auditor may give an inappropriate audit opinion on financial statements. It has three components (see Figure 10.2).

Figure 10.2

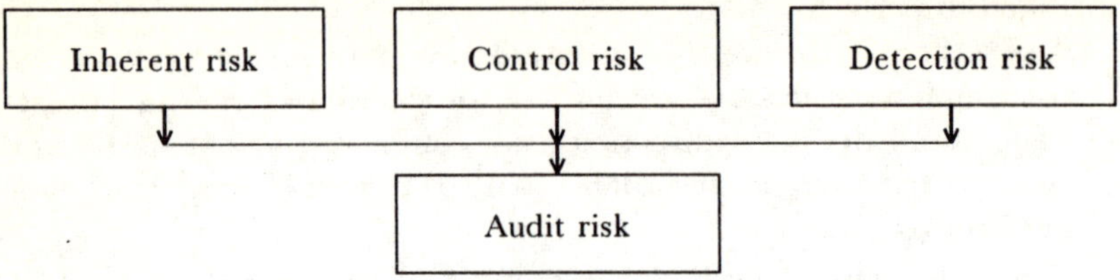

(a) *inherent risk* is the susceptibility of an account balance or class of transaction to material misstatement, irrespective of related internal controls;
(b) *control risk* is the risk that a material misstatement could occur in an account balance or class of transactions which would not be prevented or detected and corrected on a timely basis by accounting and internal controls systems;
(c) *detection risk* is the risk that the auditor's substantive procedures (tests of detail of transactions and balances and analytical procedures) do not detect a material misstatement that exists in an account balance or class of transactions.

Therefore, when planning the audit, the prime objective is to consider the likelihood of error in the light of the level of inherent risk and the system of internal control's ability to minimise control risk. Once this is done, the level of substantive work can be determined which is necessary to gain satisfaction that the overall level of audit risk and, therefore, the risk of error in the financial statements, is sufficiently low.

In assessing inherent risk, professional judgements must be used by the auditor, taking into account prior years' experience and the knowledge of the business already gained through planning. Factors will include:

- the competence and integrity of management;
- external economic factors such as the state of the industry generally;
- complexity of the business's operations;
- related parties;
- judgemental areas and processes;
- the likelihood of fraud or error;
- the effectiveness of accounting systems.

Auditors must obtain an understanding of the entity's accounting systems and control procedures so that they can assess the effectiveness of control procedures and thus the control risk. From this, the relative balance of tests of control and substantive procedures can be determined. The performance of 'walkthrough tests', that is, tracing a small number of transactions through the accounting system and observing the application of internal control procedures, can give a good indication of the overall risk environment and assist in the assessment of both inherent and control risk.

However, the nature and extent of the procedures performed by the auditors to obtain an understanding of the systems will depend upon:

- materiality;
- the organisation's complexity;
- inherent risk considerations;
- the nature of the internal controls which exist.

Within the context of pubs and restaurants, the principal internal controls will usually be concentrated on ensuring the completeness of income, in particular cash takings, supplemented by periodic stock checks to verify that the systems for recording the sales of goods for resale are being properly operated. Margin analyses will also be used to ensure that trends in gross profit margins are moving as expected and are not affected by excessive wastage of wet and dry stocks.

The more effective the entity's accounting and internal control systems are assessed to be, the lower the auditor's assessment of control risk. Where satisfactory evidence from tests of control on the accounting and internal control systems can be obtained, the extent of substantive procedures may be reduced.

Within the smaller pub or restaurant operation segregation of duties, an important element of an effective internal control system, may not be practical. This is usually offset by direct supervisory control by the proprietor or manager using their close personal knowledge of the business and its transactions. In general, this can be a good or a bad thing. Managerial controls in this manner can be very powerful in controlling the business and giving a very high level of reliance on the integrity of the financial statements. However, sufficient audit evidence will be very difficult to obtain without adequate substantive procedures.

Once an assessment of inherent and control risk is complete the auditor can determine the nature, timing and extent of the substantive audit procedures, bearing in mind the assessment of detection risk. It is generally the case that the assessed levels of inherent and control risks can never be sufficiently low that the auditor need not perform any substantive procedures. However, in certain instances these procedures may consist entirely of analytical reviews. More usually, a minimum level of detailed transactional work is required, supplemented by verification of material assets and liabilities.

10.7 Audit procedures

The more usual substantive audit procedures for specific areas of the balance sheet and profit and loss account of a pub or restaurant are highlighted below. More detailed consideration of the accounting policies relevant to pubs and restaurants is contained in Chapter 6. The level of detailed testing in each area will, of course, have been determined by the assumed level of inherent and control risk present.

10.7.1 Tangible fixed assets

The tangible fixed assets of a pub or restaurant will usually fall into the following categories:

- freehold and leasehold buildings;
- plant and machinery;
- fixtures, fittings and furnishings.

Existence of tangible fixed assets can usually be tested by physical verification, whilst ownership is usually a straightforward exercise of reviewing purchase invoices and other documents conferring title.

The valuation of tangible fixed assets may either be at cost less accumulated depreciation or, alternatively, the entity may adopt a policy of carrying assets at valuation. It is normal for pub operators to have their properties professionally valued on a regular basis and reflect these valuations in the financial statements. If this is the case then the auditor needs to verify the independence, objectivity and professional qualifications of the valuer and ensure that the assumptions underlying the valuation are appropriate.

The auditor also needs to confirm whether the valuation is inclusive or exclusive of permanent items of plant and fixtures.

Permanent diminutions in the carrying values of tangible fixed assets should normally be reflected in the financial statements as soon as these diminutions become known. A temporary diminution may not be adjusted if there was no intention to sell the property and the assumptions to support the future upturn in value are reasonable.

If the policy of the entity is to have its properties regularly valued and to incorporate these valuations into the financial statements then the auditor should ensure that properties are selected for valuation on a rational and systematic basis. 'Cherry-picking' of properties to be revalued should be avoided. It would be a cause of concern if, for various reasons, certain properties were never externally valued.

In years between professional valuations, properties may be stated at directors' valuation. The auditor should, in such cases, assess the competence of the valuing directors and the assumptions underlying the valuation. The most sensitive of these will normally be the property's projected earnings over the next few years. The auditor must be satisfied that these projections are both reasonable and achievable.

The ASB issued a Discussion Paper entitled *Measurement of Tangible Fixed Assets* in October 1996 which considers a number of issues regarding the valuation and depreciation of fixed assets. The implications for the pub and restaurant trade are considered in detail in Chapter 6.

In the case of renovations and refurbishments, the auditor should satisfy himself that all expenditure in the nature of repairs are expensed to profit rather than capitalised. Conversely, the repairs and renewals accounts in the profit and loss accounts should be scrutinised for items of a capital nature. In cases of major refurbishments, physical inspection of the project is usually of some help in determining the most appropriate accounting treatment.

Refurbishment of properties also usually gives rise to complex taxation considerations. These are discussed in detail in Chapter 7.

Certain entities follow a policy of non-depreciation of operating properties on the grounds that they are maintained to a standard which ensures that the residual value of the properties are at least equal to their carrying value. The appropriateness of this treatment is currently being debated within the accountancy profession, but it is likely that such an approach will not be allowed at some time in the future (see Chapter 6). In the meantime, care should be taken to ensure that the programmes of maintenance expenditure are indeed capable of ensuring no significant decrease in property values. The verification of depreciation charges in general should present no undue audit difficulties.

The pub and restaurant business is capital-intensive. One means of raising funds to acquire properties is to enter into sale and leaseback transactions and other forms of finance-raising schemes with properties. Such transactions will generally fall to be considered in the light of the requirements of Financial Reporting Standard 5. This is an area which is fraught with difficulties and particular care should be taken to ensure that all relevant facts pertinent to the individual case in hand are addressed.

10.7.2 Stock

The principal stocks held by a pub or restaurant will be cutlery, crockery, glasses, food and beverages. However, even in the largest establishments it may not have a significant value and reliance may be placed on independent stocktakers to count and value wet and dry stocks. In other circumstances the auditor will need to consider whether or not to attend the year-end stocktake, but cases where attendance is deemed appropriate are rare.

For entities with relatively immaterial stock levels, a simple analytical review comparing current and previous year stockholding should be adequate in most cases. The stock turnover rates could also be calculated for larger value stock items to give some indication of net realisable value.

In restaurants operating at the top end of the range, wine stocks could be significant. In these cases stocktake attendance may be appropriate. The physical condition of the wine is also a factor. The use of an expert to assess its condition may be necessary in limited cases.

Most pubs will have agreements with brewers that supplies of beers and spirits will be subject to retrospective volume discounts. In such cases the auditor will need to ensure that wet stocks are valued at the discounted cost price and, conversely, that no advance recognition of discounts receivable is evident in the financial statements.

10.7.3 Base stock

All pubs and restaurants will have a need for low value items of fixed assets which are regularly replaced. This will include cutlery, crockery, glasses, etc. It is common in the trade for a base stock of such items to be held. The value of the base stock will usually be the cost of purchasing those items when the pub or restaurant was first opened.

The administration involved in keeping a fixed asset register of these items and depreciating them would be out of proportion to their worth, therefore they are included in stock at a fixed amount known as a base stock and any new purchases are written off as incurred. Schedule 4 to the Companies Act 1985 allows this treatment, provided the nature of the items is such that they are constantly replaced and the overall value of such stock is not material to the company's balance sheet and their quantity, value and composition are not subject to material variation.

The auditor will need to satisfy himself that the amounts capitalised are reasonable and that the items included as base stock meet the Companies Act criteria referred to above.

10.7.4 Trade debtors

A pub or restaurant is unlikely to have a material level of trade debtors given the nature of the business, with most sales being settled in cash immediately. Such trade debtors as there are will normally consist of corporate debtors and credit card companies. Payments made by credit or charge cards are guaranteed by the credit card company provided the card is validated at the point of sale, and therefore all risk of bad debt is borne by them. In such cases it is enough to ensure that after-date cash receipts clear the credit card debtor in a timely fashion. Similarly, corporate debtors should also be matched to after-date receipts.

10.7.5 Prepayments and other debtors

These are likely to include:

- rent and rates;
- insurances and insurance claims;
- maintenance contracts;
- staff floats;
- sundry debtors.

All of the above tend to be small and relatively constant and can normally be satisfactorily tested using analytical techniques such as comparing current and prior periods. Exceptional debtors may require vouching to supporting documentation and the checking of after-date receipts. In extreme circumstances direct confirmation may be appropriate.

Increasingly, pubs and restaurants treat pre-opening revenue expenditure, perhaps incurred during a period of closure for refurbishment, as a prepayment. These costs are carried forward in the balance sheet and expensed to profit over a period of time once the establishment is opened. There is no set write-off period, although the matching concept is paramount, and no pre-opening costs should be carried forward for unjustifiably long periods.

10.7.6 Cash

The audit testing of cash balances at the year end is straightforward. It should include a review of the client's bank reconciliations, ensuring that the cash book and bank statement balances agree with the reconciliation details.

Unpresented cheques and lodgements recorded in the cash book should be followed through to post-year-end bank statements to ensure they clear promptly after the year end. The cash book should also be reviewed for window dressing or other unusual transactions.

From a security point of view pubs and restaurants should not be encouraged to keep large amounts of unbanked cash receipts. Otherwise the temptation to enter into unauthorised casual purchase arrangements is exacerbated and the entity also runs the risk of greater loss through theft.

10.7.7 Creditors

The typical creditors of a pub or restaurant will comprise all or some of the following:

- suppliers of food and beverages;
- credit card commissions;
- service charges;
- rents and rates;
- repairs;
- retentions on capital projects;
- professional fees;
- PAYE;
- VAT;
- loans and overdrafts.

Most of the above are common to all businesses and the usual audit procedures may be applied. These will include reconciliations of supplier balances to statements, checking after-date payments and cut-off and analytical comparisons to previous years. The extent of these tests will depend on the auditor's assessment of audit risk.

A feature of the pub and restaurant trade is the payment of performance-related bonuses to staff. The auditor should be aware of all such bonus schemes and ensure that appropriate accruals have been made based on the relevant performance criteria. Accruals for bonus payments of staff should also include the associated PAYE and NI liabilities.

Retentions for capital building works may be significant. These should be checked to the underlying agreements and records of progress payments already made by the entity up to the end of the financial year.

VAT and PAYE creditors would normally be verified by reference to VAT returns and PAYE paying in records and payroll data. The payroll will be subject to detailed audit scrutiny as part of the audit of income and expenditure.

Rental creditors may also be material in the case of enterprises with a large number of leasehold properties. Rent-free periods should be ignored in calculating year-end liabilities, and rather, the total amount payable up to the next rent review date should be spread so that each accounting period bears an appropriate charge for property rental costs.

10.7.8 Taxation

The audit of corporation tax liabilities will involve the review of the entity's tax computation, carrying out a tax reconciliation and checking the accounting for ACT and group relief. No special considerations are necessary for pubs and restaurants.

However, given the likelihood of significant capital expenditure, deferred tax liabilities arising from the excess of capital allowances over depreciation charges may be a material item in the balance sheet. If a partial provision approach is adopted then the auditor needs to understand the entity's capital expenditure projections and concur with the reasonableness of these projections as the basis for not making a full provision.

10.7.9 Profit and loss account

By their nature the profit and loss accounts of pubs and restaurants consist of the classification and aggregation of a large number of transactions each of which, in isolation, is small but relatively uniform. In well-controlled systems with acceptable levels of audit risk the most effective audit approach is to apply analytical review techniques to gain the required audit assurances on income and expenditure.

In the simplest case, a brief overall review of revenue and costs including comparisons to budgets and prior years will give the auditor sufficient evidence to conclude that they are fairly stated. In cases where the control environment is not thought to be sufficiently strong the auditor will have to adopt a more rigorous analysis, perhaps supplemented by substantive tests of detail.

An important source of comparative information with which to carry out detailed analytical reviews are industry statistics which are readily available from a number of sources. These have the great advantage of being independently produced. However, it is important to bear in mind the market in which the pub or restaurant under review operates. For example, gross profit margins achievable by a well-renowned up-market restaurant will inevitably be higher than the average of the industry as a whole.

In the majority of cases the client may prepare many useful analytical reviews on current trading as part of his regular management accounting information. The information contained in the management accounts has not been produced independently, so before placing any reliance on this the auditor should confirm that the information is both properly prepared and consistent with information from other sources which is available.

Within a restaurant business statistics usually exist which give details of the number of covers in any particular period. A simple calculation of the number of covers multiplied by an appropriate average spend per cover derived from independent sources should give a good approximation to actual revenue in that period. If the difference between actual and this projected revenue is significant then the auditor will need to obtain explanations for the discrepancies. One reason may be a series of promotional events (for example, two meals for the price of one). In relying upon such explanations the auditor must ensure they are reasonable and open to independent corroboration.

In a pub operation it is more difficult to adopt analytical techniques to predict revenues, principally because it is difficult to maintain reliable records to measure pub 'occupancy' levels. In such cases a more effective technique may be to compare revenues with prior years and forecasts. In addition, the revenue-earning pattern of a pub follows a distinct trend over a year with a pronounced peak at Christmas and the New Year and increased activity during the summer months.

Figure 10.3

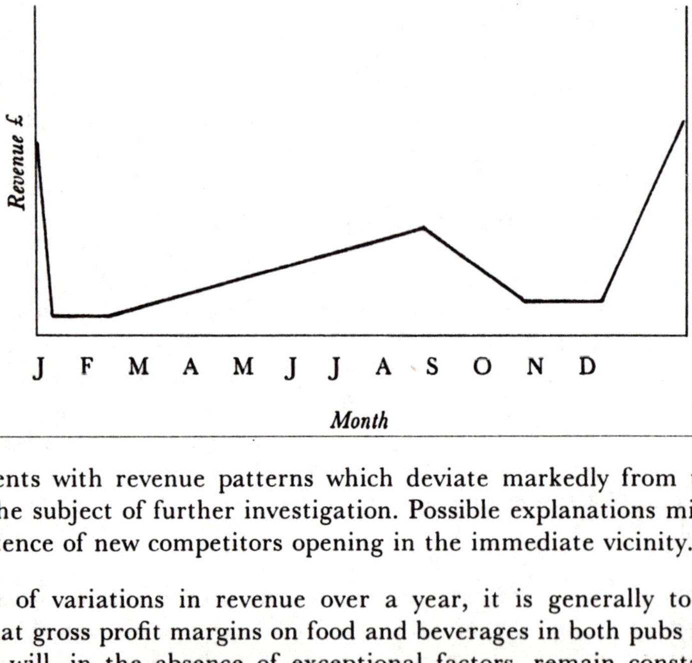

Establishments with revenue patterns which deviate markedly from this should be the subject of further investigation. Possible explanations might be the existence of new competitors opening in the immediate vicinity.

Irrespective of variations in revenue over a year, it is generally to be expected that gross profit margins on food and beverages in both pubs and restaurants will, in the absence of exceptional factors, remain constant. This can be investigated by mapping out the respective food and beverage revenues and direct expenditures over the course of a year and focusing on significant fluctuations. Unusual variations may indicate errors or problems with pilferage or wastage.

An increasingly important element of a pub's revenue is derived from gaming machines. The relaxation of restrictions on maximum prizes available have made playing these machines more attractive to customers.

In general, gaming machines are owned and operated by third parties with the pub receiving a site rent and perhaps a proportion of takings. A proof in total approach can be adopted for auditing site rent income, based on the number of machines installed and rental rates. It is also to be expected that the proportion of gaming takings will be in direct proportion to wet sales.

The expenditure of pubs and restaurants can be categorised as follows:

- food and beverages;
- salaries and wages;
- repairs and maintenance;
- entertainment;
- light and heat;
- rent and rates;
- other services.

The relationship between the cost of food and beverages and revenues has been discussed above. Next to this the largest expense heading is likely to be salaries and wages.

The pub and restaurant business is synonymous with a high level of staff turnover and the casual employee. Whilst a proportion of the staff will be long-term salaried employees, bar staff, waiters and kitchen staff tend to be casual or part-time workers, many of whom may be foreigners with work permit difficulties.

The auditor must obtain satisfaction that the payroll system in operation is adequate to record starters and leavers accurately. It is vital that all new staff are correctly entered on the payroll and that leavers are not paid for work not done. All additions to, and deductions from, the payroll should normally be administered by the bar or restaurant manager.

A high proportion of the total wages bill will be paid in cash. Again, the bar or restaurant manager should ensure that the correct amounts are paid to the right person. This should involve a witnessed payout with proof of identity and a timecard authorised as approved by a responsible official.

The use of casual workers may lead to PAYE problems. The auditor should establish that all casual workers are on the payroll and PAYE is being correctly operated.

The other principal controls which should be in place within the payroll system include:

- payroll summary reconciliations to manual ledger records;

- payment authorisation procedures and independent review;
- management review of budgeted and actual payroll costs.

Other expenditure headings can be audited by comparison to prior years and budgets. This will be sufficient for most non-direct expenses like rents and rates, insurance, light and heat, etc. Entertainment costs relate to the hire of bands, discotheques and other acts who may ask for cash payments which will not be accompanied by invoices or receipts. In such cases the auditor should ensure that these costs are accurately stated by reference to a booking schedule or similar record maintained by the entity.

10.8 Reporting

Reporting the results of the audit may take various formats. Naturally, there is the formal audit opinion given with the financial statements and addressed to shareholders. However, in addition to this there are various means of communicating audit findings to management.

A summary audit memorandum serves two distinct purposes. First, it is useful as an overall summary of the important issues arising from the audit and secondly it forms the basis of the discussions to be held with senior management at the audit clearance meeting. As a minimum, the summary audit memorandum should contain:

- a summary of the trading results and the balance sheet position at the year end;
- commentary on significant transactions;
- major judgemental areas;
- internal control weaknesses;
- outstanding audit issues yet to be resolved;
- disputed areas.

It is perfectly acceptable to include unresolved issues in the audit memorandum. The subsequent clearance of these items following discussions with management should be fully documented.

10.9 Management letter

The management letter provides a formal written document of all important matters that have arisen during the course of the audit work. As well as reporting weaknesses in accounting systems and controls, together with practical recommendations for overcoming these, the management letter should also attempt to offer constructive advice on business issues. It should also serve as a commentary on the presentation of the entity's financial statements and, if appropriate, the potential impact of forthcoming changes in accounting standards on future financial statements. Comments may also be usefully made about the auditor's perception of the business as an outsider, for example the impression given by staff at individual pubs and restaurants and the standard of premises visited.

For larger clients with a separate Audit Committee, a 'high level' version of the management letter might be prepared and presented to the Committee, for the purpose of drawing to the Committee members' attention those issues of critical importance which should be fully considered prior to formal approval of the financial statements by the board. These are likely to be matters of accounts presentation, areas subject to a high degree of judgement by executive directors and the impact of significant transactions on the financial statements. Such a letter would not normally deal with more routine operational issues which can be restricted to the more usual management letter.

Whatever comments are made, the auditor should always endeavour to be both constructive and commercial in the approach adopted in the management letter. It provides a unique opportunity to demonstrate the auditor's knowledge of the business in a way which is of positive benefit to the client.

Chapter 11 – Strategic planning

11.1 Introduction

A significant proportion of pubs and restaurants in the UK are privately owned. These are essentially small to medium-sized businesses which are run by the people who own them. This may be a proprietor, family business or a small group of individuals joining together to run a business. As such, they have all the characteristics of family and owner-managed businesses.

This chapter considers the specific needs of such businesses with regard to strategic planning. Amar Bhide writing in the Harvard Business Review[1] says that an entrepreneur's personal and business goals are inextricably linked. Whereas the manager of a public company has a fiduciary responsibility to maximise value for shareholders, entrepreneurs build their businesses to fulfil personal goals and, if necessary, seek investors with similar goals. He goes on to say that before they can set goals for a business, entrepreneurs must be explicit about their personal goals and they must periodically ask themselves if those goals have changed. His diagram, reproduced below in Figure 11.1, illustrates the thought process a business owner needs to go through.

Figure 11.1 *An entrepreneur's guide to the big issues*

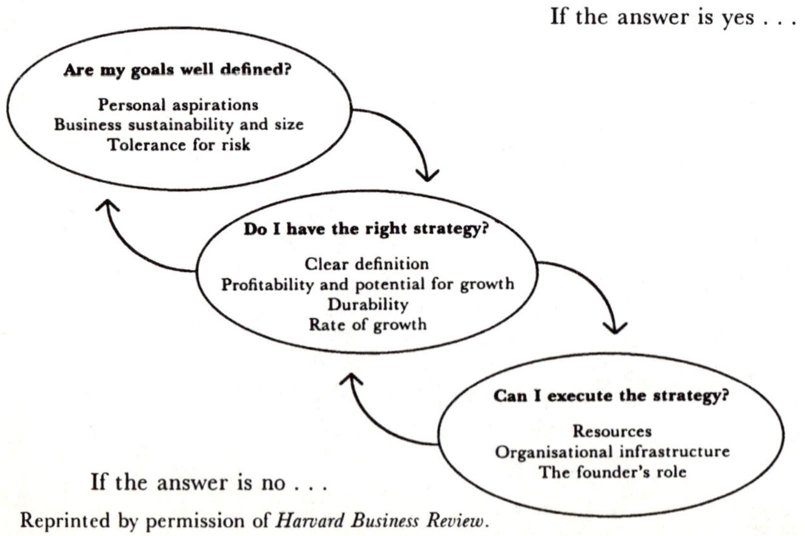

Reprinted by permission of *Harvard Business Review*.

[1] *Harvard Business Review, Vol. 74 No. 6, Nov/Dec 1996.*

11.2 A strategic business plan

A strategic business plan is a main plank in professionalising family and owner-managed businesses. Experience in helping many such businesses develop strategic plans has shown that the process is invaluable in positioning the business externally for success and identifying internal issues which must be addressed and resolved to establish the basis of continued success. Because a strategic business plan looks inwards as well as outwards, it is especially relevant to the needs of family and owner-managed businesses in addressing areas of human resources, particularly those relating to recruitment, selection, performance appraisal and reward. These areas can often cause a conflict between the interests of the owners and those of the business.

From the perspective of the owners, there can often be a desire and a tendency to achieve equality by ensuring that everyone has a job, that no-one is clearly the boss, and that everyone is paid the same. In the interest of the business, on the other hand, the ideal is to find the best talent and only bring in family members or owners who can contribute, to allocate responsibilities and establish a proper management structure and to appraise performance objectively and reward individuals based on their responsibilities and achievements. Those businesses which set explicit goals and incorporate strategies in their plans to establish a business-like approach to deal with these internal problems are the most successful.

The strategic business plan should work within a realistic time-frame, say one to three years. It should be recorded in writing and deal with the mission of the business, the goals of the owners, objectives, strategies, action programmes including consideration of how these can be implemented, and financial projections. It is important that all the owners or at least those involved in the operation of the business are fully involved in this process.

The main steps in achieving a strategic business plan are:

(a) assess the current situation of the business by carrying out a SWOT analysis (strengths/weaknesses/opportunities/threats);
(b) write a mission statement which articulates the overriding purposes of the business, its nature and principal values;
(c) state the goals in measurable terms;
(d) define the strategies, identifying the broad principles to be used in achieving the goals of the business;
(e) determine the impact on the business by assessing the level of resources required to implement the goals and strategies. This will include human as well as financial resources;
(f) discipline yourself to write the plan as a single document incorporating the mission, goals, strategies and assessment of resources along with financial budget projections;

(g) implement and monitor the plan establishing regular intervals, say quarterly, to assess performance against plan;
(h) revise the plan as required retaining flexibility needed to achieve success.

A simple checklist which can help you in identifying points to follow up is set out below in Figure 11.2. Make time to answer the checklist and follow up any points where you answer no.

Figure 11.2

1. Have you written down the goals and values for you and your business?
2. Do your co-owners share these goals and values?
3. Do you communicate well with each other?
4. Do you have contingencies if any of you are ill or die? What would happen to the business if you split up with co-owners or spouse?
5. Are you able to deal with conflicts and problems in a constructive way?
6. Do all family members or co-owners have agreed job descriptions?
7. Are their career aspirations clear and accommodated for in the business?
8. Is the reward system fair and does it encourage good performance?
9. Are there any independent directors who can be objective over problems?
10. Is there a succession plan in place which provides for both tax and transfer of power issues?

11.3 Exit routes

In establishing goals, the owners should have considered what they want to do with the business. Do they want to keep it and grow it, do they want to pass it on to family members, do they want to sell it or do they want to publicly float it off? If the intention is to keep it and grow it and to pass it on to family members, the question of succession must be considered. There are two distinct aspects to succession – succession of management and succession of owners.

11.4 Management succession

One of the main responsibilities of the head of a private business is planning for management succession. This involves both selecting and grooming a successor and describing the factors which are, in the opinion of the head of the business, the most essential to managing the company in an effective way and ensuring its success. There are a number of options available in terms of naming a successor or leader. These can range from choosing amongst existing owners, selecting a key employee or bringing in someone from the outside. There is no one method which is always right. The variable can include the nature of the business, its maturity, the qualifications of owners and the expectations and capabilities of employers and management.

In addition to selecting a successor, the head of the business must communicate the information which he considers crucial to the future of the business. At least the following areas should be addressed:

(a) *The financial picture*. The head's own assessment of the business's current position and a projection of its future financial position should be described along with financial statements, projections, tax status, banking information, lines of available credit, insurance arrangements and other relevant information.
(b) *Administration and corporate profile*. Information on any corporate records, partnership or share agreements, staff contracts, position on any legal matters outstanding and details on professional advisers should be included.
(c) *Operations and technical data*. A listing of the major equipment, quality control procedures, state of properties, maintenance contracts, capital expenditure plans should all be described.
(d) *Marketing plan*. The strategy for marketing along with information on competitors, branding or theming should be discussed.
(e) *Purchasing information*. Details of suppliers, contracts, inventories, arrangements with brewers.
(f) *Systems*. Any organisational charts, details or procedures, employee handbooks, job descriptions and management reports.

11.5 Ownership succession

The succession of management is not the only key decision for the owner – resolving the problem of the succession of ownership is just as important. It is essential to place effective ownership in the hands of those interested in and capable of providing the impetus to keep the business going. Different classes of shares and shareholder agreements could be specific objectives of owners and the needs of their families. A number of areas which can be considered include:

(a) *Separating ownership from management*. Different classes of shares can be used to safeguard the interests of families not involved in running the business. This can entitle them to income but to no voting rights except perhaps in unusual circumstances such as the sale of the business.

(b) *Restricting subsequent share transactions.* A shareholders' agreement can impose restrictions on the sale by a shareholder of their interest to outsiders.

(c) *Limiting outside investors' purchase of shares.* Existing shareholders or their families can be given the right of first refusal before any shares can be sold.

(d) *The use of trusts.* Future ownership can be settled on selected family members.

In addition to considering the ownership issues, tax planning is essential. The incidence of both capital gains tax and inheritance tax can be mitigated by proper planning. This is a vast and complex area and outside the scope of this book. Professional help is essential and this should be taken at an early stage.

11.6 Selling the business

Research has shown that, whilst a significant proportion of business owners in the UK wish to retain control for chosen successors, twice as many are looking to make a disposal at some point in the future. Grooming a business for sale is an important part of a strategic plan and, if this is the goal, the planning process needs to start many years in advance of the planned event.

The sister publication to this book, *Hotels*, published by Accountancy Books, contains practical hints on the disposal of a hotel in Chapter 10. These hints are equally applicable to pubs and restaurants and can be consulted if a disposal is being contemplated.

11.7 Going public

A strategic plan may contemplate going public as a means of raising further funding or providing an exit route for the owners. In the UK, in addition to flotation on the main Stock Exchange market, companies can be floated or traded on the Alternative Investment Market (AIM) or OFEX. Flotation on the main market is only suitable for large and mature companies and is not considered in this chapter. Some practical information and guidance on AIM and OFEX is given below.

11.8 The Alternative Investment Market

11.8.1 What is AIM?

In June 1995, the Alternative Investment Market was launched by the London Stock Exchange in a fanfare of publicity to act as a new public market for small, young and growing companies. It has two principal functions:

(a) to enable smaller companies to raise low cost capital to fund further growth;
(b) to replace the Stock Exchange's existing second-tier markets, the Unlisted Securities Market (USM) and the Rule 4.2 matched trading facility.

There is absolutely no restriction on the type of business that may be admitted to the AIM. The potential AIM entrant does not need to have reached a particular size or be able to demonstrate a lengthy trading record. In addition, it is not required to place a minimum percentage of its shares in public hands.

11.8.2 Taxation

One aspect of AIM that is frequently overlooked is the potentially significant taxation advantages membership can bring to investors. Shares in AIM companies will be classified as 'unquoted' securities for tax purposes and as a result the following reliefs may be available:

(a) owners of shares will be able to take advantage of inheritance tax and property tax reliefs;
(b) capital gains tax rollover relief on reinvestment and holdover relief on gifts of assets will be available;
(c) income and capital gains tax reliefs for investors under the Enterprise Investment Scheme and for investors in venture capital trusts.

11.8.3 Admission to AIM

Nominated advisers and brokers

The application process for companies wishing to join AIM has been made simple to encourage entrants. In particular, the Stock Exchange has delegated responsibility for vetting entrants to a nominated adviser authorised as such by the Exchange. The adviser will be a stockbroker, banker, lawyer or other financial professional experienced in corporate finance, whose function is to reassure the market that the information published by the company is accurate and to ensure that the company's directors are aware of their responsibilities under the AIM rules.

As well as a nominated adviser, the AIM entrant must also appoint a nominated broker. The broking firm has an important role to play in bringing buyers and sellers of shares together if there is no recognised market maker and in ensuring an orderly market in the company's shares by providing relevant and useful information on the company to the public.

Conditions to be satisfied at all times

A company traded on AIM must meet the following criteria at all times. It must:

(a) appoint and retain a nominated adviser and a nominated broker;
(b) be legally established under the laws of its country and be a public limited company or equivalent able to issue securities to the public;
(c) publish accounts that conform to UK or US generally accepted accounting principles;
(d) agree to abide by a code of conduct such as set out in the Model Code for AIM companies relating to trading whilst in possession of price-sensitive information.

Directors and employees of companies trading for less than two years must demonstrate commitment to the entrant by agreeing not to sell any interests they have in the company's securities for at least one year from the date of joining AIM.

Admission procedures

Every application to AIM must by supported by:

(a) an admission document or prospectus for which the directors take full responsibility;
(b) an application form signed by the directors;
(c) a declaration of compliance with the AIM rules signed by the nominated adviser and a letter from the nominated broker confirming his appointment.

The prospectus must be drawn up to contain all the information required by the Public Offers of Securities (POS) Regulations 1995. It should also contain all such information as investors would reasonably require to make an informed assessment of the company's financial position and prospects. These include the following:

(a) a description of the securities to be traded on AIM;
(b) the company's trading history and financial position;
(c) details of management including their directorships over the past five years, any unspent conviction and all bankruptcies, receiverships or liquidations of companies where they were directors and any public criticisms by statutory or regulatory authorities;
(e) substantial shareholders;
(f) a working capital confirmation by the directors that the company has sufficient working capital to meet its present requirements.

If the prospectus contains a profit forecast, perhaps to increase the marketability of the company's shares, the company's auditors must confirm that this has been properly compiled. The assumptions underlying the profit forecast must also be stated.

Figure 11.3 *Ten matters to consider when thinking about joining AIM*

1. Consider the alternatives. Venture capital including VCTs, private capital including EIS, medium-term loans, factoring, sale and leaseback, trade sale or investment.

2. Plan to enter AIM shortly after the company's statutory accounts are finalised. The figures published will then be audited, current and no profit forecast will be required. Establish a timetable and stick to it.

3. Prepare a detailed business plan to send to prospective nominated advisers and others. The plan must be professionally presented, tell the full story of the company and address all the important issues. The plan should set out the prospects for the company and why any new share capital is required.

4. Interview five or six prospective nominated advisers. They will usually make an hour or so available at no cost. Each will have interesting ideas and different views on the project which will require changes and improvements to the business plan.

5. Do not select a nominated adviser on the basis of cost alone. They are essential to a successful entry to AIM and have an ongoing role with the company. It is important that you trust them and feel you can work closely with the individuals concerned.

6. Start the pre-flotation grooming process. This might include the commissioning of an accountant's long form report which can be updated nearer the date of the flotation. The objective is to tidy up the company, for example to remove surplus assets, settle outstanding liabilities, agree corporation tax computations, etc.

7. Consider recruitment of senior managers/directors with relevant qualifications and suitable experience to strengthen the management team. Identify possible non-executive directors. It is best if directors and senior management are on board before the company is floated.

8. Put in place service contracts, share option schemes, formal agreements with distributors, manufacturers, customers, landlords and others.

9. Select other members of the professional team – accountants, solicitors, brokers, public relations experts, printers, etc. Obtain estimates of fees and meet the people who will be working on the assignment.

10. Do not take your eye off the business of the company. Your company needs to be actually or potentially profitable to be attractive to AIM investors.

11.9 OFEX

OFEX is a facility managed by J P Jenkins Limited to allow trading in the shares of unquoted companies. It is neither regulated nor a market but a mechanism whereby Stock Exchange member firms can affect much business off-Exchange. Under OFEX, participating companies are provided with an independent market maker, screen-based prices and a comprehensive company information and announcement service.

11.9.1 General requirements for entry

If the company is established, signed copies of the last three years' reports and accounts are required to be provided – the latest set must be unqualified. If the company is a 'start-up', fully qualified projections and a business plan must be produced by recognised advisers. Supporting documentation must also be made available. All documentation must be submitted by a company's advisers, i.e., a member of a recognised professional body such as the company's auditors.

11.9.2 The role of OFEX

OFEX is not a competitor to AIM as it is not in itself a market. It is principally designed to cater for those companies whose shares were previously traded under Stock Exchange Rule 4.2, but companies can and have raised small amounts of money on OFEX. These have typically ranged between £250,000 and £1,500,000. One of the main uses of OFEX is that it gives companies a stable period for reorganisation in order to groom themselves for AIM or the main market, whilst at the same time establishing a share price.

As with AIM, the decision to go on OFEX should be a planned process and it is essential that proper professional advice is taken at a very early stage.

11.10 Conclusion

This chapter has attempted to set out some of the broad principles of strategic planning and to emphasise that with all family and owner-managed businesses, the needs of the owners and those of the business are inextricably linked. Planning is essential to resolve the inherent conflicts which arise for such businesses.

Appendix 1 — Management information pack

Management accounts

Month 13

Dog and Duck

	CURRENT PERIOD							*YEAR TO DATE*							
	Act	*%*	*Bud*	*%*	*Var*	*%*	*Last yr*	*Act*	*%*	*Bud*	*%*	*Var*	*%*	*Last yr*	*Var*
SALES															
Bar	**45,078**	88.6	54,875	84.5	(9,797)	(17.9)	**53,810**	**696,283**	86.4	729,405	85.5	(33,122)	(4.8)	**751,594**	(55,311)
Food	**2,994**	5.9	6,150	9.5	(3,156)	(51.3)	**4,857**	**58,529**	7.3	74,440	8.7	(15,911)	(27.2)	**74,174**	(15,645)
Accommodation	–	–	–	–	–	–	–	–	–	–	–	–	–	–	
AWP	**2,541**	5.0	3,500	5.4	(959)	(27.4)	**3,131**	**45,769**	5.7	44,200	5.2	1,569	3.4	**42,515**	3,254
Telephone	**183**	0.4	220	0.3	(37)	(16.8)	**198**	**2,870**	0.4	2,585	0.3	285	9.9	**2,502**	368
Other	**96**	0.2	200	0.3	(104)	(52.0)	**142**	**2,023**	0.3	2,405	0.3	(392)	(19.5)	**2,355**	(342)
Total sales inc vouchers	**50,891**	100.0	64,945	100.0	(14,054)	(21.6)	**62,139**	**805,465**	100.0	853,035	100.0	(47,570)	(5.9)	**873,140**	(67,675)
GROSS PROFIT															
Bar	**27,616**	61.3	37,315	68.0	(9,699)	(26.0)	**39,015**	**468,881**	67.3	495,996	68.0	(27,115)	(5.8)	**507,484**	(38,603)
Food	**1,933**	64.6	3,628	59.0	(1,695)	(46.7)	**2,782**	**34,215**	58.5	43,920	59.0	(9,705)	(28.4)	**43,156**	(8,941)
Accommodation	–	–	–	–	–	–	–	–	–	–	–	–	–	–	–
AWP	**2,541**	100.0	3,500	100.0	(959)	(27.4)	**3,131**	**(45,769)**	100.0	44,200	100.0	1,569		**42,515**	3,254
Telephone	**183**	100.0	220	100.0	(37)	(16.8)	**198**	**2,870**	100.0	2,585	100.0	285		**2,502**	368
Other	**96**	100.0	200	100.0	(104)	(52.0)	**142**	**2,013**	100.0	2,405	100.0	(392)		**2,355**	(342)
Total GP inc vouchers	**32,368**	63.6	44,863	69.1	(12,495)	(27.9)	**45,269**	**553,749**	68.8	589,106	69.1	(35,357)	(6.4)	**598,012**	(44,264)

LABOUR COSTS															
Weekly	**6,231**	12.2	8,168	12.6	1,937	23.7	**6,932**	**88,883**	11.0	105,871	12.4	16,988	16.0	**106,279**	17,396
Salaried staff	**1,958**	3.8	1,154	1.8	(804)	(69.7)	**1,310**	**15,759**	2.0	15,002	1.8	(757)	(5.0)	**17,029**	1,270
	8,189	16.1	9,322	14.4	1,133	(46.0)	**8,242**	**104,642**	13.0	120,873	14.2	16,231	11.0	**123,308**	18,666
Manager	**1,755**	3.4	3,089	4.8	1,334	43.2	**13,170**	**39,801**	4.9	40,157	4.7	356	0.9	**49,523**	9,722
Payroll total	**9,944**	19.5	12,411	19.1	2,467	(2.8)	**21,412**	**144,443**	17.9	161,030	18.9	16,587	11.9	**172,831**	28,388
Contribution before operating costs	**22,424**	44.1	32,452	50.0	(10,028)	(30.9)	**23,849**	**409,296**	50.8	428,076	50.2	(18,780)	(4.6)	**425,173**	(15,877)
Controllables	**1,044**	2.1	4,499	6.9	3,455	76.8	**2,158**	**43,949**	5.5	61,873	7.3	(17,924)	(40.8)	**44,712**	(763)
House operating profit	**21,380**	42.0	27,953	43.0	(6,573)	(23.5)	**21,691**	**365,347**	45.4	366,203	42.9	(856)	(0.2)	**380,461**	(15,114)
Non-controllables	**26,107**	51.3	3,725	5.7	(22,382)	(600.9)	**30,857**	**70,618**	8.8	48,425	5.7	(22,193)	(31.4)	**75,459**	13,607
Net house contribution	**(4,727)**	(9.3)	24,228	37.3	(28,955)	(119.5)	**(9,166)**	**294,729**	36.6	317,778	37.3	(23,049)	(7.3)	**305,002**	(10,273)

CONTROLLABLES	Act	%	CURRENT PERIOD Bud	%	Var	%	Last yr	Var	Act	%	YEAR TO DATE Bud	%	Var	Last yr	Var
OPERATING															
Cleaning materials	**32**	3.1	77	1.7	45		**183**	151	**931**	2.1	1,001	1.6	70	**1,186**	255
Disposals	**87**	8.4	154	3.4	67		**418**	331	**2,183**	5.0	2,002	3.2	(181)	**2,796**	613
Light bulbs	**62**	5.9	27	0.6	(35)		**77**	15	**476**	1.1	351	0.6	(125)	**386**	(90)
China and glass	**71**	6.8	146	3.2	75		**288**	218	**1,084**	2.5	1,898	3.1	814	**2,182**	1,098
Utensils	**12**	1.1	14	0.3	2		**30**	18	**822**	1.9	182	0.3	(640)	**586**	(236)
Laundry	**60**	5.8	62	1.4	2		**11**	(49)	**624**	1.4	806	1.3	182	**641**	17
Window cleaning	**80**	7.7	77	1.7	(3)		**100**	20	**1,040**	2.4	1,001	1.6	(39)	**1,050**	10
Uniform purchases	**–**		58	1.3	58		**–**	–	**112**	0.3	754	1.2	642	**–**	(112)
Maintenance contracts	**209**	20.1	92	2.0	(117)		**34**	(176)	**701**	1.6	1,196	1.9	495	**1,142**	441
Equipment hire	**154**	14.8	50	1.1	(104)		**25**	(129)	**632**	1.4	650	1.1	18	**550**	(81)
Repairs – equipment	**15**	1.4	154	3.4	139		**267**	252	**3,093**	7.0	2,002	3.2	(1,091)	**2,952**	(142)
Repairs – Refrigeration	**54**	5.2	77	1.7	23		**646**	592	**585**	1.3	1,001	1.6	416	**725**	139
	837	80.2	988	22.0	151		**2,080**	1,242	**12,285**	28.0	12,844	20.8	559	**14,197**	1,912
PROPERTY															
Repairs – property	**103**	9.9	150	3.3	47		**(67)**	(171)	**3,308**	7.5	2,870	4.6	(438)	**2,274**	(1,034)
Repairs – electrical	**(207)**	(19.8)	73	1.6	280		**234**	441	**1,796**	4.1	1,229	2.0	(567)	**942**	(853)
Repairs – plumbing	**–**	–	58	1.3	58		**–**	–	**551**	1.3	754	1.2	203	**233**	(318)
Electricity	**617**	59.1	726	16.1	109		**414**	(203)	**10,203**	23.2	10,978	17.7	775	**10,485**	281
Gas	**(612)**	(58.6)	304	6.8	916		**(1,894)**	(1,282)	**3,587**	8.2	4,598	7.4	1,011	**2,503**	(1,084)
Other fuels	**–**	–	–	–	–		**–**	–	**–**	–	–	–	–	**–**	–
Gardening services	**33**	3.2	–	–	(33)		**75**	42	**148**	0.3	–	–	(148)	**330**	182
Pest control	**(54)**	(5.2)	27	0.6	81		**16**	70	**471**	1.1	351	0.6	(120)	**322**	(149)
Staff training	**–**	–	–	–	–		**–**	–	**–**		–	–	–	**–**	–
	119	(11.4)	1,338	29.7	1,457		**(1,223)**	(1,104)	**20,063**	45.6	20,780	33.6	717	**17,088**	(2,974)

PROMOTIONS															
Music and entertaining	**592**	56.7	1,154	25.7	562	**62**	(530)	**3,316**	7.5	15,002	24.2	11,686	**922**	(2,394)
Equipt hire	**–**	–	142	3.2	142	**36**	36	**388**	0.9	1,846	3.0	1,458	**496**	108
Advertising	**270**	25.9	250	5.6	(20)	**447**	177	**1,324**	3.0	3,250	5.3	1,926	**2,519**	1,195
Promotional printing	**(1,292)**	(123.7)	192	4.3	1,484	**328**	1,620	**763**	1.7	2,496	4.0	1,733	**2,839**	2,077
											1			
	(430)	(41.2)	1,738	38.6	2,168	**874**	1,303	**5,791**	13.2	22,594	36.5	16,803	**6,775**	985
ADMINISTRATION														
Telephone	**684**	65.5	231	5.1	(453)	**337**	(347)	**3,423**	7.8	3,003	4.9	(420)	**3,029**	(394)
Printing and stationery	**14**	1.3	62	1.4	48	**25**	11	**1,416**	3.2	806	1.3	(610)	**2,510**	1,094
Postage	**5**	0.5	12	0.3	7	**12**	6	**88**	0.2	156	0.3	68	**71**	(17)
Travel	**–**	–	33	0.7	33	**9**	9	**144**	0.3	429	0.7	285	**306**	162
Staff motor running	**–**	–	–	–	–	**–**	–	**–**	–	–	–	–	**–**	–
Equipt hire – swipe, etc.	**15**	1.4	31	0.7	16	**33**	18	**240**	0.5	403	0.7	163	**422**	182
Credit card commission	**37**	3.5	8	0.2	(29)	**12**	(25)	**312**	0.7	104	0.2	(208)	**129**	(182)
Staff recruitment	**–**	–	–	–	–	**–**	–	**123**	0.3	–	–	(123)	**49**	(74)
Other	**–**	–	58	1.3	58	**–**	–	**66**	0.1	754	1.2	688	**137**	71
	755	72.3	435	9.7	(320)	**427**	(328)	**5,811**	13.2	5,655	9.1	(156)	**6,651**	840
Total controllables	**1,044**	100.0	4,499	100.0	3,455	**2,158**	1,114	**43,949**	100.0	61,873	100.0	17,924	**44,712**	763

NON-CONTROLLABLES	*Act*	%	*Bud*	%	*Var*	%	*Last yr*	*Var*	*Act*	%	*Bud*	%	*Var*	*Last yr*	*Var*
			CURRENT PERIOD								*YEAR TO DATE*				
PROPERTY															
Rent	–	–	–	–	–		–	–	–	–	–	–	–	–	
Rates – general	**3,003**	11.5	2,900	77.9	(103)		**2,487**	(516)	**37,803**	53.5	37,700	77.9	(103)	**37,899**	96
Rates – water and sewage	**152**	0.6	154	4.1	2		**10,791**	10,639	**2,292**	3.2	2,002	4.1	(290)	**12,616**	10,323
Council tax	**529**	2.0	–	–	(529)		**372**	(158)	**975**	1.4	–	–	(975)	**984**	9
Cesspool cleaning	–	–	–	–	–		–	–	–	–	–	–	–	–	–
Refuse removal	**126**	0.5	131	3.5	5		**94**	(32)	**1,593**	2.3	1,703	3.5	110	**1,558**	(35)
Insurances	**229**	0.9	229	6.1	–		**229**	–	**2,977**	4.2	2,977	6.1	–	**2,977**	–
EHO repairs	–	–	–	–	–		–	–	–	–	–	–	–	–	–
Staff accommodation	–	–	–	–	–		–	–	–	–	–	–	–	–	–
	4,040	15.5	3,414	91.7	(626)		**13,973**	9,933	**45,641**	64.6	44,382	91.7	(1,259)	**56,033**	10,393
FEES															
Stocktaking fees	**397**	1.5	154	4.1	(243)		**126**	(271)	**2,035**	2.9	2,002	4.1	(33)	**1,638**	(397)
Licencing costs	**158**	0.6	50	1.3	(108)		–	(158)	**842**	1.2	650	1.3	(192)	**97**	(745)
Legal fees	–	–	19	0.5	19		–	–	–	–	247	0.5	247	–	–
Architects/surveyors	–	–	–	–	–		–	–	**360**	0.5	–	–	(360)	–	(360)
PPL & PRS licences	**(227)**	(0.9)	88	2.4	315		**(599)**	(372)	–	–	1,144	2.4	1,144	**333**	333
Valuers' fees	–	–	–	–	–		–	–	–	–	–	–	–	–	–
	327	1.3	311	8.3	(16)		**(473)**	(800)	**3,237**	4.6	4,043	8.3	806	**2,069**	(1,169)
DEPRECIATION	**21,740**	83.3	–	–	(21,740)		**17,357**	4,383	**21,740**	30.8	–	–	(21,740)	**17,357**	4,383
Total non-controllers	**26,107**	100.0	3,725	100.0	(22,382)		**30,857**	13,516	**70,618**	100.0	48,425	100.0	(22,193)	**75,459**	13,607

PAYROLL COSTS																
WEEKLY																
Bar	**3,743**	7.4	6,383	9.8	2,641	41.4	**4,354**	611	**53,176**	6.6	82,666	9.7	29,49-0	35.7	**70,088**	16,912
Other	**733**	1.4	–	–	(733)		**870**	137	**9,703**	1.2	–	–	(9,703)		**11,598**	1,895
Security	**1,240**	2.4	1,385	2.1	145	10.5	**1,360**	120	**17,480**	2.2	18,005	2.1	525	2.9	**18,803**	1,323
Cleaning (inc contracts)	**420**	0.8	400	0.6	(30)	(7.5)	**428**	(2)	**5,730**	0.7	5,200	0.6	(530)	(10.2)	**3,936**	(1,794)
Holiday pay	**86**	0.2	–	–	(86)	–	**(80)**	(166)	**2,794**	0.3	–	–	(2,794)		**1,853**	(941)
Relief staff	**–**	–	–	–	–	–	**–**	–	**–**	–	–	–	–		**–**	–
SALARIED	**6,231**	12.2	8,168	12.6	1,937	23.7	**6,932**	700	**88,883**	11.0	105,871	12.4	16,988	16.0	**106,279**	17,396
	1,958	3.8	1,154	1.8	(804)	(69.7)	**1,310**	(648)	**15,579**	2.0	15,002	1.8	(757)	(5.0)	**17,029**	1,270
	8,189	16.1	9,322	14.4	1,133	12.2	**8,242**	52	**104,642**	13.0	120,873	14.2	16,231	13.4	**123,308**	18,666
MANAGER																
Package	**2,768**	5.4	2,550	3.9	(218)	(8.5)	**13,170**	10,402	**36,061**	4.5	33,150	3.9	(2,911)	(8.8)	**41,319**	5,257
Quarterly bonus	**(738)**	(1.5)	385	0.6	1,123	291.8	**–**	738	**2,147**	0.3	5,005	0.6	2,858	57.1	**5,000**	2,853
Monthly bonus	**(275)**	(0.5)	154	0.2	429	278.4	**–**	275	**649**	0.1	2,002	0.2	1,353	67.6	**2,310**	1,661
Relief manager	**–**	–	–	–	–		**–**	–	**944**	0.1	–	–	(944)		**894**	(50)
	1,755	3.4	3,089	4.8	1,334	43.2	**13,170**	11,415	**39,801**	4.9	40,157	4.7	356	0.9	**49,523**	9,722
Payroll total	**9,944**	19.5	12,411	19.1	2,467	19.9	**21,412**	11,468	**144,443**	17.9	161,030	18.9	16,587	10.3	**172,831**	28,388

Appendix 2 – Summary of financial ratios

Listed below are the key ratios which could be used to analyse the results of a company.

1 Performance ratios

(a) Return on employed capital $\frac{\text{Net profit before tax and interest}}{\text{Fixed assets and current assets}} \times 100$

(b) Return on net assets $\frac{\text{Net profit before tax and interest}}{\text{Net assets}} \times 100$

Where net assets = fixed assets and current assets − current liabilities.

(c) Profit margin $\frac{\text{Profit before tax and interest}}{\text{Sales}} \times 100$

(d) Return on equity $\frac{\text{Profit after tax}}{\text{Shareholders' funds}}$

Shareholders' funds are share capital plus reserves.

(e) Net asset turnover $\frac{\text{Sales}}{\text{Net assets}}$

This can be analysed between $\frac{\text{Sales}}{\text{Net assets}}$ $\frac{\text{Sales}}{\text{Working capital}}$

(f) Stock turnover Sales

Where net assets = fixed assets & current assets − current liabilities.

(g) Net profit margin $\frac{\text{Profit before tax and interest}}{\text{Sales}} \times 100$

(h) Return on equity $\frac{\text{Profit after tax}}{\text{Shareholders' funds}}$

Shareholders' funds comprise share capital plus reserves.

(i) Net asset turnover $\frac{\text{Sales}}{\text{Net assets}}$

This can be analysed between $\frac{\text{Sales}}{\text{Fixed assets}}$ $\frac{\text{Sales}}{\text{Working capital}}$

(j) Stock turnover $\frac{\text{Sales}}{\text{Stock}}$

(k) Debtors' turnover $\frac{\text{Sales}}{\text{Debtors}}$

2 Financial status ratios

(a) Debt ratio	Long-term debt / Capital employed
(b) Interest cover	Profit before interest and tax / Loan interest

(a) and (b) are known as solvency ratios

(c) Current ratio	Current assets / Current liabilities
(d) Acid test	Liquid assets (debtors and cash) / Current liabilities
(e) Earning	Shareholders' funds / Long-term capital employed and bank overdraft

3 Stock market ratios

(a) Earnings per share	Profit before tax / Number of ordinary shares in issue
(b) Price/earnings ratio	Market price per share / Earnings per share
(c) Dividend yield (net)	Dividend per share (net) / Market price per share
(d) Dividend cover	Earnings per share / Dividend per share

Ratio analysis

What do ratios mean?

1 Performance ratios

These measure how successfully a company is being run, or how well its management is utilising the assets for which it has been made responsible.

(a) Return on employed capital

This takes no account of current liabilities such as trade creditors and short-term debt such as a bank overdraft. It also calculates the return based on the profits generated before long-term debt is paid for or tax has been paid. Thus, one arrives at the return the investor is making in the business irrespective of how the business is financed and the vagaries of the tax legislation in force.

(b) Return on net assets

This has the same advantages as the ratio for return on capital, however, it does take into account short-term financing and therefore shows the actual capital tied up in the business.

(c) Profit margin

This shows the relationship which exists between the amount of profit (before the deduction of tax and loan interest) that a company is making and the amount of sales revenue needed to achieve it. If the information is available, it is an interesting exercise to calculate the gross profit margin, but to do this one needs access to more information than is shown in published accounts.

(d) Return on equity

This measures the return on the funds invested by the shareholders but takes into account the cost of financing via loan capital and the impact of taxation.

(e) Net asset turnover

The net asset turnover ratio is a measure of how well a company has used its assets. However, care needs to be taken because significant investment in fixed assets during the year will change the ratios dramatically. Thus, it may be helpful to analyse this measure by splitting the denominator into fixed assets and working capital.

(f) Stock turnover

Stock turnover shows how quickly goods move through the business, usually the quicker the turnover the better, however, there may be problems with shortages if stocks are too low. For instance, a restaurant should not run out of wine or a pub out of beer.

Ideally, stock turnover should be calculated using cost of sales figures and not sales. However, these are not normally available.

(g) Debtors' turnover

Where a company makes more cash than credit sales, debtors' turnover is unlikely to be of much use. In any event care should be taken to ensure that fluctuations in trading are taken into account.

2 Financial status ratio

(a) Debt ratio

A fairly low debt ratio gives the provider of long-term loans a fairly high level of safety. For example, if a long-term debt was 8 and capital employed was 50 then the debt ratio would be 16 per cent. This means that 84 per cent of the book value of its assets needs to be lost before it would be unable to repay its loan liability in full.

(b) Interest cover

This indicates the relative safety in loan interest payments in the same way that the debt ratio showed safety.

(c) Current ratio

This is one of the crucial liquidity ratios and shows to what extent short-term assets are adequate to settle short-term liabilities. Usually, a ratio of less than 1.0 deserves very close scrutiny. However, as stock is usually financed by creditors it is common for pubs and restaurants to have a current ratio of less than 1.0.

(d) Acid test

This is the strict test of a company's liquidity. It excludes stock in estimating the resources available to meet current liabilities, on the basis that it can take several months to convert stock into cash.

(e) Earnings

This ratio emphasises to what extent the owners are financing the business. One should note that the lower the percentage the more likely the company is to have higher interest charges that must be paid before the shareholders (owners) can be paid a dividend.

3 Stock market ratios

(a) Earnings per share

Profit after tax attributable to ordinary shareholders should be adjusted for extraordinary items, minority interests and preference dividends.

Note that one must use the number of shares *issued* not authorised.

(b) Price/earnings ratio

This needs to be treated with extreme caution when the company makes a loss, because a negative p/e will be calculated.

(c) Dividend yield

This deals purely with the proportion of the profit paid out as dividend, thus it does not take account of the capital gain that an investor may make from his shares.

(d) Dividend cover

This is just a mark of the safety of the dividend. As with dividend yield, this is normally calculated gross of tax.

Appendix 3 – Glossary of IT terms

Hardware
The physical components that make up a **system**, e.g., the monitor and the keyboard.

Software
Other words used are applications, programs or packages.

System
The generic term used to include **hardware** and **software**.

Operating system
The basic **software** of a computer. It contains all the set-up information of the computer, e.g., the commands of the keyboard and monitor. The most common operating system is **DOS**.

Processor
The actual brain of a computer. A choice of 486 or Pentium are now the standard.

RAM/Memory
Random access memory. This is memory that is used to make the **software** run quickly.

Hard disk
The physical storage for the **software** to reside on. Recommended at least 800Mb.

Expansion slots
Needed to expand the functionality of your PC. Placed at the back of your PC the standard is 4, e.g., sound cards or internal modems cards can be slotted in easily.

Directories
'Filing cabinet' within the **hard disk** that make it easier to locate files.

Byte
A measure of a program. One byte represents one character, e.g., the word 'telephone' has a size of nine bytes.

DOS
Disk operating system. Different manufacturers have brought out their own versions, but the most popular is MS DOS (Microsoft).

Windows
Microsoft operating package that allows multi-tasking operations. Different versions have been brought out, Windows 3.1, Windows 3.11, Windows 95 and Windows NT.

MAC
Apple operating package that also allows multi-tasking operations.

UNIX
Different flavours of UNIX operating packages are on the market.

Network
A method of linking computers together so that they can share the same information, **hardware** items such as printers, etc.

File server
The central computer that runs a **network** system.

Novell
A popular operating **software** needed to run a **network** system.

LAN
Local area network. A network connected by standard network cabling, e.g., in an office building.

WAN
Wide area network. A network over a large area either using modems or **ISDN** lines.

ISDN
A faster and more reliable way to pass data or voice over a larger distance than a standard telephone line, although at a cost.

Appendix 4 – Statement of requirements

1 Hardware environment

Number	*Requirements*	*Weighting*	*Response*
1	The EPOS should operate in the case of power failure for at least 15 minutes		
2	The cable run between the CPU and the EPOS should reach at least 100 metres without boosters		
3	The number of EPOS to be installed should be 20		
4	The EPOS should be water-resistant		
5	There should be a spare EPOS, bill printer and kitchen printer left on site as spare		
6	The kitchen printers must be able to print on duplex rolls		
7	The tape streamer should be ARC Serve with DAT tapes		
8	The foot print of the EPOS should be no bigger than 310mm wide & 300mm long		
9	The EPOS should be able to have a customer display that can be rotated 180 degrees		
10	The EPOS should have an integrated credit card reader with online authorisation		

Appendix 5 – Suppliers of EPOS and food and beverage control systems

Company Name	*Contact*	*Position*	*Telephone*	*Fax*
Accounting Answers Ltd	Mr Karl Thacker	Sales & Marketing	01703 667 644	01703 667 763
Checkout Computer Systems Ltd	Mr John C Bowen	Director of Sales & Marketing	01582 471 112	01582 471 118
Counter Solutions	Mr Andrew Motley	Sales & Marketing Director	01773 530 303	01773 530 404
Fretwell Downing Data Systems Ltd	Mr Charles C Mobbs	Sales Director	0114 281 6000	0114 281 6001
GE Information Services Ltd	Mr David J Mead	Sales Executive	01932 776 000	01932 776 020
Innsite Hotel Services Ltd	Mr Philip J Davidson	Sales & Marketing Director	0181 897 3071	0181 759 4017
Micros Fidelio	Mr David Jones	Sales Executive	01753 536 969	01753 536 799
NFS Europe	Mr Luis De Souza	Director	01920 485 725	01920 485 723
Pabulum Consultants Ltd	Ms Tina Isidoros	Marketing Manager	01628 476 969	01628 482 897
Remanco Systems Ltd	Mr Calum McIndoe	Sales Executive	0181 891 6453	0181 891 6882
Rural Computer Systems Ltd	Ms Jane Clapham	Sales & Marketing	01248 370 700	01248 370 389
Sulcus Hospitality Group	Mr Phillip Wanbon	General Manager	0181 681 1900	0181 760 0354
Welcome Computer Systems	Mr Ian Jennings	Operations Manager	01604 821 970	01604 843 728
XI Data Systems	Mr Timothy F Burgess	Managing Director	0113 245 2788	0113 242 3801

Appendix 6 – Comparison of accounting

	SFI	*Grosvenor*	*Morlands*	*Old English*	*Gibbs*
Goodwill written off against reserves	Y	N	Y	N	Y
Goodwill capitalised and amortised	N	Y	N	N	N
No depreciation on freehold properties	Y	Y	Y	Y	Y
Leasehold properties depreciated over remaining term of lease when it has less than # years to run	20	20	N	N	N
F/hold and long l/hold properties regularly reviewed by independent valuers, surplus taken to reserves, permanent diminution taken first to reserves and excess to P&L	Y	N	N	N	N
Revaluation policy as above except 1/3 of property valued annually	N	N	N	N	N
Revaluation policy as above except 1/5 of property valued annually	N	N	N	N	N
Property valued no further details	N	Y	Y	Y	Y
Temporary diminutions in value offset against revaluation reserve as a pool, if pool exhausted balance taken to P&L	Y	N	N	N	N
F A @ cost includes interest cost of capital on major developments	Y	N	N	N	N
Construction and major hotel development pre-opening and start-up costs deferred and amortised over 5 years	N	N	N	N	N
Pre-opening costs capitalised	N	N	N	N	N
Pre-opening cost expensed when the outlet opens	N	N	N	N	N

policies

Greenhalls	*Scottish & Newcastle*	*Whitbread*	*Regent Inns*	*Yates Bros*	*JD Witherspoon*	*Tom Cobleigh*	*Century Inns*	*Enterprise Inns*	*Greene King*
Y	Y	Y	Y	Y	N	Y	N	N	Y
N	N	N	N	N	N	N	N	N	N
Y	Y	Y	Y	Y	Y	Y	Y	Y	Y
50	30	20	20	20	20	Lease term	N	N	N
N	N	Y	N	N	Y	N	N	N	N
N	N	N	N	N	Y	N	N	N	N
N	N	Y	N	N	N	N	N	N	N
Y	Y	N	Y	Y	N	Y	N	N	Y
N	N	N	N	N	Y	N	N	Y	N
Y	N	Y		N	Y		N	N	N
Y	N	N	N	N	N	N	N	N	N
N	N	N	Y	N	Y	N	N	N	N
N	N	N	N	Y	N	N	N	N	N

Appendix 7 – Extract from RICS 'Approval and Valuation' Manual

'The best price at which the sale of an interest in a property would have been completed unconditionally for cash consideration on the date of valuation assuming:

(a) a willing seller;
(b) that, prior to the date of valuation, there had been a reasonable period (having regard to the nature of the property and the state of the market) for the proper marketing of the interest, for the agreement of the price and terms and for the completion of the sale;
(c) that the state of the market, level of values and other circumstances were, on any assumed date of exchange of contracts, the same as on the date of valuation;
(d) that no account is taken of any additional bid by a prospective purchaser with a special interest; and
(e) that both parties to the transaction had acted knowledgeably, prudently and without compulsion.'

For existing use value, the Appraisal and Valuation Manual includes these additional assumptions:

'(f) the property can be used for the foreseeable future only for the existing use; and
(g) that vacant possession is provided on completion of the sale of all parts of the property occupied by the business . . .'

Appendix 8 – Extract from ASB Discussion Paper *Measurement of Tangible Fixed Assets*

Valuation of non-specialised property (Chapter 3)

16 Where an entity elects to revalue its non-specialised properties it is proposed that full external professional valuations should be carried out on each non-specialised property at intervals of no more than five years. In the intervening years, the current value of each non-specialised property should be determined by means of an interim valuation carried out by either:

(a) an external professional valuer; or
(b) the directors, following the advice of a valuer holding a recognised professional qualification who could be an employee or officer of the entity and has recent post-qualification experience in the location and category of the non-specialised properties concerned.

However, external professional valuers should always carry out the interim valuation in a year in which:

(a) there have been significant changes to the physical structure of the non-specialised property; or
(b) there is an indication that the value of the non-specialised property in question has moved significantly out of line with values of non-specialised properties of the same general type and location; or
(c) insufficient evidence is available to the company's internal valuers about the state of the market for non-specialised properties of that type and location.

17 Detailed guidance on the procedures to be followed during a full external professional valuation and an interim valuation is provided in paragraphs 3.5–3.8. The RICS has indicated that it is likely that the costs of an interim valuation would be significantly lower than the costs of a full external professional valuation.

Basis of valuation of property (Chapter 4)

18 The Discussion Paper discusses the available options and proposes guidance on the basis of valuation to be used in financial statements for different types of property. It examines the different bases of valuation that are defined by the RICS for accounting purposes, and considers how they relate to the cost of replacement. The two main bases of property valuation used by professional valuers are Open Market Value (OMV) and Existing Use Value (EUV), which is an extension of OMV relevant to

owner-occupied non-specialised property. Only in a limited number of cases will OMV and EUV be materially different from each other. There are two possible ways of valuing non-specialised properties in the financial statements:

(a) value the non-specialised property at EUV in the balance sheet (and therefore also for the purposes of determining depreciation), but give further information on the OMV in the notes to the financial statements where materially different; or

(b) value the non-specialised property at OMV in the balance sheet, but disclose EUV in the notes to the financial statements where materially different.

The Board's preliminary view is that method (a) is preferable; not only does the balance sheet value correspond more closely with the cost of replacement, but the consequential depreciation charge based on the EUV is a more appropriate measure of the service potential consumed by the entity.

Depreciation of tangible fixed assets (Chapter 5)

19 Chapter 5 initially considers the nature and purpose of depreciation. It concludes that depreciation should be viewed as a measure of the cost of the economic benefits of the tangible fixed asset that have been consumed during the period.

20 The main practical issues that arise with the application of SSAP 12 are addressed. It is proposed that:

(a) the estimate of a tangible fixed asset's useful economic life should take into account reasonably expected technological changes, but should not assume a limitless extension through maintenance, refurbishment, overhaul or replacement of components;

(b) where major components of a tangible fixed asset need to be replaced at regular intervals they should be accounted for as separate assets and depreciated over their individual useful economic lives;

(c) a change in the estimated useful economic life of a tangible fixed asset should be accounted for prospectively over the remaining useful economic life of the tangible fixed asset;

(d) the residual value should be estimated on prices prevailing at the date of the acquisition or revaluation (where this has taken place). Where there is sufficient objective evidence of reasonably expected technological changes the estimate of residual value should take these changes into consideration; and

(e) where the residual value is material it should be reassessed annually to take into consideration reasonably expected technological changes. The residual value should not, however, be reassessed to take account of changes in price unless the tangible fixed asset is also revalued. A change in the residual value of a tangible fixed asset should be accounted for prospectively over the remaining useful economic life of the asset.

21 Where a tangible fixed asset is revalued, its future depreciation is based on the revalued amount and it is proposed that its residual value should be estimated based on prices prevailing at the revaluation date. An increase in value is not sufficient justification for not depreciating an asset. No change is proposed in the existing prohibition against split depreciation.

22 Since it is normally uneconomic to provide a limitless extension to the life of a property through maintenance and refurbishing, it is proposed that there should be a general requirement for depreciation of properties.

Appendix 9 – Table 1 from Schedule A, Capital Allowances Act 1990

(1) *Assets included in the expression "building"*	*(2)* *Assets so included, but expenditure on which is unaffected by the Schedule*
A Walls, floors, ceilings, doors, gates, shutters, windows and stairs.	1 Electrical, cold water, gas and sewerage systems – (a) provided mainly to meet the particular requirements of the trade, or (b) provided mainly to serve particular machinery or plant used for the purposes of the trade.
	2 Space or water heating systems; powered systems of ventilation, air cooling or air purification; and any ceiling or floor comprised in such systems.
B Mains services, and systems, of water, electricity and gas.	3 Manufacturing or processing equipment; storage equipment, including cold rooms; display equipment; and counters, check-outs and similar equipment.
	4 Cookers, washing machines, dishwashers, refrigerators and similar equipment; washbasins, sinks, baths, showers, sanitary ware and similar equipment; and furniture and furnishings.
C Waste disposal systems.	5 Lifts, hoists, escalators and moving walkways.
	6 Sound insulation provided mainly to meet the particular requirements of the trade.
D Sewerage and drainage systems.	7 Computer, telecommunication and surveillance systems (including their wiring or other links).
	8 Refrigeration or cooling equipment.

(1) *Assets included in the expression "building"*	*(2)* *Assets so included, but expenditure on which is unaffected by the Schedule*
E Shafts or other structures in which lifts, hoists, escalators and moving walkways are installed.	9 Sprinkler equipment and other equipment for extinguishing or containing fire; fire alarm systems.
	10 Burglar alarm systems.
	11 Any machinery (including devices for providing motive power) not within any other item in this column.
F Fire safety systems.	12 Strong rooms in bank or building society premises; safes.
	13 Partition walls, where moveable and intended to be moved in the course of the trade.
	14 Decorative assets provided for the enjoyment of the public in the hotel, restaurant or similar trades.
	15 Advertising hoardings; and signs, displays and similar assets.
	16 Swimming pools (including diving boards, slides and structures on which such boards or slides are mounted).

Appendix 10 – Customs & Excise mark-up exercise

Product	*Selling price*	*Purchase price*	*Mark-up*		*Average mark-up*	*Purchases of total*	*Average weighted mark-up*
	£	£	£	£	£	%	%
(a)	(b)	(c)	(d)		(e)	(f)*	(g) (e × f)
Best bitter	2.20	1.04	1.16	111.54			
Strong bitter	2.48	1.18	1.30	110.17	111.15	33.15	36.85
Guest bitter	2.16	1.02	1.14	111.76			
				333.47 ÷ 3			
Australian lager	2.34	1.10	1.24	112.73			
German lager	2.48	1.18	1.30	110.17	111.45	35.85	39.95
				222.90 ÷ 2			
Bottled lager	2.46	1.10	1.36	123.64			
	1.96	1.00	0.96	96.00	109.82	12.06	13.24
				219.64 ÷ 2			
Brandy	1.70	0.84	0.86	102.38			
Whisky	1.28	0.62	0.66	106.45			
Vodka	1.28	0.62	0.66	106.45	105.64	8.04	8.49
Gin	1.28	0.62	0.66	106.45			
Rum	1.28	0.62	0.66	106.45			
				528.18 ÷ 5			
Sherry	1.84	1.00	0.84	84.00			
Wine	1.88	0.90	0.98	108.89	96.44	1.89	1.82
				192.89 ÷ 2			
Juices and mixers	1.02	0.42	0.60	142.86			
Coke	0.92	0.36	0.56	155.56	149.21	9.01	13.44
				298.42 ÷ 2			
						100%	**113.79%**

Notes

* Percentages obtained from analysis of annual purchases

1 Calculated from analysis of supplies

Appendix 11 – Standard audit work programme

Client .... File no. ....

Audit programme – tangible fixed assets Year ended ....

	WP ref	Comments/ results	Initials
1 Obtain/prepare summary of tangible fixed assets.			
2 Physically inspect assets (book to physical).			
3 Confirm property title.			
4 Vouch additions (book to invoices, etc.)			
5 Consider the reasonableness of any revaluations made in the year.			
6 Consider whether there have been any diminutions in value and ensure correct treatment.			
7 Ensure profit or loss on disposal is correctly calculated and accounted for.			
8 Vouch disposals (initial records to book).			
9 Check depreciation, if possible by proof in total.			
10 Review depreciation policy taking into account reasonableness of residual value.			
11 Consider the need for any exceptional write-down of fixed assets, including those carried at valuation.			
12 Confirm proper treatment of leased assets.			

	WP ref	*Comments/ results*	*Initials*
13 Confirm correct distinction between capital and revenue expenditure (especially repairs).			
14 Consider capital commitments.			
15 Agree/reconcile amounts disclosed in the accounts with the nominal ledger.			

Client .... File no. ....

Audit programme – Stock Year ended ....

	WP ref	*Comments/ results*	*Initials*
1 If stock is significant to the client's business, physically examine the stock.			
2 Test count records: (a) for completeness; (b) for subsequent alterations; (c) both to and from details noted at the count; (d) for correct casts and extensions; (e) both to and from any final stocksheets.			
3 Test casts and extensions of stock sheets.			
4 Test stock valuation by reference to purchase invoices or other cost records.			
5 Confirm valuation is on an acceptable basis, consistent with last year.			
6 Test provisions and write-downs are adequate but not excessive.			
7 Consider acceptability of any professional stocktakers.			
8 If current replacement cost differs significantly from book value, review the calculation.			
9 Agree/reconcile amounts disclosed in the accounts with the nominal ledger.			
10 The results and conclusions of all work are fully recorded in the working papers and cross-referenced to this programme.			

Appendix 11

Client .... File no. ....

Audit programme – Stocktake attendance Year ended ....

	WP ref	*Comments/ results*	*Initials*
A Before the count			
1 Obtain the client's stocktaking instructions and assess whether they are adequate. Inform the client of any deficiencies.			
2 Are we likely to be able to rely on managerial controls or comprehensive internal controls to reduce the extent of our test counts?			
3 Determine the nature and approximate monetary value of the stock to be counted. Note any high value or key stock lines that should be counted on a 100% basis. Consider also any items that were high value in the previous year.			
4 Determine the sample sizes for test counts.			
5 Where stocks are stored in bulk and cannot be measured accurately, assess the effectiveness of methods used by attending with suitably experienced staff.			
B During the count			
1 Review the stockholding areas to ascertain the nature, location and size of the stocks to be counted			
2 Note whether the client's staff are following the stocktaking instructions. If not, consider whether we need to extend our test counts.			
3 Ensure that all stock is included in the counting and that all areas are systematically cleared.			

	WP ref	*Comments/ results*	*Initials*
4 Ensure that any defective, obsolete and slow-moving items are identified and recorded as such on the stock sheets.			
5 Consider need for speciality.			
6 Exercise the physical condition.			
7 Ensure that any items that do not belong to the client are excluded from the count.			
8 Ensure that all differences disclosed by double counts are investigated and resolved.			
9 Record the following test counts in sufficient detail to enable the items selected to be traced to the final stock summary: (a) high value and key items (to test for both overstatement and understatement); (b) a sample selected from the physical stock items (understatement test); (c) a sample selected from a client's count records (overstatement).			
10 Review procedures for dealing with internal and external movement of goods during the stocktake.			
11 Record purchases/stock and sales/stock cut-off information (e.g., serial numbers of the last GRNs and despatch notes).			
12 Examine the serial numbering or other control of count records and note the details.			
13 Where work in progress is being examined, ensure that adequate information is recorded relating to the degree of completion.			

	WP ref	*Comments/ results*	*Initials*
14 Ensure against subsequent alteration of the stocktaking records by photocopying the stock sheets and recording the number of sheets used.			
15 Note below any additional tests that are considered necessary:			
16 The results and conclusions of all work are fully recorded in the working papers and cross-referenced to this programme.			

Client .... File no. ....

Audit programme – Debtors Year ended ....

	WP ref	*Comments/ results*	*Initials*
1 Obtain/prepare summary of debtors.			
2 Agree credit card and other trade debtor balances by reference to cash received after date or by circularisation.			
3 Test debt or sales and income/stock cut-off.			
4 Vouch prepayments and sundry debtors to supporting records.			
5 Confirm terms of amounts due from directors (and connected persons) and consider the legality and disclosure.			
7 Consider classification of material credit balances.			
8 Agree/reconcile amounts disclosed in the accounts with the nominal ledger.			
9 The results and conclusions of all work are fully recorded in the working papers and cross-referenced to this programme.			

Client .... File no. ....

Audit programme – Cash at bank and in hand/bank overdrafts Year ended ....

	WP ref	*Comments/ results*	*Initials*
1 Obtain or prepare, and test, bank reconciliations.			
2 Obtain bank confirmations and agree balances to reconciliation.			
3 Review other information included in bank confirmations.			
4 Count cash balances, and reconcile them to relevant records; in particular, examine vouchers for authenticity and date.			
5 Ensure that there is no significant window dressing by reviewing material receipts and payments before and after the year end.			
6 Agree/reconcile amounts disclosed in the accounts with the nominal ledger.			

Client	File no. ....
Audit programme – Creditors	Year ended ....

	WP ref	*Comments/ results*	*Initials*
1 Obtain/prepare summary of creditors.			
2 Reconcile trade creditors to suppliers' statements, paying particular regard to action required on reconciling items.			
3 If impossible to perform to sufficient extent, consider other procedures to verify trade creditors (e.g., direct contact with supplier, or review of constituent document).			
4 Review after-date payments, invoices and unmatched goods received documentation for evidence of additional current year liabilities.			
5 Analytically review supplier retrospective discounts and perform test checks on calculation.			
6 Test purchases/stock and expenses cut-off.			
7 Review of accruals and sundry creditors for omissions, and test calculations.			
8 Agree PAYE/NI creditor.			
9 Ensure VAT is properly reconciled.			
10 Test accuracy of directors'/loan accounts and confirm terms.			
11 Consider classification and recoverability of material debit balances.			
12 Ensure commitments and contingent liabilities are accurately identified and disclosed.			
13 Agree/reconcile amounts disclosed in the accounts with the nominal ledger.			

Client .... File no. ....

Audit programme – Taxation Year ended ....

	WP ref	*Comments/ results*	*Initials*
1 Prepare/review the corporation tax computation.			
2 Determine the latest position regarding the agreement to previous years' corporation tax computations. Identify and action any adjustments.			
3 Prepare or review the deferred tax computation.			
4 Reconcile the total tax charge in accounts with the profit before tax multiplied by the applicable corporation tax rate.			
5 Reconcile the directors' remuneration in the accounts with that paid in the year.			
6 Note any contentious areas in the current year's tax computation.			
7 Highlight any disclosures in the accounts that may have tax consequences.			
8 Agree/reconcile amounts disclosed in the accounts with the nominal ledger.			

Client .... File no. ....

Audit programme – Capital, reserves and statutory books Year ended ....

	WP ref	*Comments/ results*	*Initials*
1 Agree the authorised capital with the Memorandum of Association.			
2 Agree the allotted capital with the register of members.			
3 Ensure changes in share capital are properly authorised.			
4 Review all movements in reserves.			
5 Ensure dividends have been approved, correctly accounted for and paid out of distributable reserves.			
6 Copy (or take extracts of) minutes and all other statutory registers; follow up all matters relevant to the audit and accounts.			
7 Consider need for a company search (e.g., for charges).			
8 Consider the basis, legality and disclosure of transactions with related parties.			

Client	File no. ....
Audit programme – transactions	Year ended ....

	WP ref	*Comments/ results*	*Initials*
A Sales/income (Primary objective – understatement)			
1 Test that all despatches of goods or provisions of services result in sales being completely and accurately recognised in appropriate sales and VAT accounts in the nominal ledger.			
2 Test that other income (including purchase returns if material) is completely and accurately recognised in income and VAT accounts).			
B Purchases/expenses (Primary objective – overstatement)			
1 Test that amounts recorded in purchases, expenses and VAT account(s) (including sales returns if material) in the nominal ledger represent valid purchases and have been accurately recorded.			
2 Test accruals for overstatement and prepayment for understatement.			
C Wages and salaries (primary objective – overstatement)			
1 Test persons included in the payroll exist and are only included once.			
2 For selected individuals (including directors), test gross pay per nominal ledger payroll accounts is correctly calculated and authorised. *(Note: the sample should include the person responsible for preparing the payroll.)*			
3 Test that deductions from pay have been properly accounted for and paid over.			

	WP ref	*Comments/ results*	*Initials*
4 Test net pay from payroll to payments records.			
5 Vouch directors' remuneration for disclosure in the accounts.			
D Journals and nominal ledger			
1 Ensure all balances brought forward in client's books agree with the previous year's accounts; agree also reversal of closing accruals.			
2 Test any significant journal entries generated by the client.			
3 Check casts in nominal ledger, cash books and other accounting records.			
4 Agree/reconcile amounts disclosed in the accounts with the nominal ledger.			

Index

Entries in this index are referenced to paragraph number.